WESTMAR COLLEGE

W9-BMI-369

WESTMAR COLLEGE

# BETWEEN
## STATE AND NATIO

MARTHA DERTHICK

*with the assistance of Gary Bombardier*

# BETWEEN STATE AND NATION

## Regional Organizations of the United States

THE BROOKINGS INSTITUTION

*Washington, D.C.*

353.9292
D438

JK
325
.D46

*Copyright © 1974 by*
THE BROOKINGS INSTITUTION
*1775 Massachusetts Avenue, N.W., Washington, D.C. 20036*

*Library of Congress Cataloging in Publication Data:*
Derthick, Martha.
  Between state and nation: regional organizations
of the United States.

  Includes bibliographical references.
  1. Federal government—United States—Case studies.
2. Regionalism—United States—Case studies.
3. Regional planning—United States—Case studies.
I. Bombardier, Gary, joint author.    II. Title.
JK325.D46    353.9'292    74-727
ISBN 0-8157-1812-8
ISBN 0-8157-1811-x (pbk.)

9 8 7 6 5 4 3 2 1

90358

Board of Trustees

Douglas Dillon
*Chairman*

John E. Lockwood
*Vice Chairman*

Donald B. Woodward
*Chairman, Executive Committee*

Vincent M. Barnett, Jr.
Louis W. Cabot
Edward W. Carter
William T. Coleman, Jr.
George M. Elsey
John Fischer
Kermit Gordon
Gordon Gray
Huntington Harris
Roger W. Heyns
Luther G. Holbrook
William McC. Martin, Jr.
Robert S. McNamara
Arjay Miller
Barbara W. Newell
Herbert P. Patterson
J. Woodward Redmond
H. Chapman Rose
Warren M. Shapleigh
Gerard C. Smith
J. Harvie Wilkinson, Jr.

*Honorary Trustees*
Arthur Stanton Adams
William R. Biggs
Eugene R. Black
Robert D. Calkins
Colgate W. Darden, Jr.
Marion B. Folsom
Huntington Gilchrist
John Lee Pratt
Robert Brookings Smith
Sydney Stein, Jr.

THE BROOKINGS INSTITUTION is an independent organization devoted to nonpartisan research, education, and publication in economics, government, foreign policy, and the social sciences generally. Its principal purposes are to aid in the development of sound public policies and to promote public understanding of issues of national importance.

The Institution was founded on December 8, 1927, to merge the activities of the Institute for Government Research, founded in 1916, the Institute of Economics, founded in 1922, and the Robert Brookings Graduate School of Economics and Government, founded in 1924.

The Board of Trustees is responsible for the general administration of the Institution, while the immediate direction of the policies, program, and staff is vested in the President, assisted by an advisory committee of the officers and staff. The by-laws of the Institution state, "It is the function of the Trustees to make possible the conduct of scientific research, and publication, under the most favorable conditions, and to safeguard the independence of the research staff in the pursuit of their studies and in the publication of the results of such studies. It is not a part of their function to determine, control, or influence the conduct of particular investigations or the conclusions reached."

The President bears final responsibility for the decision to publish a manuscript as a Brookings book or staff paper. In reaching his judgment on the competence, accuracy, and objectivity of each study, the President is advised by the director of the appropriate research program and weighs the views of a panel of expert outside readers who report to him in confidence on the quality of the work. Publication of a work signifies that it is deemed to be a competent treatment worthy of public consideration; such publication does not imply endorsement of conclusions or recommendations contained in the study.

The Institution maintains its position of neutrality on issues of public policy in order to safeguard the intellectual freedom of the staff. Hence interpretations or conclusions in Brookings publications should be understood to be solely those of the author or authors and should not be attributed to the Institution, to its trustees, officers, or other staff members, or to the organizations that support its research.

# Foreword

REGIONAL ORGANIZATIONS, units with jurisdictions encompassing several states, are an invention designed to improve the working of the American federal system. The Tennessee Valley Authority is the oldest and much the best known of such organizations, but there are many others, most of which were set up in the 1960s to plan and coordinate the economic development of depressed areas, such as Appalachia, or to coordinate planning for the development of river basins.

Despite their diverse forms and increased numbers, regional organizations in the United States remain experiments. They may help to resolve interstate conflicts or promote interstate cooperation. They may enable the federal government, a group of states, or the federal government and the states together to pursue public purposes for homogeneous areas that do not conform to established jurisdictions. They may also be a means of decentralizing federal administrative activities and improving coordination of such activities. How well regional organizations serve these objectives, how they may be improved, and whether to extend them are at issue.

This study classifies and compares various kinds of regional organizations and evaluates their effectiveness. It seeks to judge from their performance whether regional organizations should be established across the nation or whether regional activity should continue to be organized, as in the past, on an ad hoc basis, function by function and region by region.

The author, Martha Derthick, is a senior fellow in the Governmental Studies program at Brookings. Her associate in this project, Gary Bombardier, who is now a staff member of the Subcommittee on Intergovernmental Relations of the House Committee on Government Operations, prepared the chapter on Federal Regional Councils. Research assistance was provided by Janis Humphrey at the outset of the project and Joy Silver throughout. The latter did much of the interviewing of state officials and examination of regional files. Lawrence D. Brown made many helpful suggestions. In addition, the author wishes to thank the many persons, government officials for the most part, who made files available, gave interviews, offered criticism of chapter drafts, or participated in a seminar at Brookings at which preliminary findings were discussed. To name any of these persons risks omitting some unfairly and might imply agreement of some with views they do not share.

The project also benefited from the contributions of an advisory committee consisting of George Bell, James W. Fesler, Arthur Maass, James L. Sundquist, David B. Walker, and Edwin W. Webber, and from the comments of Jesse Burkhead.

The manuscript was edited by Elizabeth H. Cross; the index was prepared by Patricia P. B. Wells.

The Brookings Institution is grateful to the National Area Development Institute for acting as sponsor of the work, and to the Ford Foundation for a grant making such sponsorship possible. The views expressed are the author's and should not be attributed to either of these organizations, to the members of the advisory committee, or to the trustees, officers, or other staff members of the Brookings Institution.

KERMIT GORDON
*President*

*October 1973*
*Washington, D.C.*

# Contents

BETWEEN
STATE AND NATION

# [1]

# The Logic of
# Regional Organization

ONE of the recurring problems of government is how to perform functions that do not fit neatly into fixed geographic jurisdictions. Attempts to meet the problem have resulted in a number of improvisations in the United States, so-called regional organizations, some of which are the subject of this book. Their origins can be briefly stated.

In 1933 a newly elected president with an interest in regional planning believed that a government corporation should develop the Tennessee River and conserve the forests and soil of the valley, an area that extends into seven states. He proposed the *Tennessee Valley Authority* (TVA).

In the early 1950s New York City began developing the headwaters of the Delaware River in upper New York State to increase its municipal water supply. Officials in Philadelphia and other downstream communities were alarmed about their own supplies from the Delaware. Pennsylvania sued New York, and in 1954 the Supreme Court decreed an allocation of Delaware River water and appointed a river master. None of the states liked having the Supreme Court manage their water supply. In 1961 they formed the *Delaware River Basin Commission* (DRBC) to negotiate their differences and to develop the river. The United States joined the organization too, becoming a signatory to an interstate compact for the first time.

During the 1960 election campaign the Conference of Appalachian Governors called on the candidates to recognize the Appalachian region's need of help. President Kennedy, who had been much affected by the sight of Appalachian poverty during the campaign, responded by naming a federal-state committee to plan a program of special aid. Congress enacted this program in 1965 for the benefit of eleven (later, thirteen) states and created the *Appalachian Regional Commission* (ARC), a joint federal-state body, to plan and coordinate it.

As soon as the program for the Appalachian states was enacted, senators from other parts of the country, eager that their states should receive similar benefits, combined to sponsor Title V of the Public Works and Economic Development Act of 1965, which authorized joint federal-state commissions for regions that lagged behind the rest of the nation. By 1972, there were seven *Title V commissions*, whose chief function was planning the economic development of large areas throughout the country, from New England to the Northwest and from the southeastern Atlantic coast to the desert areas of the Southwest.

In the late 1950s a number of expert study groups and public officials believed that an organizational form was needed to coordinate planning for the major river basins, which normally extend into several states. Various federal interagency committees, created by executive action, existed for this purpose, but evaluators inside and outside the government criticized them sharply. The result was Title II of the Water Resources Planning Act of 1965, which authorized the creation of federal-state commissions for river basin planning as a standard form. By 1972, there were seven *Title II commissions*, covering most of the northern and western parts of the country.

By now there are enough regional organizations in American government and their forms are sufficiently varied to invite description and comparative analysis, in an attempt to reach conclusions that will be useful in considering the future of regional organizations. The organizations described are "regional" in the sense that their jurisdictions cover all or parts of several states.[1] This definition of region is arbitrary, of course. When persons in this

1. When an organization cuts across a state boundary, this alone does not make it regional for purposes of this analysis. It must do so on such a scale as to encompass all or parts of more than two states. Thus the Port of New York Authority is excluded. Although it certainly meets the criterion of a "leading case" set forth below, by this definition it fails to be regional.

country speak of a regional organization, they usually mean a unit that cuts across the existing boundaries of government to embrace some underlying social, economic, or natural entity. A region may be big or little; as a practical matter, regional organization generally seems to entail enlarging the scale of existing local or state governments. This study does not cover "substate" regionalism. It excludes local development districts, metropolitan governments, and all other attempts to consolidate or federate local units except those that have resulted from the activity of suprastate regional organizations.[2]

There has never been a sustained movement for regional organization that left its impress across the United States. Regionalism (it is not quite accurate to use so concrete a term as "regional organization") is one of those ideas that grips a few minds or much of an academic discipline, as it gripped sociologists and planners in the 1930s and economists and planners in the 1960s, but then disappears for a while.[3] It has been much subject to intellectual fad and fashion. Perhaps because the fashion has never gripped political scientists, the "regional idea" has not taken shape as a specific set of proposals for regional organization. There has been no consensus on what functions should be performed regionally nor on what the best regional forms might be. The most careful analysis of regional problems and functions, done in the 1930s by the National Resources Committee, reached the thoroughly pragmatic conclusion that the selection of an organizational type should depend on the

2. Those who wish to compare American experience with that of other countries may consult E. Kalk, ed., *Regional Planning and Regional Government in Europe* (The Hague: International Union of Local Authorities, 1971). On recent English experience, see Jesse Burkhead, "Federalism in a Unitary State: Regional Economic Planning in England," Occasional Paper 10 of the Metropolitan Studies Program (Syracuse University, Maxwell School, 1973; processed). In this country, the Advisory Commission on Intergovernmental Relations is preparing a comprehensive, three-volume report on substate regionalism, which complements the commission's Report A-39, *Multistate Regionalism* (Washington: ACIR, 1972), the subject matter of which is very like that in this book.

3. See, for example, John Friedmann and William Alonso, eds., *Regional Development and Planning* (M.I.T. Press, 1964); John R. Meyer, "Regional Economics: A Survey," *American Economic Review*, vol. 53 (March 1963), pp. 19–48; Merrill Jensen, ed., *Regionalism in America* (University of Wisconsin Press, 1952); Benton MacKaye, *The New Exploration: A Philosophy of Regional Planning* (Harcourt, Brace and World, 1962); Howard W. Odum and Harry E. Moore, eds., *American Regionalism* (Holt, 1938); *The Papers and Proceedings of the Regional Science Association* (1954 to present).

functions to be assigned, the area of operation, the constitutional powers required, and the incidence of benefits and costs.[4]

Whereas interest in regional forms has been intermittent and visionary, confined ordinarily to a few who have a taste for reform and refuse to be discouraged, opposition is ubiquitous if often inarticulate. It exists in the federal and state governments and government agencies whose functions and prerogatives would be challenged by the introduction of a rival organizational type. Regional organizations are excrescences on the constitutional system, unusual things that must be superimposed on the universe of functionally specialized federal and state agencies. The odds are against their being formed and, if formed, against their flourishing.[5]

For the most part, actual regional organizations have been improvised. In most cases their forms and functions have responded to opportunities of the moment and to the idealism and interests of their founders, tempered by political conditions at the time of their founding. In 1973, regional organizations in the United States remained anomalies or experiments or both. Whether to improve them and how, whether to extend them and in what form, are at issue, particularly in the field of economic development. The Nixon administration proposed in the early 1970s to end federal support for the regional commissions for economic development. The backers of the Appalachian Regional Commission countered by proposing that the form be repeated nationwide. Congress renewed the life of the Appalachian Regional Commission in 1971 and the administration withdrew its proposal in that case, but the future of the Title V commissions remains in doubt.[6] Organizational forms to manage water resources have been at issue for much of this century. As the variety of actual forms increases, the issues get more

4. National Resources Committee, *Regional Factors in National Planning* (1935), p. viii. For a similar conclusion, more recently arrived at, see Jefferson B. Fordham, *A Larger Concept of Community* (Louisiana State University Press, 1956), pp. 41–76. Political scientists have shown little serious interest in questions of space or area. Two notable exceptions are James W. Fesler, *Area and Administration* (University of Alabama Press, 1949), and Arthur Maass, ed., *Area and Power* (Free Press, 1939).

5. Roscoe C. Martin et al., *River Basin Administration and the Delaware* (Syracuse University Press, 1960), chap. 17.

6. In June 1973 Congress renewed authorization for the Title V commissions for one year, and the President signed the bill, saying that he continued to believe that support of the Title V commissions should be a state responsibility but that he was "willing to continue a limited amount of Federal funding for their projects during this one year of transition." White House press release, June 19, 1973.

complicated. In a massive report, the National Water Commission in 1972 found the federal-interstate compact commission to be the preferred institutional arrangement for water resources planning and management in multistate regions, yet only two such compacts exist, the compact commissions have had a hard time getting established, the executive branch opposed both of them, and the prospects for the form do not seem promising. At the same time, the National Water Commission did not repudiate the Title II commissions, which it said were "new and unique regional institutions," to be preferred to informal interagency committees, and "should be given a chance to develop joint coordinated comprehensive plans for their regions." Nor for that matter did the commission reject federal corporations. While it acknowledged that corporations of the scope and type of TVA were unlikely, it thought there might be "isolated situations" in which water resources projects might best be carried out by such an organization.[7] In the tradition of American government, this expert commission was eclectic and pragmatic.

When it comes to regional organizations, what works at all and what works best remain unsettled, but these questions are much more open to answers from observation than ever before. The great increase in the number and variety of regional organizations in the 1960s offers a considerable body of experience to examine.

## The Case for Regional Organization

At its most daring, the case for regional organization argues that the state governments are artificial creations, obsolete and too numerous, which should be replaced by larger governments rationally adapted to the "natural" or sociocultural features of American society.[8] In this radical form, as proposals for regional government, proposals for regional organization have no chance of adoption. The Constitution stipulates that states may not be joined to form

7. *Water Policies for the Future: Final Report to the President and to the Congress of the United States by the National Water Commission* (1973), chap. 11.

8. See William B. Munro, *The Invisible Government* (Macmillan, 1928), pp. 151–59; William Y. Elliott, *The Need for Constitutional Reform* (Whittlesey House, 1935), pp. 191 ff. For a more recent proposal, see the draft constitution prepared by Rexford G. Tugwell at the Center for the Study of Democratic Institutions, appearing in *Center Magazine*, vol. 3, September 1970.

a new state except with the consent of their legislatures and of Congress. Such actions would probably have to be approved in a popular referendum. It is hard to imagine that the people or legislature of a state would abolish it, and still harder to imagine that whole groups of states would voluntarily replace themselves with regional governments. Nothing remotely like that has happened so far. Nothing like it occurs in the cases to be described. On the contrary, state governments demonstrate their powers of survival.

In its more modest and pragmatic form, the main argument for regional organizations is that they are needed to respond to the problem of "scale" that arises when functions spill over state boundaries without, however, requiring nationwide action. The problem of scale may arise when actions in one state jurisdiction substantially affect the welfare of a neighboring jurisdiction, as when New York City's withdrawal of water from the Delaware River in upper New York State threatened cities downriver in Pennsylvania. As an economist would put it, adjustment of jurisdictional boundaries becomes necessary to encompass "externalities."[9] Rivers obviously invite regional organization, for they make their way to the ocean without regard to man-made boundaries of government. It is not surprising that three of the cases to be covered are organizations with a concern for water resources, or that some of the most powerful current arguments for regional organization come from specialists in water quality management.[10] The scale problem also arises when common social or economic characteristics or natural features extend across jurisdictional boundaries so that government activities ought to encompass the homogeneous area. This is the logic underlying the regional commissions for economic development, which are supposed to serve areas that have economic deprivation in common.[11]

9. An economist might also add that small units should be enlarged to capture whatever economies of scale can be realized in program planning and administration.

10. Allen V. Kneese and Blair T. Bower, *Managing Water Quality: Economics, Technology, Institutions* (Washington: Resources for the Future, 1968); Marc J. Roberts, "Organizing Water Pollution Control: The Scope and Structure of River Basin Authorities," *Public Policy*, vol. 19 (Winter 1971), pp. 75–141.

11. Most theoretical analyses of the scale problem have been addressed to metropolitan areas. See especially Vincent Ostrom, Charles M. Tiebout, and Robert Warren, "The Organization of Government in Metropolitan Areas: A Theoretical Inquiry," *American Political Science Review*, vol. 60 (December 1961), pp. 831–42; and Edward C. Banfield and Morton Grodzins, *Government and Housing in Metropolitan Areas*

As approaches to the scale problem—that is, as means for carrying out public functions on a regional scale—regional organizations may be divided into those with operating, management, or regulatory functions, and those that are for planning and coordination only. The Tennessee Valley Authority and the Delaware River Basin Commission fall into the first group; the Appalachian Regional Commission, the Title V commissions, and the Title II commissions into the second. At first glance anyway, making comparisons across these two categories is implausible and unfair. It would be absurd to stack the accomplishments of a Title II commission, which has the right only to prepare coordinated plans, against those of the Tennessee Valley Authority, a corporation with sweeping rights of ownership, development, and manufacture. Things so unlike cannot reasonably be compared. However, each category may be divided into subtypes, between which comparisons can be made.

While the TVA and the DRBC have similar functions, they are dissimilar in form. The DRBC is multipartite and representative; TVA is unitary and autonomous. The DRBC consists of representatives of four states and the United States; TVA was created by the United States and its governing board consists of three presidential appointees. Since their functions are so similar and their forms so different, comparison will entail judging the relative merit of the forms. Among the planning and coordinating organizations, distinctions of form are not so immediately apparent. All are representative. The ARC, Title V commissions, and Title II commissions are made up of representatives of the federal government and participating state governments, yet there is a significant conceptual difference between them, which is manifested in their form. The Title II commissions contain, besides a presidentially appointed chairman, a representative of each of the federal departments with an interest in river basin planning. They were conceived of as a way of bringing interested governments and government agencies together as peers in a common forum to prepare coordinated development plans. The organizations that will ultimately carry out the plans cooperate in the planning. In the ARC and the Title V commissions, the federal government is represented only by one presidential appointee, the federal cochairman. The federal execu-

(McGraw-Hill, 1958), chap. 2. More generally, see Arthur W. Macmahon, *Administering Federalism in a Democracy* (Oxford University Press, 1972).

tive agencies are not represented directly although some of them are expected to carry out the regional commissions' plans. The rationale for these commissions is that an independent coordinator, newly introduced into a milieu of hitherto uncoordinated organizations, can define regional goals for these other organizations to pursue. This latter type of organization will be called a "catalyst," to be distinguished from the "forum of peers." Neither of these subtypes has the right to pursue independently the goals it defines. Whereas the forum of peers derives from agencies that have operating functions, the catalyst has no such relation to the agencies yet is supposed to influence their conduct. The question is which of these two types of planning and coordinating organizations is preferable.

While regional organizations are justified primarily as responses to the scale problem—that is, to a lack of fit between the areal jurisdictions of governments and the demands of governmental functions—none of them is justified in that way alone. They are also advanced as solutions to what may be called the problems of "coordination" and of "centralization."

The coordination problem pervades American government. Familiarly stated, the problem is that the functions of federal government agencies overlap, with the result that the agencies compete for program and project opportunities, waste funds, embarrass themselves and the President by fighting publicly, and while doing more or less the same things, do them for different purposes. The classic case, which was abundantly documented by political scientists and presidential commissions in the 1940s and 1950s, is water resources development.[12] The Army Corps of Engineers, the Bureau of Reclamation of the Department of the Interior, and the Soil Conservation Service of the Department of Agriculture all build works for using and conserving water. A generation ago, they more than once independently made major plans for developing the same basin and then fought publicly over which plan would be carried out. Under sharp criticism and the threat of action by the Executive

12. See especially Arthur Maass, *Muddy Waters* (Harvard University Press, 1951), chap. 5; Henry C. Hart, *The Dark Missouri* (University of Wisconsin Press, 1957), chaps. 5–8; and Commission on Organization of the Executive Branch of the Government, *Reorganization of the Department of the Interior*, A report to the Congress (March 1949), with app. L, "Task Force Report on Natural Resources," and app. Q, "Task Force Report on Public Works."

Office of the President, the agencies themselves worked out a means —the interagency committee, formed both at the Washington level and in several of the major basins—to lessen their conflicts. These committees also became a means for coordination between development agencies and agencies with an interest in pollution control, conservation, and recreation. The committees thus created evolved into a statutory form, the Title II commissions. That several of the cases deal with water resources is due not just to the regional character of river basin development, but also to the severity of the coordination problem in that field. The Title II commissions were formed as a response to the coordination problem quite as much as to the problem of scale.

More recently, grants-in-aid for social and economic purposes have given rise to a somewhat different formulation of the coordination problem. Here too the problem in its familiar form persists. Different agencies give grants for similar purposes with the result that their activities overlap, causing confusion among local applicants and inefficiencies and inconsistencies in federal administration. Beyond that, the various federal agencies are said to be failing to collaborate to ameliorate social conditions. In this formulation of the coordination problem, the object of federal activity is not a project for which different agencies compete; it is a complex social "problem"—the underdeveloped region, the slum, the ghetto, the deprivation of a family, the delinquency of a child—the "solution" to which requires concentrated, collaborative attention by a series of federal agencies. Failures to coordinate mean that government action is ineffective (rather than inefficient). It becomes necessary to foster collaboration of federal agencies in the field, as near as possible to the problem that is the alleged target of coordinated activity.[13]

Whichever perception of the coordination problem prevails, it is combined with another, related perception, which is that agencies specialized by function are too powerful. Not only do they fight with each other in unseemly fashion and fail to cooperate in problem-solving; they are too committed to narrow, programmatic spe-

---

13. For an extended statement of the problem and evaluation of one attempt to respond, see Abt Associates, Inc., "A Study of the Neighborhood Center Pilot Program" (prepared for Bureau of the Budget), 4 vols. (Cambridge, Mass.: Abt Associates, 1969; processed).

cialties and indifferent to direction from "generalists" who allegedly see social problems in all their complexity and can weigh the relative value of specialized programs. An organization specialized by area rather than function is conceived as a setting within which generalists can influence functional specialists. The area may be defined on any geographic scale—the neighborhood, the city, a metropolitan area, and so on. In these particular cases, it is defined as a suprastate region.

To enlarge the possibilities for analytical comparison, the cases of regional organization include one that is *primarily* a response to the coordination problem, the Federal Regional Councils, which were created by executive action in the late 1960s and which bring together the regional directors of the major federal grant-in-aid agencies in each of the ten standard federal administrative regions. For the time being at least, these councils are not conceived of as responses to the scale problem; there is no presumption that a common regional interest requires an organized response by government. In their case, the region is merely a convenient level or point at which to organize certain federal administrative activities, including coordination of grant-in-aid administration.[14]

Apart from their common emphasis on area rather than function, regional organizations respond to the coordination problem in different ways. The most frequent way is the single federal agent, a presidential appointee, who in three cases (the DRBC, the ARC, and the Title V commissions) is the sole federal member of a federal-state organization and is supposed to speak there for all interested federal agencies. This approach is also embodied in modified form in the Title II commissions, which combine a federal chairman, who is a presidential appointee, with representatives of federal agencies. A second approach, represented by the Federal Regional Councils and again the Title II commissions, is the interagency coordinating council, although the Title II commissions contain states as well as federal agency representatives and have as chairman

14. For an analysis of the logic of federal coordination at the regional level, see Charles L. Schultze, *The Politics and Economics of Public Spending* (Brookings Institution, 1968), pp. 132 ff.; Schultze's testimony in *Reorganization of Executive Departments*, Hearings before the House Committee on Government Operations, 92 Cong. 1 sess. (1971), pp. 260–63; and James L. Sundquist, *Making Federalism Work: A Study of Program Coordination at the Community Level* (Brookings Institution, 1969), chap. 7, especially pp. 272–77.

a single federal agent. A third approach is transfer of the coordination function to another level of government. The task of properly relating federal expenditures to objectives and to one another is that of the state's chief executive. Reliance on the governor is to some degree implicit in all the joint (federal-state) organizations, but only the ARC has explicated it as an approach to the federal government's coordination problem and has designed grant-in-aid administration specifically to enhance the governor's coordinating role. Finally, there is the multipurpose agency (TVA) within which are contained functions that are normally carried out by more than one federal agency.

One purpose of this study is to compare the results of these different responses to the need for coordination—their effectiveness in reducing conflict and inconsistency among federal executive agencies and in concerting federal agency actions in pursuit of common objectives. Only TVA does not depend on harmonizing federal agency actions but is supposed to improve coordination by the comprehensiveness of its own purposes. Precisely because it does not depend on other executive organizations and can treat coordination of different functions and purposes autonomously, it may well prove the most effective coordinator.

The organizations are engaged in such different activities and the criteria of successful coordination are so imprecise that no more than rough comparisons can be made. But it should be possible to generalize about the most common technique of coordination, to compare it with other techniques, and to use the experience of regional organizations generally to reflect on the nature of coordination within the federal government. Though regional organizations are an atypical form, they may nonetheless illuminate typical features of American government.

As federal activity expands, making American government as a whole more centralized, centralization evokes a critical response. At least since the New Deal, it has been said that government in the United States is too centralized.[15] One alleged consequence of this

15. Much of the literature on regionalism contains this theme. In 1935, Elliott anticipated "a degree of federal centralization unheard of in past practice and totally contrary to the theory of our constitution." His proposal for regional commonwealths "would revive our drooping federalism and stay the present march of centralization in Washington." *Need for Constitutional Reform*, pp. 186, 193. See also Odum and Moore, *American Regionalism*, p. 242. In general, scholarly literature on federalism

is a loss of citizen interest and participation in government; the voters, it is said, cannot control a government in Washington and cease to care. These regional organizations have not usually been justified as responses to this particular problem. It is hard to see how they could be, since none is responsible to an electorate and except for TVA they are barely visible to any public. Only diligent and attentive citizens know that they exist.[16] They are often justified, however, as responses to a different element of the centralization problem, which is Washington's alleged inability to govern the country. Federal laws and regulations are uniformly applicable but not uniformly adaptable to the wide variety of local conditions and needs. Federal bureaucracies move slowly, amid rising amounts of red tape. The founders of the ARC were reacting to this centralization problem when they called for a program specially designed for the region. For example, they argued that the federal highway program was unsuited to Appalachia because it made construction contingent on the volume of traffic, whereas Appalachian roads should be located to induce traffic and thereby stimulate economic growth. The ARC has deliberately sought to keep its own grant-in-aid guidelines simple and flexible so that they may easily be adapted to individual states.

The particular centralization problem to which regional organizations are meant to respond should perhaps be thought of as a "central bureaucracy" problem. These organizations are not meant to stay the expansion of federal activity. They are federal in origin or embody a federal presence. Their presumed advantage is that they assure some flexibility and adaptiveness in federal executive actions, by constituting either an alternative to line agencies for per-

has been descriptive rather than normative, concerned more with the origins of the federal system and its characteristics than with prescriptions for federal-state relations. See, for example, Morton Grodzins, *The American System* (Rand McNally, 1966); Daniel J. Elazar, *American Federalism: A View from the States* (Crowell, 1966); and Aaron Wildavsky, ed., *American Federalism in Perspective* (Little, Brown, 1967). The complaint of excessive centralization comes mainly from popular sources or interest groups, although a series of official or semiofficial reports in the 1950s, notably that of the Commission on Intergovernmental Relations, recommended reductions in federal activity or ways to limit its expansion. See Grodzins, *American System*, chap. 12.

16. According to two Gallup polls in 1945, 60 to 67 percent of the nation's population had heard of the Tennessee Valley Authority. Hadley Cantril, ed., *Public Opinion, 1935–1946* (Princeton University Press, 1951). It seems unlikely that a national poll-taker would have occasion to ask the question about other regional organizations.

forming federal executive functions or a medium for influencing such agencies.

Of itself, the regionalism of the organizations counteracts centralization. Regional organizations are alike in that they embody some dispersion of federal authority to agencies with provincial jurisdictions, although this does not necessarily mean that they have offices in provincial locations. The TVA, DRBC, and Title II commissions have headquarters in their regions, the ARC is located in Washington, and most of the Title V commissions have offices in both. Beyond the common regionalism of the organizations, several different strategies of decentralization may be distinguished. The most common, found in the DRBC, the ARC, Title V commissions, and Title II commissions, is "jointness": federal and state members are combined in one organization so that federal executive decisions may be accessible to state influence and plans for the two levels of government or grant-in-aid regulations may be made cooperatively. In TVA's case, the organization is purely federal but has a high degree of authority and flexibility so that it may adapt operations to local conditions. Finally, there is the strategy represented by the Federal Regional Councils. Within federal line agencies having national jurisdictions, authority is delegated to field officials at common locations, and these officials are brought together in a coordinating forum, the interagency council.[17]

As with strategies of coordination, these techniques of decentralization will be compared for what they may show about the relative merits of particular regional organizations. The effectiveness of the regional organizations as agents of decentralization may be judged by a combination of two criteria: the *amount of federal authority* the regional organization has, and the *accessibility* of that authority to nonfederal interests. By these standards, the DRBC seems likely to be the most effective, since it combines a broad grant of federal authority with a joint structure, which guarantees the member states access to the regional organization's decisions. TVA can match the DRBC in scope of authority and other organizations can match its jointness, but it is unique in combining the two.

17. As elements of the central government, regional organizations are instruments of decentralization. For the states, they are instruments of centralization, in that they aggregate state activity. This aggregation of state activity is one aspect of the organizations' response to the problem of scale.

Again precise comparisons of techniques or organizations cannot be made, but the most common technique, jointness, will be appraised and compared with other techniques, and the experience of regional organizations will be applied to analysis of federal-state relations.

## Why These Organizations Were Chosen

If defined broadly, the universe of regional organizations is very large. It might be said to include federal administrative units with regional jurisdictions, of which there are hundreds. Presumably it includes the many informal interagency coordinating committees that have planned river basin development in the past two decades and commissions that have been created by interstate compacts.[18] It ranges from an autonomous, sharply defined organization such as TVA to far less autonomous, transitory, and ill-defined organizations. The universe includes a variety of legal types. Regional organizations may be created by interstate compacts, parallel state legislation, federal legislation, federal and state legislation combined, or executive action. The universe changes with time.

Among regional organizations, those chosen for analysis represent efforts at structural reform of at least a limited sort. Unlike, say, regional administrative units of federal executive agencies, they are not typical, well-established elements of government. At least in the short run and maybe in the long, these organizations are deviations from the norm. Among the efforts at regional organizations as reforms, those that have the greatest actual or potential impact on American government seem the most interesting. This led to selection of two categories—"leading" and "generalized" cases.

18. On river basin coordinating organizations, see Gary Warren Hart, *Institutions for Water Planning—Institutional Arrangements: River Basin Commissions, Inter-Agency Committees, and Ad Hoc Coordinating Committees* (National Technical Information Service for the National Water Commission, 1971); on interstate compact commissions, Frederick L. Zimmermann and Mitchell Wendell, *The Interstate Compact since 1925* (Council of State Governments, 1951), especially pp. 13–29; Weldon V. Barton, *Interstate Compacts in the Political Process* (University of North Carolina Press, 1965); Edward J. Cleary, *The ORSANCO Story: Water Quality Management in the Ohio Valley under an Interstate Compact* (Resources for the Future, 1967); Richard H. Leach and Redding S. Sugg, Jr., *The Administration of Interstate Compacts* (Louisiana State University Press, 1959); Marian E. Ridgeway, *Interstate Compacts: A Question of Federalism* (Southern Illinois University Press, 1971).

The TVA, the DRBC, and the ARC are leading cases in that each has formal authority or other organizational resources that distinguish it from the rest.

TVA is in a class by itself. Created to develop and conserve the Tennessee Valley, it has become the largest producer of electric power in the country and the exclusive supplier of electricity to an area of 90,000 square miles. It owns nearly $4 billion in capital assets. Including those who are temporary, it has more than 20,000 employees, which makes it bigger than some federal departments, and its budget is more than $1 billion a year. Although many proposals to reproduce the TVA have been introduced in Congress, none has passed.

When the DRBC was created in 1961 by the United States, New York, Pennsylvania, New Jersey, and Delaware, the federal government joined an interstate compact for the first time. The compact gives the commission broad powers "to encourage and provide for the planning, conservation, utilization, development, management, and control of the water resources of the basin." The commission has a staff of fifty-five and a budget of $1.5 million.[19] The DRBC, unique for almost a decade, is so no longer. A commission modeled after it was created for the Susquehanna basin in 1970.

Although technically the ARC has no operating functions and is a planner and coordinator only, in practice it makes policy for and to some extent administers a major program of federal aid to the Appalachian region, an area now defined as including 397 counties in states ranging from Mississippi to New York. Appropriations for this program are currently over $300 million a year. The commission has a staff of over a hundred. The ARC has a number of imitators in the Title V commissions, but they are smaller and less well financed. Like the TVA and the DRBC, the ARC stands out.

The other three organizations are generalized cases in that the authorizing actions created a class of organizations rather than a single organization. The generalized cases are all very much weaker —that is, they have much less authority and other organizational resources—than the leading cases.

Like the ARC the Title V commissions are authorized to prepare

19. By contrast, the Ohio River Valley Water Sanitation Commission, the most nearly comparable interstate compact commission, had a budget in 1971 of $375,600 and a staff of thirteen.

comprehensive and coordinated plans, but unlike the ARC they have never been able to acquire large spending programs of their own. Appropriations for the Title V program in fiscal year 1972 were $39 million, an average of less than $8 million a commission. The average staff size is twenty-three.

The Title II commissions, in contrast to the TVA and DRBC, are strictly planning and coordinating organizations. They have no operating, management, or regulatory functions. The average size of staff is eleven, and their budgets have been $300,000 to $400,000.

Of the six cases, only the Federal Regional Councils are not authorized by law, receive no appropriations, have no staffs except what the member agencies assign to them, and have no offices of their own. Calling them organizations at all is stretching a point. They are forums within which member organizations meet for purposes of coordinating federal grant-in-aid administration. They are also the only one of the six that covers the whole country.

The leading cases presumably are the regional organizations that have the deepest impact on American society and are therefore most worth appraising in detail. If regional organizations matter at all, the leading cases should show whether and how. On the other hand, the generalized cases presumably have the widest impact, and if regional organizations are to be extended, their experience may provide a better basis for predicting what the results are likely to be.

The next six chapters will describe the cases of regional organization, covering their origins, their main activities on behalf of their regions, their functioning as agents of coordination and decentralization, and the outcome of attempts to duplicate or extend them.[20] While these accounts may be of interest to a reader who wants to know about any of the organizations for its own sake, because they are constructed with particular analytical purposes in mind, the accounts are selective.

With the conspicuous exception of TVA, most of these organizations have been in existence a short time and are at least a step removed from the field of action. Except for TVA, they are composed of representatives of other organizations or of whole governments; they either have no right to carry out operating functions or are unable, as is true of the DRBC, to exploit what rights they

20. For easy reference, summary data about the organizations are given in the Appendix.

have; and they are very small. Hence this is not an account primarily of government in action, but rather of governments trying to organize to improve their actions. It is a study of attempts to revise habitual modes of action.

# [2]

# The Tennessee Valley Authority

By ANY TANGIBLE MEASURE, such as revenue, employment, or capital assets, the TVA is by far the most important regional organization in the United States. A public corporation, TVA was created by Congress in 1933 "to improve the navigability and to provide for the flood control of the Tennessee River; to provide for reforestation and the proper use of marginal lands in the Tennessee Valley; to provide for the agricultural and industrial development of said valley; to provide for the national defense by the creation of a corporation for the operation of Government properties at and near Muscle Shoals in the State of Alabama."[1] The statute enumerates many specific powers, most having to do with the holding of real property, the production and use of fertilizer and other nitrogen products, and the production, distribution, and sale of electric power.

Most of TVA's operations take place in the Tennessee basin, an area of 41,000 square miles that includes a large part of Tennessee and smaller parts of Kentucky, Mississippi, Alabama, Georgia, North Carolina, and Virginia. TVA supplies electric power for a much larger area, 91,000 square miles, in the same states.

## Origin and Conception

Early in the fall of 1933, a few months after the TVA act was passed, the three newly appointed board members sought to learn from a presidential adviser, Rexford G. Tugwell, what the President thought the TVA ought to be. Were they to constitute a govern-

1. 48 Stat. 58.

18

ment, a planning and coordinating agency, or a public corporation devoted to certain specific tasks? A reading of the law and most of the history of the law would have supported the third interpretation. Tugwell, on the other hand, suggested that the Authority "must approximate a government and perhaps in important matters supersede the states."[2] Conceptions of the Authority's purpose differed, and for several years would continue to differ within the Authority itself.

During the 1920s, a congressional block led by Senator George Norris of Nebraska sought to create a public corporation to hold and operate certain government facilities at Muscle Shoals, Alabama, on the Tennessee River. These properties consisted of two nitrate plants, which the federal government had built during World War I to produce explosives, and a large dam to supply power for the plants. The plants were intended to manufacture fertilizer in peacetime, but they lay idle after the war while the government tried to arrive at a plan for their disposition. Norris was determined that the right to generate power at Muscle Shoals, which was an excellent site for that purpose, should remain in public hands. Besides winning support from a small number of progressives who shared his ideological aim, Norris's proposal for a "Muscle Shoals Corporation of the United States" had support from the South, a region where farming depends heavily on fertilizer and which therefore sought a cheap, abundant supply of it. The essential issue in the long debate over Muscle Shoals was whether the facilities should be owned publicly or privately. Republican presidents twice vetoed Norris's bills. By 1930 the Senate Committee on Agriculture and Forestry—of which Norris was chairman and which had jurisdiction because of the plants' capacity to make fertilizer—was growing weary of the question. "Muscle Shoals is an old friend," it reported. "After more than 10 years of investigation, discussion, and consideration it is still with us. Up and down the ragged road of legislative consideration we have traveled together through many weary and discouraging epochs of parliamentary mysteries and doubts. Senators have been born into and have died out of its various controversies, and, like Jarndyce v. Jarndyce, it is still with us."[3]

---

2. R. G. Tugwell and E. C. Banfield, "Grass Roots Democracy—Myth or Reality?" *Public Administration Review*, vol. 10 (Winter 1950), pp. 47–49.

3. S. Rept. 19, *Congressional Record*, vol. 72, pt. 6, 71 Cong. 2 sess. (1930), p. 6408.

The election of 1932 made enactment of Norris's bill certain by bringing to office a president who would sign it. More, this particular president enlarged the conception of the new organization. It would be something greater than a corporation with specific tasks to perform. "It is clear that the Muscle Shoals development is but a small part of the potential public usefulness of the entire Tennessee River," he declared. "Such use, if envisioned in its entirety, transcends mere power development; it enters the wide fields of flood control, soil erosion, afforestation, elimination from agricultural use of marginal lands, and distribution and diversification of industry. In short, this power development of war days leads logically to national planning for a complete river watershed involving many States and the future lives and welfare of millions. It touches and gives life to all forms of human concerns."[4] The Muscle Shoals Corporation of the United States had become the Tennessee Valley Authority.

The change in conception, though mainly rhetorical, altered the content of the bill. The preamble was lengthened, more or less to paraphrase the President's message, and two sections were added to lay the basis for national planning in the Tennessee Valley. One of these authorized the President to make such general plans for the basin as might be "useful to the Congress and to the several States in guiding and controlling the extent, sequence, and nature of development." The second instructed him to recommend legislation to the Congress from time to time to realize a wide range of public purposes in the valley, including flood control, navigation, generation of electric power, proper use of marginal lands, reforestation, and "the economic and social well-being of the people."[5] Yet most of the powers of the corporation—as distinguished from the President, who was the beneficiary of these two sections—remained as Norris had drafted them. On its face, the statute made the Authority more the instrument of public ownership that Norris had sponsored than the national agency for regional planning that Roosevelt spoke of.

4. *The Public Papers and Addresses of Franklin D. Roosevelt*, vol. 2: *The Year of Crisis, 1933* (Random House, 1938), p. 122. For a detailed account of Roosevelt's role in the founding of TVA, see Frank Freidel, *Franklin D. Roosevelt: Launching the New Deal* (Little, Brown, 1973), pp. 350–54.

5. Secs. 22 and 23.

While Norris had consistently favored development of the Tennessee for a variety of purposes—navigation, flood control, and power—his bills did not envision a single new organization with comprehensive powers for developing the river. Authorization for construction would have remained with the secretary of war. With building dams as with generating power, Norris's prime concern was that a public agency be in control. Under the revisions of 1933, flood control and navigation were included among the specific tasks of the new corporation, which was empowered to "construct dams, reservoirs, power houses, power structures, transmission lines, navigation projects, and incidental works in the Tennessee River and its tributaries." Thus the TVA displaced the Corps of Engineers in the valley. Besides owning and operating the federal property already built at Muscle Shoals, TVA would carry out development all along the river.[6]

The creation of a single agency with wide-ranging development powers for a whole river basin fulfilled an ideal of the conservation movement. "Each stream is essentially a unit from its source to the sea," the National Conservation Commission had declared in 1908. Development should encompass the whole unit, not just isolated projects, and plans should extend "to all uses of the waters and benefits to be derived from their control." The National Waterways Commission reiterated these themes in 1912, and during the New Deal they would find expression in the work of the National Resources Board and its successors.[7] And yet, although TVA was the first and most important embodiment of the ideal, as such it

6. 48 Stat. 61; and Preston J. Hubbard, *Origins of the TVA: The Muscle Shoals Controversy, 1920–1932* (Vanderbilt University Press, 1961), especially pp. 75–76, 193, 217, 313–14. I have tried to trace the origin of the new language by examining documents at the Franklin D. Roosevelt Library in Hyde Park, New York, and the Norris papers in the Library of Congress, and in correspondence with Arthur E. Morgan, without success. The language first appeared in H.R. 5081 of the Seventy-third Congress, as reported by the House Military Affairs Committee on April 20, 1933. A minority of that committee objected: "Flood control and navigation are matters which naturally come under the direction of the Army engineers and at no time during the hearings on this bill were any of the Army engineers called before the committee to testify on any of these matters. Neither were there any communications from the Secretary of War, or anyone connected with the Department of War, sent to the committee on this subject." H. Rept. 48, 73 Cong. 1 sess. (1933).

7. *Water Resources Activities in the United States: Reviews of National Water Resources During the Past Fifty Years*, printed for the use of the Senate Select Committee on National Water Resources, 86 Cong. 1 sess. (1959), pp. 6, 8–9, 16–21.

was an accident—the by-product of the particular issue and opportunity that arose in connection with the Muscle Shoals properties.

If there was a concept of coordination in the act of 1933, it remained implicit and very different from the concepts that informed the regional organizations that came later. In general the others have been created to resolve conflicts or concert action among different governments and government agencies. For this purpose they have brought government or agency representatives together in a common organizational setting. TVA does not do that. It is an independent actor, an instrument of ownership and development created by the federal government in pursuit of federal purposes. If, in the eyes of New Deal officials, it was to be a coordinator, it was so in the broad sense that any government or multipurpose government agency is a coordinator: it concerts a variety of individual and group actions in pursuit of the purposes it defines. If TVA was designed to resolve conflict, the conflict was the ultimate one between man and nature, not the official struggles between elements of the federal bureaucracy. Tugwell wrote in 1935 that if TVA succeeded it might "furnish a new pattern for civilization. . . . Yet the difficulties are very great. Nature has been grievously hurt and man is as yet unrepentant. The problem is a double one of repairing the damage and of conviction of sin."[8] There has always been an element of romance in TVA.

Given the differing conceptions of the TVA and the vagueness of the New Deal conception, the three-man board would have plenty of scope for choosing its course. The board would determine which conception would prevail. As it happened, TVA became a performer of specific tasks, not a comprehensive regional planner or regional government. Sections 22 and 23 of the act, the planning sections, have barely been used, and a regional planning unit created at the outset was eliminated after 1938. Among specific tasks, TVA has concentrated heavily on the generation and sale of electric power. It did not supersede the state governments. It accommodated to them and developed an organizational ideology, the "grass-roots doctrine," that made a great virtue of having done so. Tugwell, who had advised the directors to constitute a government, later would acknowledge that they had rejected his advice. "From 1936

8. Rexford G. Tugwell, *The Battle for Democracy* (Columbia University Press, 1935), p. 21.

on," he wrote, "the TVA should have been called the Tennessee Valley Power Production and Flood Control Corporation."[9]

## The Authority's Activity

The 650-mile-long Tennessee is the fourth largest river in the United States in terms of flow, and because of TVA it is the most thoroughly developed and controlled.[10] TVA has developed the main stem and its major tributaries. It has built twenty-three dams and acquired five others from the Corps of Engineers or the Tennessee Electric Power Company. These dams have turned the river into an unbroken stairway of lakes deep enough to be navigated the year round. TVA has also built more than 100 miles of connecting channels on the tributaries. The series of dams and reservoirs helps to control floods not just in the Tennessee but also in the Ohio and the Mississippi, which it flows into. The navigation channel connects the valley with ports in twenty-one states and carries about 3.5 billion ton-miles of freight each year. The major work of development is completed, yet lesser projects continue. Of TVA's request for $63.7 million in appropriations for fiscal 1973, slightly more than half was for water resources projects.[11]

TVA supplies electric power for an area of 6 million people. Initially it generated electricity at dams as one product of developing the river, but after World War II TVA's power program acquired a life of its own. It began building coal- and then nuclear-powered generating plants. In 1971 this system was the biggest in the country, generating over 91 billion kilowatt-hours, of which less than 20 percent came from water power. The geographic boundaries of the system have been stabilized by law, but the generating capacity continues to increase. Revenue from sales pays for operations and for part of construction costs. TVA finances construction

9. Tugwell and Banfield, "Grass Roots Democracy," p. 50.
10. Harry Wiersema, "The River Control System," in Roscoe C. Martin, ed., *TVA: The First Twenty Years* (University of Alabama Press and University of Tennessee Press, 1956), pp. 77–94. This is a comprehensive summary of TVA's activities. See also two pamphlets issued by the TVA: *TVA Today 1972* and *Facts about TVA Operations 1969.*
11. *Public Works for Water and Power Development and Atomic Energy Commission Appropriation Bill, 1973,* Hearings before a Subcommittee of the House Appropriations Committee, 92 Cong. 2 sess. (1972), pt. 3, pp. 1117 ff.

also through bond issues. Of more than $1 billion in TVA expenditures in fiscal 1971, $930 million went for the power program. Of that, $476 million was capital outlay.

TVA conducts research on fertilizer, manufactures it in limited quantities, and distributes it for demonstration and experimental use on farms. Under TVA ownership, the World War I nitrate plant at Muscle Shoals has become a national fertilizer development center. Most of the demonstration farms are located in the Tennessee Valley, but TVA's fertilizer program operates in the rest of the country as well. Agricultural colleges in nearly every state collaborate with TVA on educational projects, and several hundred fertilizer plants throughout the country are licensed to use its developments. TVA spent $19.5 million in fiscal 1971 on the fertilizer program.

TVA does a good many other things too, but they are relatively minor compared to these three and often are incidental to them. It has long had a forestry program under which it distributes seedlings and promotes conservation. It has given planning assistance to state and local governments, usually those that were disrupted by its development projects. It has developed recreation lands and other public facilities for state and local ownership and management, again usually as a by-product of developing the river. It developed and manages one very large recreation area, Land between the Lakes, astride the Kentucky-Tennessee border. It undertakes local flood protection projects. It has a program of tributary area development through which it aids rural communities with small investments of its own, assistance in getting help from other federal agencies, and encouragement for self-improvement. Early in its life, it built a new town—Norris, Tennessee.

In sum, TVA's activities are varied yet specialized. Tugwell was not far wrong when he said TVA was a power production and flood control corporation. This specialization has disappointed those who like him hoped that TVA would be something more. It has not approximated a regional government, and in no important respect has it superseded the states or their local governments.

The simplest explanation for TVA's failure to take on a wider range of functions and to perform them more aggressively is that a majority of the original board did not believe it should. The chairman, Arthur E. Morgan, was committed to the New Deal's vision of the TVA as a comprehensive social reformer. The other two members—Harcourt A. Morgan, who was in charge of the agricultural program, and David E. Lilienthal, in charge of the power program—were pursuing purposes that conflicted with Arthur Morgan's and impelled the organization in other directions. The two-man majority prevailed. Persistently defeated within the Authority and publicly hostile to the men who were defeating him, Arthur Morgan was removed from office by the President in 1938.

Arthur Morgan lost control of the TVA as soon as it was organized. At the very first meeting he and Lilienthal clashed over the strategy of relations with utility companies. Lilienthal, a young lawyer who had started a career in utility regulation, was eager for a fight. Morgan was not—the new social and economic order he sought must come about by "the democratic process of voluntary general agreement." Harcourt Morgan was a mediator on this occasion, but before long Arthur Morgan alienated him too with "visionary" plans for the TVA. Arthur Morgan proposed, for example, that TVA develop a general social and economic plan for the valley, begin an ambitious program to create public forests, and sponsor a study of the proper functions of the real estate man in an organized society, after which it would refuse to deal with real estate men who did not adopt TVA's policy. He also suggested a separate coinage for the valley, and a change in the laws of land ownership so that land could be taken away from farmers who misused it. Harcourt Morgan was a pragmatic man whose life had been spent in the region in the service of its farmers and agricultural schools. He thought Arthur Morgan's schemes "impracticable" or "clearly outside the scope of our responsibility under the law." [12] At this point, within two months of the Authority's first meeting, Lilienthal and Harcourt Morgan combined to limit Arthur Morgan's authority and discretion within the organization, and ultimately to defeat his conception of what it should be and do.

Lilienthal committed TVA to a major power program and led

12. Arthur M. Schlesinger, Jr., *The Coming of the New Deal* (Houghton Mifflin, 1959), p. 327; *The Journals of David E. Lilienthal*, vol. 1: *The TVA Years, 1939–1945* (Harper and Row, 1964), p. 39; *Investigation of the Tennessee Valley Authority*, Hearings before the Joint Committee on the Investigation of the Tennessee Valley Authority, 75 Cong. 3 sess. (1939), pp. 99–103, 105 ff. On the conflict within the board, see also Thomas K. McCraw, *Morgan vs. Lilienthal: The Feud within the TVA* (Loyola University Press, 1970).

the ensuing campaign against the private utilities ("the most brazen crowd in the country").[13] This choice was advantageous to TVA politically, for it stirred the public's imagination and evoked the President's support.[14] The battle against the utilities for control of the power market in the valley helped build a large and stable constituency. TVA became a symbol for the progressive coalition, and as long as that coalition survived nationally, TVA could count on support in Congress. The generation and sale of power were also advantageous to TVA financially. TVA was authorized to keep revenue from power sales. Concentrating on the power program has enabled it to be largely self-sustaining, though it continues to receive appropriations (about $60 million a year as of the early 1970s) for other functions, and it has sometimes had to request appropriations also for the construction of new generating facilities when income was insufficient for that purpose.

Harcourt Morgan committed the organization to working through state and local institutions, a practice that Lilienthal later articulated as the "grass-roots" philosophy of TVA. Morgan stated the case for this as early as October 1933 in a memorandum on the section of the TVA act that gives the President authority to make surveys and plans for development of the valley. It is one of the sections that were added in 1933 in the expectation of making TVA a national agency for regional planning. The President had delegated his authority to the TVA, and Harcourt Morgan in effect proposed that TVA delegate it in turn. He suggested that "plans will be futile unless in their formulation the people of the Valley and their agencies have participated. For the Authority to proceed in

13. *Journals*, vol. 1, p. 150.

14. Lilienthal wrote in his diary (ibid., p. 107):

"Why is it that the 'water control,' the 'save the soil' and the 'unified program of land and water' aspect of TVA is such a sad failure, so far as capturing the general public imagination is concerned? And why has the power program, from the time Senator Norris used that issue, years ago, been such a success, so far as public interest and concern goes?

"Isn't the answer that all the eloquence about land and water omits two factors almost essential to wide public interest of a lively kind, to wit, emphasis upon human beings and a fight? In my activities 'crusading' on the power issue, when we were surrounded by a 'ring of steel,' and the getting of a market presented a problem indeed, I sensed the crucial importance of stressing the *human* factor, the concrete picture of men and women benefiting from low electric rates, etc. . . . And, of course, the utility companies furnished the 'fight' element."

the making of surveys and plans without such work being in collaboration with and in harmony with the existing agencies, will
necessarily breed antagonism [and] distrust."[15] What Harcourt
Morgan preached for TVA's planning, he practiced in its agricultural program, for which he was responsible. This helped win acceptance of TVA in the region.[16]

The strategic choice that the first directors fought over was not
simply a matter of what the TVA should become or do. Just as important, it was a choice of which organizations to challenge. Arthur
Morgan, like Tugwell, would have challenged state and local governments. One of TVA's functions, he suggested in 1933, was to
remedy the chaos of local government.[17] Lilienthal sought to challenge private organizations, the public utility companies, and this
was far more realistic both legally and politically. TVA bought the
utilities' properties in the valley with congressional consent. It could
not legally buy the state and local governments as it bought the
property of the Tennessee Electric Power Company. It might have
spent money independently for functions that had traditionally
belonged to them, but it is unlikely that Congress would have made
appropriations for such activities.

It is arguable that if at least one other member had shared Arthur
Morgan's conception of TVA it would have evolved very differ-
ently, yet in view of the advantages to the organization of the course
the board majority chose, it would be wrong to interpret their
choice as simply the expression of personal beliefs. In retrospect,
it seems clear that the Lilienthal–Harcourt Morgan majority responded realistically to the legal and political environment of the
TVA and to the needs of the new organization, and that any but
an eccentric set of directors would sooner or later have chosen a
similar course, even if not all would have pursued it with equal
commitment and competence. It was a peculiarity of Arthur Morgan as chairman that he was so little guided by the needs of the

15. Memorandum, Harcourt Morgan to Arthur E. Morgan and Davil E. Lilienthal,
Oct. 3, 1933, quoted in app. A to George Jacob Gordon, "Intergovernmental Relations
in the Tennessee Valley" (Ph.D. dissertation, Syracuse University, 1971).

16. Philip Selznick, *TVA and the Grass Roots* (Harper and Row, Torchbook,
1966), makes the classic argument of this point.

17. Arthur E. Morgan, "Purposes and Methods of the Tennessee Valley Authority,"
*Annals of the American Academy of Political and Social Science*, vol. 172 (March 1934),
pp. 52–53.

organization and so incensed at Lilienthal's skillful use of propa-
ganda on the organization's behalf.[18]

In any case, it was not an accident that the board produced the
result it did. If President Roosevelt had believed it possible and
desirable to make TVA an aggressive performer of regional functions and reformer of state and local governments, he could have
appointed to the board three men who shared that purpose. That
it was thought necessary to appoint a man (Harcourt Morgan, as it
happened) who was closely identified with the institutions of the
region and who would most probably resist their radical reform or
replacement shows the power that state and local interests have in
national politics.

## Coordination

The distinctive virtue of TVA as coordinator is that it incorpo-
rates functions that have usually been performed by more than one
federal agency. Lilienthal wrote that it was TVA's "unified approach" that broke with tradition:

There was . . . nothing particularly novel about the individual tasks
entrusted for execution to this new agency. There were long-established
precedents for government activity in flood control and navigation, in
forestry and agriculture, and in research. Public power systems were not
an innovation. The new thing about TVA was that one agency was
entrusted with responsibility for them all, and that no one activity
could be considered as an end in itself.[19]

This arrangement should have solved the federal government's
coordination problem in natural resources within TVA's area of
jurisdiction *if* TVA had superseded the federal line agencies functioning there. In fact the only major agency that TVA substantially
displaced was the Corps of Engineers, which lost the right to develop
the Tennessee River.[20] Other federal departments continued to
perform their usual functions in the valley with the result that
TVA's presence gave rise to a new coordination problem, that of

18. *Investigation of the Tennessee Valley Authority*, Hearings, pp. 6 ff.
19. David E. Lilienthal, *TVA: Democracy on the March* (Harper, 1944), p. 58.
20. The Corps was not displaced altogether. It has retained functions relating to
navigation. For example, it has designed locks for some of TVA's dams and it operates
and maintains navigation facilities.

harmonizing the regional agency's acts with those of line agencies having national jurisdictions.[21]

This new coordination problem occurred mainly in the field of agriculture. Formally, the problem was dealt with by a memorandum of understanding concluded in 1934 by the chairman of TVA, the secretary of agriculture, and the presidents of the seven land-grant colleges in the valley states. The parties agreed to clear joint activities through a tripartite committee. According to Philip Selznick's interpretation, the agreement was "a device for the control of TVA—or at least its relevant activities—by the Department of Agriculture, which was at that time dominated by men committed to the land-grant college system."[22] Formal agreement or no, Harcourt Morgan was committed to carrying out TVA's agricultural program through the land-grant colleges and state extension services rather than to asserting a claim to leadership or independent activity. In practice, the coordination problem was resolved by TVA's deferring to the Department of Agriculture and its state clients.

Conflict nonetheless developed between TVA and Agriculture as a result of the Authority's resistance to admitting the Soil Conservation Service (SCS) to the valley. Until 1940 it was Agriculture's policy to refrain from undertaking erosion control within TVA's area. The SCS, newly established within the department in 1935, was excluded from that part of the country. Eventually local interests sought to invite the SCS to northern Alabama, and the Department of Agriculture, under new leadership, changed its policy. There followed a long jurisdictional dispute between SCS and TVA as SCS slowly established itself in the Tennessee Valley. Where there had been one soil conservation program, now there were two.[23]

There could be no unified regional program unless TVA did displace federal agencies across the full range of its activities; but even this would leave open the question of how much integration of federal purpose could be achieved within one organization per-

21. *Ten Rivers in America's Future*, Report of the President's Water Resources Policy Commission (the Cooke Commission), vol. 2 (1950), pp. 734–37, 751–53.

22. *TVA and the Grass Roots*, pp. 95–96.

23. Ibid., pp. 169–79; Norman I. Wengert, *Valley of Tomorrow* (University of Tennessee Press, 1952), especially chap. 7; and Robert J. Morgan, *Governing Soil Conservation* (Johns Hopkins Press, 1965), pp. 124–32.

forming many functions. The interagency coordination problem might simply be transmuted into an intra-agency problem.

To a degree this happened in TVA, whose early years were marked by intense conflict within the governing board. A "unified approach" did not produce consistency of purpose. Activities were specialized, and each did tend to become an end in itself. TVA's chief forester, a contestant in the conflict, described the internal differences as follows in 1938:

There are decided differences of opinion within the TVA as to just what the TVA is or should be. Three views exist and fight persistently for acceptance:

1. That TVA is a federally owned and operated electric power utility corporation. All else is quite secondary and is only permitted to exist because (a) it, like dam construction, must go on if electric power is to be generated; or (b) the other activities are so generally popular and worthwhile that it takes more courage on the part of the advocates of this "power concept" openly to throw it overboard, than to pay lip service to it and quietly work under cover to hamstring it and keep it insignificant.

2. That the TVA is an adjunct to local agencies, such as the land-grant colleges and extension services of the seven valley states. Except for dam construction and similar work, which manifestly is quite impossible for the local and state agencies to perform, the advocates of this concept believe that the Authority itself has nothing in the way of a job to do; that it should merely get money from Congress, pass it on to local and state agencies, and let them do everything in their own way, with personnel of their own choosing. Knowing little or nothing of either forestry or wildlife this group holds firmly to early pioneer ideas of land ownership, land use, and conservation. It thinks of forests as small scattered farm woodland tracts. It thinks of foresters as extension workers to be called in for advice and suggestions by the county agricultural agents and farm owners. As the farm woods is, in their minds, only a minor part of the farm, so the forester or the wildlife expert is only a minor technician, quite unfit for large responsibility in land management and policy determination. One can imagine the attitude of this group toward the many important problems of forestry and wildlife management confronting the TVA.

3. That the TVA is a unique effort on the part of the people of the United States, through the federal government, to solve the major problems of a great watershed. The advocates of this third concept propose to approach the job with a scientific attitude. They have been assembled

from all over the U.S.; they are spending most of the money—and are doing most of the work. To them the TVA is simply a large federal organization, with a very clearcut, definite job. They believe that the other federal and state organizations are important, and that the TVA should coöperate with them fully, but that TVA should not turn over to them, however, the work of the TVA itself.[24]

These differences derived in large part from the beliefs of the board members, each of whom had charge of administering a portion of the Authority's work. It is not a coincidence that the number of competing conceptions was three. They ramified through the organization and threatened morale and effectiveness.

These internal strains were reduced after 1937–38. The dissenting board member, Arthur Morgan, was removed, and some of his most loyal followers left. Board members gave up administrative functions and concentrated administrative responsibility in a general manager, to whom the staff reported and who received policy guidance from the board. The forestry relations department, which had been allied with Arthur Morgan, was brought under the supervision of a chief conservation engineer, who also had charge of the agriculture program. The organization was divided into three main parts, which were responsible for the design and construction of river developments, the power program, and the agriculture and forestry programs. Following the reorganization, a number of written interdepartmental agreements were negotiated to refine the definition of jurisdictions and to limit conflict.[25]

This organization has survived with few changes. (One change was the reestablishment of the division of forestry as a separate unit directly responsible to the general manager.) Its principal characteristic is decentralization. The construction, power, and agriculture programs each operate with a high degree of independence and in different locations—Knoxville for construction, Chattanooga for power, and Muscle Shoals for agriculture. Forestry is outside of Knoxville in Norris, the new town that Arthur Morgan built. The office of the general manager imposes a minimum of

24. E. C. M. Richards, "The Future of TVA Forestry," *Journal of Forestry*, vol. 36 (July 1938), pp. 644–45, quoted in Selznick, *TVA and the Grass Roots*, pp. 148–49.

25. C. Herman Pritchett, *The Tennessee Valley Authority* (Russell and Russell, 1971), chap. 6; Marguerite Owen, *The Tennessee Valley Authority* (Praeger, 1973), pp. 58–67; Gordon R. Clapp, "The Problems and the Methods of General Management in a Multiple-Purpose Regional Agency" (TVA, May 22, 1941; processed).

central supervision. It contains no planning staff and only a small budget review staff.[26] Thus the mode of coordination within TVA has not been integration through strong central direction. Friction among the parts has been reduced by giving freedom to each.

The fact that intra-agency differences persisted does not mean that no gains in coordination were secured by consolidating functions within a single organization. Particularly in the design and management of the river control system, lodging authority within one organization appears to have had beneficial results. "It is clear enough," a leading student of federal resource administration concluded in 1950, after observing TVA, "that a great river system of control structures cannot be satisfactorily operated on the basis of inter-agency agreements, written or oral." He cited from TVA's experience "the intricate sequences in the manipulation of the system of reservoirs that may be involved in mastering a single flood-menacing storm, or to trace the seasonal schedules and inter-relationships among the units of the system for electric power production, malaria control and the spawning of fish." He concluded, however, that it was not necessary to combine management of watershed land with management of the river, and argued against duplicating the Authority as a nationwide form for the administration of natural resources.[27]

## Decentralization as Doctrine and Practice

If the essence of the federal government's centralization problem is organizational rigidity, TVA was well designed to be a cure. TVA's founders chose the corporate form precisely because it would give exceptional freedom and flexibility. President Roosevelt called for "a corporation clothed with the power of government but possessed of the flexibility and initiative of a private enterprise." Congress echoed him.[28]

26. Donald C. Kull, *Budget Administration in the Tennessee Valley Authority* (University of Tennessee Press, 1948).

27. Charles McKinley, "The Valley Authority and Its Alternatives," *American Political Science Review*, vol. 44 (September 1950), pp. 614 ff. For a description of basin management systems, see Roscoe C. Martin et al., *River Basin Administration and the Delaware* (Syracuse University Press, 1960), chap. 16.

28. Pritchett, *Tennessee Valley Authority*, pp. 222–23.

The statute guaranteed the Authority's freedom in several ways. Members of the corporation were given long terms—nine years (with initial appointments of three, six, and nine years). The board was to direct the exercise of all powers of the corporation, and these were stated in broad terms. In selecting employees, the board need not observe the civil service laws of the United States; it could set up its own merit system. Although it was required to pay the Treasury the net proceeds from the sale of power or other products, it was authorized to withhold whatever it deemed necessary for operations or new construction. That was a very important exception. As one student of the Authority has written, "This language was so broad as to ensure that, during the construction period at least, there would be no net revenues."[29]

Unlike some public corporations, TVA is not sustained entirely by its own revenue. Revenue from power sales, although it passed $10 million in 1940 and rose sharply thereafter, has never been enough to finance all of TVA's activity. The act authorized "all appropriations necessary," and Congress's annual appropriations acts have also been cast in brief and permissive terms. Because Congress has not designated amounts for each function, the Authority has enjoyed broad discretion in the use of appropriated funds. Moreover, such funds have usually been available until spent in contrast to the usual practice of putting a time limit on their expenditure.[30]

Granted that TVA has had great freedom, how is freedom used? Whose interests or purposes are served? How does an organization so blessed get its bearings?

The "grass-roots" doctrine, formulated by David Lilienthal, was TVA's answer to these questions. The doctrine was an attempt to reconcile the nation's need for a powerful central government with democracy's dependence on citizen participation. Lilienthal argued that the federal government must exercise broad legislative powers

29. Ibid., p. 235.

30. Arnold R. Jones, "The Financing of TVA," *Law and Contemporary Problems,* vol. 26 (Autumn 1961), pp. 724–40. Operating expenses of the power program have been financed from power revenues, which are used only for the power program. Other sources—appropriations or revenue from the sale of bonds—have been used for the construction of power facilities. Both operating and capital costs of nonpower activities (flood control, navigation improvement, fertilizer and munitions development, agriculture, forestry, and other resource development programs) are financed from appropriations, although income from the sale of fertilizer and chemical products helps support that program.

but that administration could be decentralized. For decentralization to occur, two criteria must be met. Men in the field must have the power of decision: "A decentralized administration is one in which the greatest number of decisions is made in the field." And there must be popular and local-government participation: "A decentralized federal administration must develop as far as possible the active participation of the people themselves. It must utilize the services of state and local agencies, supplementing and stimulating, not duplicating, their staff or equipment." Lilienthal stated that TVA met these criteria while remaining fundamentally an instrument of national purpose.[31]

As a description of TVA's behavior, the doctrine is suspect if only because it had strategic origins. Within the President's staff a proposal had developed for putting TVA under the jurisdiction of the Department of the Interior. Lilienthal reacted with his attack on the evils of centralized bureaucracy. Besides giving purpose and a profound significance to TVA's activity, this propelled TVA into a new fight in 1939, just when the inspiriting fight against the utility companies had ended. Lilienthal's diaries are perfectly explicit on the origin of the grass-roots doctrine. "This untoward experience," as he called the proposal to deprive TVA of its autonomy, "was responsible for one of the best pieces of thinking and writing I have done on this job, the Grass Roots speech before the Southern Political Science Association."[32]

31. Lilienthal, *The TVA: An Experiment in the "Grass Roots" Administration of Federal Functions*, address before the Southern Political Science Association, Nov. 10, 1939, Knoxville, Tennessee.

32. *Journals*, vol. 1, p. 150. Two days after the grass-roots speech, he wrote: "I am all excited these days, excited about TVA and the way it is working out, and by the fascinating place in it I have, the function of keeping it on its toes, eager and on the *qui vive*. This is quite in contrast with my feeling of a few months ago. The change has been due to the wholly unexpected effort to put us into the Department of the Interior. . . . That aroused my fighting impulses, and made it necessary for me to do some intensive thinking about a particular issue. . . . All of this has been exhilarating. It has been great to touch off other people, to argue and match ideas, especially since it involved a field of thinking which is relatively fresh, not only to me but to anyone. The latest product was a speech I made day before yesterday before the Southern Political Science Association called 'The TVA: An Experiment in the "Grass Roots" Administration of Federal Functions.' . . . It did the organization good, is being talked over a good deal, but best of all, as one fellow put it . . . it made people proud they were working for TVA, because what we are doing is really important. I hope it will stir up controversy in Washington; it certainly was intended to, and I shall be disappointed if it doesn't" (pp. 142–43).

As a description of TVA's conduct, the doctrine also has the defect of being too general. This is the nature of such doctrine, but the defect is accentuated in TVA's case by the actual variety of organizational behavior. The fact is that how TVA has conducted relations with others has depended on which program TVA was conducting. Each has its own pattern of politics and administration.

Before the grass-roots doctrine was enunciated in comprehensive terms, the Authority itself drew a clear distinction between the functions that were federal in nature and therefore proper for it to execute and those that were local in nature and therefore properly left to the people of the valley and their state and local governments. "Control of the Tennessee River is under the authority and direction of the Federal Government," TVA's annual report said in 1936. "The planning of the river's future is entrusted to the TVA." On the other hand, the TVA had "no power or desire to impose from above a comprehensive plan for the social and economic life of the Valley." "The planning of the Valley's future must be the democratic labor of many agencies and individuals."[33]

This distinction survived in practice. Like any major public works developer, TVA has often had to proceed in spite of protests from people whose lands were to be bulldozed or inundated. Nor has TVA engaged state and local governments in development decisions. One scholar, after analyzing ten development decisions by TVA in the fields of navigation, flood control, and electric power, concluded that "the pattern of intergovernmental relations which emerges from these events is not one of partnership, nor of continuing interaction between levels of government in working out joint policy, nor of shared responsibility. It is a pattern of firm federal control of basic programs under accountability to the Executive and the Congress, with intermittent attempts to make common cause with state agencies concerning fringe issues."[34] In these development issues, deference has been shown to state and local governments only indirectly. TVA might have used control of the shoreline around the reservoirs to develop a recreation system of its

33. *Annual Report of the Tennessee Valley Authority for the Fiscal Year Ended June 30, 1936*, p. 2.

34. Elliott Roberts, *One River—Seven States: TVA-State Relations in the Development of the Tennessee River* (University of Tennessee, Bureau of Public Administration, 1955), p. 90.

own rather than making land available to state and local governments. This it has not done.[35]

On the other hand, the grass-roots doctrine was real enough in the agriculture program, which TVA has administered through agricultural experiment stations of the state universities and county agents of the state agricultural extension services. "Officials of the extension service," according to Selznick, "constitute the operating organization which brings the TVA fertilizer and soil conservation program to the rural population."[36] TVA has contracted with state agencies for the demonstration services. It imposes few guidelines or restrictions on their conduct and reimburses them for personnel and equipment. As time passed, TVA extended its agricultural activities outside the valley, but its basic administrative technique —reliance on land-grant universities and affiliated agricultural organizations—remained the same. For TVA, the price of the grass-roots doctrine was acceptance of certain policies and practices that might have been overturned had the Authority defined its agricultural policy autonomously or in response to its progressive supporters at the national level. The benefits of the agriculture program tended to go to the bigger, more prosperous farms. Owners rather than tenants benefited. Negro agricultural colleges did not participate.[37]

TVA's development of the river and its relations with farmers fitted the established pattern for federal agencies. For aid to agriculture, the federal government historically had operated through grants-in-aid to state and local agencies. So did TVA. In constructing public works for navigation and flood control, federal agencies historically had acted independently. So did TVA. In the forestry and power programs, however, either there was no adequate precedent in federal government activity or TVA tried to depart from it.

In forestry, TVA began by trying to depart from tradition. Historically, the Forest Service of the Department of Agriculture administered forest lands set aside from the public domain as preserves. After 1911 it also had authority to purchase lands for preservation, which enabled it to create national forests in the East.

35. Owen, *Tennessee Valley Authority*, p. 220, records a TVA proposal to undertake a recreation program directly. This was inexplicably abandoned.
36. *TVA and the Grass Roots*, p. 131.
37. Ibid., passim.

TVA's initial plan for a forestry program called for massive federal purchases in the valley, some seven million acres, half a million of which TVA proposed to retain for use as a demonstration of scientific forest management. It also proposed to ask for authority to regulate the practices of owners of private forest land. Though endorsed by the full board in 1934, these policies were Arthur Morgan's only. They were revised in 1937 as the two-man majority took control of TVA and they were abandoned in 1941, but the forestry division remained something of a dissident within TVA, distinguished from the agricultural division by a commitment to direct action. Agricultural officials tried to persuade forestry officials to work through the land-grant colleges and extension services, and to a degree they did so, but they also established relations directly with forestry and conservation agencies. Rather than subsidize their state and local collaborators, as did TVA's agricultural relations division, TVA's foresters preferred to educate the public directly to the need for conservation and for supporting state and local programs. They have been less closely tied to any client group than have TVA's agricultural officials.[38]

In its power program, for which there was no real precedent, TVA was able to evoke support from a national majority *and* to work through local organizations, a combination that was crucial to establishing the program.

For all its freedom and flexibility, TVA could not have carried out the power program without the support of the President and Congress, which if nothing else was needed to protect freedom and flexibility. This federal corporation did not develop into the nation's biggest producer of electric power while no one was looking. President Roosevelt's reappointment of Lilienthal to the board in 1936 and removal of Arthur Morgan two years later constituted a general endorsement of the course TVA was taking. Lilienthal con-

38. Owen, *Tennessee Valley Authority*, pp. 31–34, 100–01, 220; Selznick, *TVA and the Grass Roots*, pp. 147–51; J. O. Artman, "Forestry," in Martin, ed., *TVA: The First Twenty Years*, pp. 177–92. It is perhaps an exaggeration to say that TVA sought to depart from tradition in the federal conduct of forestry programs. TVA foresters had good relations with members of the Forest Service and shared with them an overriding commitment to professional objectives. TVA's ambitious initial proposals were not framed as a criticism of the Forest Service, but in support of shared professional aspirations. They brought no response, however, from the headquarters of the Department of Agriculture. Owen, *Tennessee Valley Authority*, p. 32.

sulted with the President about the power program, and the White House was involved in negotiations with the private utilities. When TVA bought the Tennessee Electric Power Company in 1939, it had to get the consent of Congress to financing the purchase. Construction of a steam plant at Johnsonville, Tennessee, with which TVA embarked on a peacetime expansion of generating capacity, confirmed the Authority's commitment to supplying all the power needs of its region. President Truman approved the budget request, and a newly elected Democratic Congress appropriated funds in 1949, after a long debate. In the 1950s, when a Republican administration opposed appropriations for new generating facilities, Congress authorized TVA to issue revenue bonds for that purpose, a proposal that had been debated for several years. By 1960, TVA's power program was securely established, a legacy of the New Deal–Fair Deal period which had survived the test of a hostile Republican presidency. In supplying public power to the Tennessee Valley region, TVA was carrying out national policy—controversial policy, certainly, but fully confirmed by repeated debates and majority decisions.[39]

In administration of the power program, the grass-roots doctrine applied. Instead of retailing power the Authority disposes of it wholesale to approximately 160 municipal governments and rural cooperatives. Lilienthal called this "the most far-reaching instance of a grass-roots partnership between local agencies and TVA," adding that "responsibility for those municipal and co-operative systems . . . is lodged with the people themselves," who "determine their own standards of efficiency of service and level of rates."[40] Along with customers, retail distributors of TVA power have formed an important base of support whenever TVA's power program was under attack in national politics. TVA's grass-roots partners have joined the Authority in protests to Congress. This has helped to mobilize the congressional delegation from TVA's service area. Whereas the sponsor of TVA in 1933 had been a senator from Nebraska who was a national leader of the progressive movement, its defenders have usually been congressmen from rural districts of Tennessee, Alabama, and Mississippi whose constituencies

39. Congressional Quarterly, *Congress and the Nation, 1945–1964* (Washington, 1965), pp. 908–31.

40. *TVA: Democracy on the March*, pp. 133–36.

are served by TVA power. Any proposal that threatens the size of TVA's revenues or its right to reinvest them in power operations runs counter to the valley's interest in having cheap, publicly subsidized power, and this interest is thoroughly organized at the local level through the medium of distributors.

The progressive majority that supported TVA nationally was committed on principle to the goal of the power program—a large volume of sales at low rates. TVA appealed to progressives as a demonstration of the superiority of public over private production of power. In general, TVA's grass-roots constituency shares these goals too, out of self-interest, except that local governments, which are TVA's grass-roots partners in the power system, also have an interest in realizing taxes from utility operations or in realizing profits from sales. TVA has kept enough control over its local partners to make sure that programmatic goals are thoroughly protected. Its contracts with municipal and cooperative distributors sharply limit their discretion, and in pursuit of low rates, TVA has accepted conflict with state and local governments over a wide range of matters. It resists state taxation of local electric service, tries to keep its own payments to state and local governments in lieu of taxes low, occasionally forces rate reductions, and zealously guards against any sign that local governments are making a profit out of power sales. Far from dealing directly with the people or with the people's elected governments, TVA has encouraged the formation of appointed, largely autonomous power boards which will be free of "politics." A political scientist at the University of Tennessee has written, "A suggestion today that TVA's power operations have increased citizens' participation or have encouraged anything resembling a town meeting would evoke laughter anywhere in the Valley."[41]

TVA's relations with its grass-roots partners have been very different in the power program than in the agricultural program. In agriculture, according to Selznick, activity came to be valued to the degree that it involved the state universities and extension service. Grass-roots cooperation became an end in itself.[42] In the power program the dominant goals have remained programmatic; if co-

41. Victor C. Hobday, *Sparks at the Grass Roots* (University of Tennessee Press, 1969), especially pp. 39–40.
42. Selznick, *TVA and the Grass Roots*, p. 132.

operation with local institutions conflicted with such goals, cooperation has been sacrificed.

In sum, there has been no consistent pattern of decentralization in TVA's operations, no uniform striking of the balance between responses to central and local influences. The different pattern of client-and-constituency relations each program has had suggests that decentralization in TVA has depended more on factors external to the organization than on internal factors. Decentralization was not determined by the organization's form or its grass-roots ideology, which would have affected all activities equally. That different programs had different client groups and different ideas about how to deal with them limited the possibilities for internal coordination. The specialized functional alliances that are so prominent a feature of federal-state-local relations were to some extent reproduced within the Tennessee Valley in the operations of the federally created regional authority: the agriculture division dealt with the extension service, the foresters dealt with forestry and conservation agencies, and the power division dealt with local power boards, while the engineers and dam-builders went ahead and built their dams.

Whatever the consequences of TVA's freedom and flexibility for outsiders, for members of the Authority these were rewarding attributes of the organization. Decentralization has meant that policy makers are relatively accessible to the staff and able to react to proposals. A recent account of TVA by a long-time employee makes the point with the story of a recreation specialist who spotted the possibility for developing Land between the Lakes while on a flight from Paducah to Knoxville:

The next morning he voiced his concern to the head of the office in which he worked, then to the General Manager and with his endorsement to the Board, which authorized an immediate exploration of the possibilities. Few government employees have such easy access to those with the power to decide. Few can present their proposals directly to the head of the agency that employs them. That they can in TVA is one result of the location of headquarters in the region, not at the nation's capital. In the centralized agencies of government, it takes time for an idea to work its way from the "field," as offices outside Washington are described, to the site of decision, and there may never be a confrontation between the proposer and the deciders.[43]

43. Owen, *Tennessee Valley Authority*, p. 140.

Just as the staff member in TVA is near the policy makers, he is also near the visible products of his work—the dams and lakes, the reforested slopes, the industries humming and houses lighted with low-cost power. The sense of being away from the bureaucracy and dealing with visible problems, and of having power to deal with them on the scene, in part accounts for the high morale that has characterized TVA.

## The Impact of the TVA

TVA proudly measures its own success by flood damage that has not occurred; transportation charges that have been saved by shippers who use the navigation channel; grass and forage crops that grow where land once was bare or planted with crops that depleted the soil; acres of land that have been reforested; man-made lakes with 10,000 miles of shoreline and 600,000 acres of water surface available for recreation; and dramatic rises in the use of electricity and reductions in its cost. TVA reported in 1972 that "the average home in this area now uses nearly 15,000 kilowatt-hours of electricity a year, 25 times as much as in 1933 and twice the present national average." The average electric rate in the area was 1-1/4 cents a kilowatt-hour; in 1933 the rate was 5-1/2 cents. Whereas only 3 percent of farms were served with electricity in 1933, now virtually all are.[44]

To the question of how much of this would have happened anyway, TVA replies with a story of a newspaper editor. When a visitor to the valley asked if the changes would have occurred without TVA, the editor thought for a while, then said, "Well, they didn't."[45] Scholarship has not done much better, nor can it. There is no way to answer the question. Economic development would have proceeded without TVA but presumably at a slower pace. It is virtually certain that this extraordinary regional organization— partly because of its form, which facilitated rapid and decisive action, and partly because of the federal subsidies for which it was a

44. *TVA Today 1972*, p. 17. However, recent rises in TVA's electric rates have stirred criticism in the valley. See the remarks of Tennessee Representative Joe L. Evins, *Congressional Record*, daily ed. (May 7, 1973), pp. E2947–48.

45. Owen, *Tennessee Valley Authority*, p. 215.

channel—contributed to development of the region more than usual forms of organization would have.

The only available scholarly evidence is consistent with this conclusion. According to an economic appraisal done in the early 1960s, since TVA's creation economic development has been more rapid in the Tennessee Valley than in the nation or the Southeast as a whole. Manufacturing employment gained 119 percent in the valley between 1929 and 1960, while the gain was 101 percent in the Southeast and only 55 percent in the nation. Manufacturing wages and sales were up 807 percent in the valley, 720 percent in the Southeast, and 443 percent in the nation. The analyst estimated, on the basis of locational characteristics of new and expanded industries, that TVA programs were "a significant factor behind one-third of the new industrial jobs and at least one-half of the increased value added by industry."[46]

TVA is well known to the people of the region, and generally regarded there and beyond as a success ("the most spectacularly successful of all New Deal enterprises," Henry Steele Commager called it[47]). TVA's own morale has been sustained by a perception that the organization is something very special—the New Deal's first act of daring, and an experiment that worked.

## Duplicating the TVA

Although the Authority is well established and widely regarded as a success, it has no imitators in the United States and no one is proposing that it be imitated. In retrospect, creation of TVA appears as a singular event in American political experience.

Numerous proposals for more regional authorities were made in the 1930s and 1940s. Almost every year for nearly twenty years after passage of the TVA act, bills were introduced in Congress for authorities in other valleys. Three times these bills got to the committee hearing stage—in 1937, when President Roosevelt submitted a proposal for regional planning bodies to cover the entire country;

46. Stefan H. Robock, "An Unfinished Task: A Socio-Economic Evaluation of the TVA Experiment," in John R. Moore, ed., *The Economic Impact of TVA* (University of Tennessee Press, 1967), pp. 114–15.

47. Commager, in Introduction to Lilienthal, *Journals*, p. xxxi.

in 1945, when Senator James Murray of Montana pushed for creation of a Missouri Valley Authority; and in 1949, after President Truman had proposed a Columbia Valley Authority. The bills of 1937 and 1949 did not emerge from committee. The bill of 1945 was reported on adversely by two different committees. None was ever voted on. None had strong support from any important source, even the sponsoring presidents. Interest was confined to a few very liberal members of Congress with a strong commitment to public development of power; to occasional supporters within the regions for which new authorities were proposed; and to the officials and regional supporters of TVA, who apparently feared that TVA would be politically vulnerable if it remained unique. All proposals were strongly opposed either publicly or privately by the federal agencies whose jurisdictions would have been invaded and by their allies in Congress. Less intense opposition arose from governors. Had the proposals seemed at all likely to pass, the private utility companies would have mounted major campaigns against them.

That regional authorities more or less on the model of TVA should have been opposed by established administrative and legislative organizations is not surprising. TVA was a radical departure from customary arrangements for natural resources development; in retrospect, the surprising thing is not the failure to duplicate TVA but that so drastic a departure from the normal mode of federal organization should have occurred at all.

The circumstances of TVA's creation in 1933 were quite special, however. The existence of federal properties at Muscle Shoals was a singular situation, and it gave rise in the 1920s to a singular question: should these properties be owned and operated by a public corporation created specially for that purpose? A congressional majority said yes, but that was not to say that river basin development generally should be taken away from established federal construction agencies and given to new, highly autonomous corporations. It is not clear that Congress understood in 1933 that this was what it was doing in the Tennessee Valley. The bills that had been considered at such length in the 1920s did not give the Muscle Shoals Corporation sweeping development powers; they would not have displaced the Corps of Engineers. The legislative paragraph that accomplished that unusual result was one of the last-minute additions, and in the emergency atmosphere of the Hundred Days it did not get much attention from Congress. Besides, though the Corps had plans for the Tennessee Valley, work there was not high on its list of priorities.[48] In general, the Corps's functions were less fully developed than they were later to become, after the flood control acts of 1936 and 1944. The Tennessee Valley was therefore a bureaucratic vacuum, which the new Authority filled. The Missouri and Columbia valleys were not vacuums; there the Bureau of Reclamation and the Corps of Engineers were at work and had plans for much more work. Unwilling to create more authorities, Congress was also unwilling in the early 1940s to extend TVA's jurisdiction over development to the neighboring Cumberland valley. The Corps of Engineers has developed the Cumberland.

In 1933 the implications of TVA for existing federal development agencies were unclear.[49] As its proponents said, the Authority was an experiment. Federal bureaus and congressional committees learned from observing the experiment that to repeat it would not be in their interests. TVA's strength as a regional development organization was the scope of its authority and its freedom from others' control; but these very characteristics were bound to make repetition of the form politically difficult. Autonomy does not attract organizational allies. Those compromises of its autonomy that TVA made were made within the region, with state agencies. This helped to build support for TVA in its immediate environment but not to build national support for more TVAs.

Even if it had been politically feasible to reproduce the form of TVA, it would probably have been impossible to reproduce the results. The personal interest of President Roosevelt, the extraordinary idealism and commitment of TVA's initial leadership, the special circumstances of the depression, the relative homogeneity and compactness of the region, the steady development of federal line agencies' functions throughout the country—all these made it unlikely that another authority in another place at another time would work as well. Nor could another authority be expected to have the same freedom and flexibility. In the Government Corporation Control Act of 1945, Congress laid down restrictions on the

---

48. Hubbard, *Origins of the TVA*, p. 275.

49. Although at least one member of Congress did perceive them. See the remarks of Representative Chester C. Bolton, *Congressional Record*, vol. 77, pt. 3, 73 Cong. 1 sess. (1933), pp. 2341–42.

general form. And unless the results of reproducing the form were certain to be very beneficial, the case for reproduction could not be very strong. Even sympathetic analysts of TVA concluded that attempts to create more such organizations would give rise to serious problems of presidential control, to conflict with federal line agencies, and to interregional rivalries. Those who argued the merits of TVA did not argue with equal enthusiasm the case for reproducing it.[50]

50. C. Herman Pritchett, "The Transplantability of the TVA," *Iowa Law Journal*, vol. 32 (January 1947), pp. 327–38; McKinley, "The Valley Authority and Its Alternatives"; and Owen, *Tennessee Valley Authority*, pp. 234–37.

# [3]

# The Delaware River Basin Commission

UNLIKE the Tennessee Valley Authority, which is exclusively federal, the Delaware River Basin Commission was created jointly by four states and the United States. Since 1961, the compact on which it rests has been law for New York, New Jersey, Pennsylvania, Delaware, and the United States. The purposes of the compact are stated in broad terms, and so are the powers of the commission. The compact is "to encourage and provide for the planning, conservation, utilization, development, management and control of the water resources of the basin." The commission is required to ("shall"):

develop and effectuate plans, policies and projects relating to the water resources of the basin. . . . adopt and promote uniform and coordinated policies for water conservation, control, use and management in the basin. . . . encourage the planning, development and financing of water resources projects according to such plans and policies.

It is authorized to ("may"):

Plan, design, acquire, construct, reconstruct, complete, own, improve, extend, develop, operate and maintain any and all projects, facilities, properties, activities and services, determined by the commission to be necessary, convenient or useful for the purposes of this compact.

. . . borrow money for any of the purposes of this compact, and may issue its negotiable bonds . . . in respect thereto.[1]

---

1. *Delaware River Basin Compact* (DRBC, 1967), Articles 1, 3, and 12. The powers and duties of the commission are spelled out at length in the compact, first in general terms and then for particular functions—water supply, pollution control, flood protection, watershed management, recreation, hydroelectric power, and regulation of

## Origin and Conception

"Something new in American government has been invented on the Delaware," two students of American federalism wrote not long after the DRBC was formed. "For the first time anywhere in the United States, a major interstate basin is to be served by a governmental agency which is at once a part of the government of each of the affected states and the United States Government. . . . In place of the competition, overlapping, duplication and jurisdictional no man's lands which have characterized the separate efforts of a multitude of local, state and federal agencies, a unified program may be substituted."[2]

According to one of its founders, the DRBC began with two main functions: to "settle existing disputes [over allocation of water] between the States of Delaware, New Jersey, New York, and Pennsylvania," and to "establish a Federal-state partnership for the purpose of developing the Delaware River in an orderly manner and in accordance with a comprehensive plan."[3] To serve the first purpose, it brought the four basin states together. To serve the second, it combined them with the federal government. Moreover, because the federal government would be represented by a single member rather than by members of each of its water resources agencies, the founders of the DRBC believed they had achieved a breakthrough in intrafederal coordination. They believed that in the Delaware basin they were doing for the federal government what it had never been able to do for itself: integrating the actions of its water resources agencies.

---

withdrawals and diversions. Regulating navigation is the only important water-related function over which the commission lacks jurisdiction. With respect to all functions, the authorizing language is broad. For example, for flood protection, the commission "may plan, design, construct and operate and maintain projects and facilities, as it may deem necessary or desirable for flood damage reduction." On hydroelectric power: "The commission may develop and operate, or authorize to be developed and operated, dams and related facilities and appurtenances for the purpose of generating hydroelectric power and hydroelectric energy." Articles 6 and 9.

2. Frederick L. Zimmermann and Mitchell Wendell, "New Horizons on the Delaware," *State Government*, vol. 36 (Summer 1963), p. 157.

3. *Delaware River Basin Compact*, Hearings before Subcommittee No. 1 of the House Judiciary Committee, 87 Cong. 1 sess. (1961), p. 48. The formulation is that of Arthur C. Ford, president of the Board of Water Supply of New York City.

A movement for regional cooperation in the Delaware basin got under way in the mid-1950s, not long after the Supreme Court had issued a decree settling a dispute among New York, Pennsylvania, and New Jersey over rights to the water of the Delaware. This was the second time in three decades that such a dispute had gone to the Court, and conflict threatened to continue. New York City, which draws about half of its water supply from the Delaware, was developing the river's headwaters in upstate New York. Philadelphia, which depends wholly on the river, feared that its supply was threatened. All parties wanted a method for settling disputes that would be more accessible to their influence and less fraught with uncertainty than resort to a judicial institution of the central government. Simultaneously, the fortunes of electoral politics facilitated cooperation. Three of the four basin state governors and both of the big city mayors concerned happened to be liberal Democrats. In 1956 they formed the Delaware River Basin Advisory Committee (DRBAC), made up of civic leaders in the basin, to consider problems of the Delaware. Some of them, particularly the reform mayor of Philadelphia, Joseph Clark, hoped for a valley authority on the model of TVA.[4]

A major flood in 1955 gave further impetus to the committee's work. Following the flood, the Corps of Engineers began a survey of the Delaware, in the course of which state officials experienced the frustrations of dealing with a large number of federal development agencies. This heightened their interest in an organization that promised to simplify relations with the federal government. Also, a major development program seemed likely to follow from the Corps's plan, and that raised the question of how development would be administered.

The suggestion of a federal-interstate compact came from a study group at Syracuse University, hired to consider alternative forms of organization. In the early 1950s, the Council of State Governments had suggested the participation of the federal government in interstate compacts, but not until the proponents of intergovernmental cooperation in the Delaware basin seized on the idea did it get strong backing within any region. Officials in the basin decided in the fall of 1959 that they would prepare a federal-interstate com-

4. DRBAC files at DRBC headquarters, Trenton, N.J., and interview with a DRBAC official, W. Brinton Whitall, March 26, 1973.

pact, rejecting the recommendation of the Syracuse group that they begin by asking Congress to create a federal development agency by statute. The Syracuse group reasoned that a federal-interstate compact commission would be appropriate in the long run, after major development had been accomplished, but that a purely federal agency on the model of TVA would be preferable in the short run, because it could be created more quickly, would get more generous federal funding, and would be better suited to execute development.[5] State officials wanted from the start an organization to which their governments would belong.

Officials in the basin recognized that their main difficulty would be in getting federal participation. Interstate compacts had a long history as a form of cooperation between states, but for the federal government actually to join such a compact with the states would be a major departure in intergovernmental relations, raising fundamental questions of constitutional principle.[6] Federal officials often participated in negotiation of interstate compacts and in the work of interstate organizations, but they had never done so in a way that would bind the federal government.[7] When the New England states in 1958 sounded out the federal executive departments about joining a compact, they were rebuffed. The Department of Justice questioned the constitutionality, and departments with responsibility for water resources also objected.[8] The New England proposal was

5. Roscoe C. Martin et al., *River Basin Administration and the Delaware* (Syracuse University Press, 1960), is a published version of the study. See especially chapters 7 and 18. The study was commissioned by the Water Resources Foundation of the Delaware River Basin, which cooperated with the DRBAC, and financed by the Ford Foundation.

6. For an argument in support of the constitutionality of the Delaware compact, see Frank P. Grad, "Federal-State Compact: A New Experiment in Co-Operative Federalism," *Columbia Law Review*, vol. 63 (May 1963), pp. 825–55.

7. Frederick L. Zimmermann and Mitchell Wendell, *The Interstate Compact Since 1925* (Council of State Governments, 1951), chap. 6; Wallace R. Vawter, "Interstate Compacts—The Federal Interest," in Commission on Organization of the Executive Branch of the Government, *Report on Water Resources and Power* (June 1955), vol. 3, pp. 1683–1723; Martin et al., *River Basin Administration*, pp. 137–41.

8. The Northeastern Resources Committee, an intergovernmental and interagency planning body, which prepared the proposal, went ahead anyway and submitted the compact to Congress in 1960. Regional officials of the federal agencies had cooperated in the drafting, although their agency headquarters were against it. When the proposal came before Congress, all the interested executive agencies opposed it. Also, not all the New England states had approved it, which weakened whatever chances it had. *Northeastern Compact*, Hearings before the House Committee on Public Works, 86

merely for a planning and advisory organization, and the federal departments could be expected to have stronger objections to a compact organization with greater powers, such as was to be proposed for the Delaware.

Knowing that the executive branch was unlikely to assent, officials of the DRBAC considered forming a compact commission with state membership only, but they decided that the federal government was too important to be left out. Without its participation, a regional organization would be insignificant. "As long as the federal government refrains from joining the compact agency," one of them wrote, "then roughly 80 per cent of the overall 'job' of water resources development will remain outside the control of the basin agency. . . . If it is decided to proceed with an interstate agency then my long-term prediction is that we shall have a rather disorganized kind of river basin development here at an unnecessarily high level of cost, and that the interstate agency will become a pleasantly innocuous entity that is referred to in the press once a year following its annual picnic held at a place called Pocono Manor."[9] Deciding to try for federal participation in the compact, they also decided to omit federal participation in the drafting for fear it would turn into obstruction. Except for a few informal contacts, basin officials kept Washington at a distance while they worked.

The executive branch did indeed object to joining the compact.

---

Cong. 2 sess. (1960). See also Frederick L. Zimmermann, "The Role of the Compact in the New Federalism," *State Government*, vol. 43 (Spring 1970), pp. 128–35.

9. W. Brinton Whitall to Walter M. Phillips, Jan. 20, 1960; DRBC files, Trenton. In a memorandum for the DRBAC, "Reasons for Having the Federal Government a Primary Party to the Delaware Basin Compact," Dec. 4, 1959, Whitall and a colleague, Blair Bower, identified eleven reasons for federal membership in the compact commission. They argued that it would give the agency important responsibilities and a program of broad scope and significance; enable the basin agency to coordinate the programs of federal agencies; improve coordination between federal agency and state agency programs; facilitate access to federal funds, both for development projects and the basin agency's budget; convey federal legal powers to the basin agency; encourage a higher level of competence and performance on the part of the agency's staff; improve the agency's access to data and technical resources of the federal agencies; improve program efficiency by integrating all available government powers in one agency; by integrating a variety of programs in one agency, make them more immune to the pressures and blandishments of client groups; and make federal activity more open to state influence. The memorandum is in Whitall's files, DRBC, Trenton.

In a long memorandum solicited by the White House, the Department of Justice argued that the compact might "tie in fact the hands of the federal government—[it might] inhibit the free exercise of delegated constitutional powers in a forbidden way." Justice found it necessary "to consider the constitutionality of a delegation of federal authority to a 'federal agency' in which the federal government has a minority voice."[10] While Justice did not find this arrangement unconstitutional, it plainly doubted its wisdom. Collectively, the agencies put forth their position in the spring of 1961 at a meeting with the basin's senatorial delegation and two of the four governors. On behalf of the executive branch, Secretary of the Interior Stewart Udall announced that the states should proceed with the compact but that the federal government did not want to join. The executive branch maintained that the proposal would require the federal government to yield certain of its constitutional powers to "a third form of government" responsible to neither the federal government nor the states. "It is our bedrock position," Udall concluded, "that cession is the very essence of your proposal and that this would end up by operating river basins under sort of an Articles of Confederacy and that the constitutional system that we have simply does not permit it."[11]

Proponents of the compact reacted angrily at what they took to be an abrupt, callous, and thoroughly negative rejection of "a

10. "Memorandum for the Honorable Frederick G. Dutton, Re: Delaware River Basin Compact," April 25, 1961, by Nicholas deB. Katzenbach; Lee C. White files, John F. Kennedy Library, Waltham, Mass. Speaking specifically of constitutionality, this memorandum states: "If the compact here proposed is viewed as unconstitutional, it is because it is found to be inconsistent with the underlying political scheme embodied in the Constitution. In our opinion, the Compact does not clearly violate any specific provisions of the Federal Constitution. The Constitution is silent with regard to federal adherence to an interstate compact; it neither endorses nor proscribes a hybrid commission as a mechanism for achieving joint federal-state objectives. . . . In short, if Congress and the President find this compact an appropriate means for promoting and protecting the national interest, we believe it unlikely that the federal government would find itself barred by a judicial finding of unconstitutionality. But, the President and the Congress have constitutional responsibilities also, and it is incumbent upon them to consider the scheme contemplated by the Compact in the light of the political scheme envisioned by the Constitution itself."

11. "Official Report of Proceedings before the Department of the Interior in the Matter of: Delaware River Compact Meeting, Washington, April 13, 1961," pp. 4–13, 31 (hereafter cited as "Official Report"). This transcript is in the DRBC files, Washington.

proposition that we have given our blood and guts to." [12] They challenged the federal delegation to develop and defend its claim that the compact was unconstitutional, and, failing to get a satisfactory response, they ascribed federal opposition to bureaucratic timidity and self-interest. In a thrust at the new administration, Joseph Clark, now a senator from Pennsylvania, said he wondered what had happened to the "new frontier." He had expected "imaginative, positive thinking" from the Kennedy administration. [13]

The challenge to the President brought a response from the President's representatives. Both Lee C. White, a special counsel to the President, and Elmer B. Staats, deputy director of the Bureau of the Budget, suggested that discussion continue in an effort to preserve the compact and meet federal objections. [14] Thereafter, representatives of the federal agencies and of the region met several times. Having perceived that the White House favored approval of the compact and that it had powerful support in Congress, the federal agencies gave in on the fundamental question. They agreed that the federal government would become a signatory, but they proposed a series of reservations to safeguard federal interests. Congress approved the compact, with reservations, in September. It barely considered the principle of jointness. The issue was raised by only one opponent, Representative William Cramer, a minority member of the House Public Works Committee, who argued that federal membership in the DRBC would be "a bad precedent." Cramer feared that the federal government would be morally committed to expenditures voted by the state-dominated commission. "There is no limitation with regard to what the Federal cost will be under this proposal," he declared. [15]

The compact was "an almost unbelievable innovation," in the eyes of two sympathetic observers. [16] To have won approval so quickly and against the ingrained opposition of the federal execu-

12. Ibid., pp. 13 ff. The quotation is from Governor Robert B. Meyner of New Jersey; ibid., p. 72.

13. Ibid., pp. 56–57.

14. Ibid., pp. 61 ff. More than ten years later, White recalled that he was stung by Clark's remarks. The transcript confirms this. "I must say," he replied then, "that there is no more mortal thrust that you could make than to call us orthodox" (p. 61). Jarred by this challenge, White began to ask himself, "What the hell—why not try it [the compact]?" Interview, July 25, 1972.

15. *Congressional Record*, vol. 107, pt. 9, 87 Cong. 1 sess. (1961), p. 11813.

16. Zimmermann and Wendell, "New Horizons on the Delaware," p. 163.

tive agencies was a strategic triumph. Success inevitably had its price. Although most of the federally inspired revisions were technical, one was potentially of great importance. This was Article 15.1(s), which gave the federal member a veto.

The essence of the compact commission is that it should make policy simultaneously for all five member governments. It would do this by adopting a comprehensive plan for the water resources of the basin, to which all the signatories are bound. The compact provides that "no project having a substantial effect on the water resources of the basin shall hereafter be undertaken . . . unless it shall have been first . . . approved by the commission."[17] The reservation added at the request of the federal executive agencies states that the federal government will not be bound by any provision of the comprehensive plan unless the federal member has concurred in it. Further, "whenever the President shall find and determine that the national interest so requires, he may suspend, modify or delete any provision of the comprehensive plan to the extent that it affects the exercise of any powers, rights, functions, or jurisdiction conferred by law on any officer, agency or instrumentality of the United States."[18] Drafters of the compact had sought to acknowledge federal sovereignty by stating the right of Congress to withdraw or to revise the terms of the compact, but the executive branch found this insufficient.

Even with the reservations ("the minimum necessary protection of Federal interests," the executive branch called them), the federal agencies did not say they approved the compact. They merely refrained from opposing it. They told Congress that they would have opposed it but for the uniqueness of the situation in the Delaware basin. After a long history of disagreement, the states had united behind a proposal for intergovernmental cooperation, and the federal administration "would be loath to stand in the way." Since the Delaware case was unique, it should not set a precedent, the agencies said.[19]

17. Article 3.8.

18. Officials of the commission point out that technically this protection of federal prerogatives does not constitute a veto. A negative vote by the federal member does not prevent the commission from acting. It only exempts the federal government from being bound by the action.

19. *Delaware River Basin Compact*, Hearings before the Senate Committee on Public Works, 87 Cong. 1 sess. (1961), pp. 24–30.

## Resolving Interstate Conflict: The Case of the Drought

For the state and city governments, the main purpose of the compact was to resolve conflicting claims to the water of the Delaware. "In essence," the city solicitor of Philadelphia told Congress, "it is a peace treaty."[20] At the state level, much the hardest part of the compact negotiations was that covering water allocations. In the end, the parties agreed to respect the terms of the Supreme Court's decree of 1954, which had authorized New York City to make diversions of a certain amount but required it to make releases from its reservoirs so as to maintain a certain level of flow in the river. Without adequate flow, salty ocean water would move up the estuary and contaminate the municipal supply of Philadelphia. In case of a drought or other catastrophe, the commission might declare an emergency and, with the unanimous consent of the members and in consultation with the river master appointed by the Supreme Court, determine diversions and releases so as to meet the emergency. For the duration, it could substitute its judgment for that of the Supreme Court. Since the commission was composed of the disputants, its function was not so much to make independent judgments about allocation as to provide a setting in which they could negotiate their differences.

As a peacekeeper, the commission was put to the test promptly. Drought in the Delaware basin began in 1961 as the commission was being formed; it grew steadily worse and produced a crisis in interstate relations in the summer of 1965. On June 14, in violation of the Supreme Court decree, New York City stopped making releases from its Delaware reservoirs, which had fallen to little more than a fourth of their capacity.

The procedure set forth in the compact was followed successfully in the weeks after New York's action. The commission held a public hearing, declared an emergency, and worked out a temporary formula for diversions and releases in lieu of the court decree. New York resumed releases but at a lower level than the decree would have required. Thereafter, until the drought ended early in 1967, the commission repeatedly extended the declaration of emergency and revised the diversion-and-release formula in response to chang-

20. *Delaware River Basin Compact*, House Judiciary Hearings, p. 45.

ing conditions on the river. It sought to assure a large enough flow to protect Philadelphia against the salt front while safeguarding New York against exhaustion of its reservoirs. Despite threats from New Jersey and Pennsylvania, none of the parties went to the Supreme Court. The commission thus passed its first test. In devising terms of settlement, it had been able to draw on its powers over water resources throughout the basin and its links to other public organizations. The flow of the river had been maintained partly by arranging for releases from two privately owned reservoirs and from a federal reservoir on the Lehigh River. The benefits of a comprehensive, areal approach to river basin management were demonstrated.[21]

Though an important test of the commission, the drought was a limited, special test. The commission had responded successfully to an emergency. What it would do typically and routinely remained to be seen.

## The Commission's Activity

The DRBC's actual functions have fallen far short of its formal powers. Except for navigation control, there is virtually nothing that the DRBC is not authorized to do with respect to water resources in the basin, yet its activity has been limited and selective. After more than ten years, it is still seeking to develop a set of functions that will be stable, serve important public purposes, and not be fatally undermined by the noncooperation of member governments.

One of the principal duties of the commission, which potentially is also a major source of its influence, is to maintain the comprehensive plan for development and use of water in the basin. No project having a substantial effect on water resources may be undertaken without a finding by the commission that the project is consistent with the plan. However, the commission has not had an independent capacity for comprehensive planning. It has created a plan by reviewing and approving proposals put before it by other

21. The account of the DRBC's response to the drought draws on Richard A. Hogarty, *The Delaware River Drought Emergency*, Inter-University Case Program, no. 107 (Bobbs-Merrill, 1970), p. 44; the DRBC annual reports for 1965, 1966, and 1967; and the September 1965 issue of the *Delaware Basin Bulletin*, published by the Water Resources Association of the Delaware River Basin.

agencies, mainly the Corps of Engineers, which completed its massive survey of the Delaware just before the commission's founding. Much of the commission's routine business consists of reviewing local private and public projects, such as construction of water supply and waste treatment works, piers, dikes, docks, and power stations, which become part of the comprehensive plan upon being approved. A typical agenda for a commission meeting contains perhaps a dozen such items, which have been reviewed by the staff before the commission acts on them. The approval rate is very high, but this disguises the fact that the staff often secures changes by negotiation. With some conspicuous exceptions, such as two nuclear generating plants proposed by the Atomic Energy Commission and approved by the DRBC in 1973, most of the projects are not controversial and many are minor. Some state officials criticize the commission for failing to distinguish projects having a "substantial" effect on the basin's water resources, which the compact says it shall review, from the merely trivial. Others question whether the commission's review really brings to bear a distinctive competence rather than merely repeating the reviews of federal and state agencies. As time has passed, the commission has developed its own principles and standards.

The commission has not carried out major development activity. It was not expected to do so, despite the authority given it. Nor has it become a source of demands for federal development expenditures or a means by which the states secure federal commitments of major expenditure, a result that some opponents of federal participation in the compact feared. By the spring of 1973 the Tocks Island dam, much the biggest project proposed for the basin by the Corps of Engineers, had not yet been started, and its future remained uncertain, jeopardized variously by problems of design and cost and by opposition from environmental interests. The commission, rather than being a medium for securing federal commitments to development, has more often been a medium through which governors have protected their states against unwanted private or federal projects or project features. For example, Delaware was able to delay private construction of a large crosscountry petroleum pipeline until the commission secured safeguards against rupture. New Jersey was able to secure a change in the design and federal funding of a portion of interstate highway;

as a result of the commission's objections, the Bureau of Public Roads agreed to provide funds for elevating a bridge.

Increasingly, the commission conceives of itself as a manager of the basin's water resources. It keeps track of what the river is doing and of what men and organizations are doing to the river. While most of the commission's work is technical, it is quite varied, depending on what opportunities individual staff members see. Describing a typical day of staff activity, the commission's annual report for 1972 says:

The watershed planner would be providing assistance to one of dozens of local conservation groups with whom he is DRBC's link. . . . And the water-land use planner would be making a population analysis or be off discussing a sewerage construction grant problem with the Delaware Valley Regional Planning Commission. . . . The geologist might be in Carbon County in the Poconos checking on a groundwater contamination complaint. The problems of fish passing through a generating turbine may be under analysis by the biologist. . . . Or he might be out collecting limnological data from a dozen tributaries to determine their effects on the upper Delaware.[22]

Routinely, the staff gathers data on the flow of the river, monitors pollution spills, and alerts downstream users to spills. Also, the commission has assumed from state and local governments the obligation of reimbursing the federal government for the portion of development project costs attributable to water supply. It will control storage, allocation, and wholesaling of water at all federally developed reservoirs and will reimburse the federal government with revenue from sales.[23]

In doing less than the compact authorizes, the commission has done less than its proponents hoped and its opponents feared. The explanation appears to lie in the tension between the commission's form and its function. In function, it is a radical innovation in American government: broad powers hitherto vested in federal and state agencies are given to a compact commission with a regional jurisdiction. But the representative form of the commission tends to negate what the compact has done otherwise. The commission cannot exercise its powers unless the member governments concur, and

22. Delaware River Basin Commission, *Annual Report, 1972*, p. 22.

23. This summary of the commission's activities is based on a reading of the commission's annual reports and meeting dockets and minutes, as well as on interviews with staff members.

they and their component executive agencies are not amenable to being displaced. Also, the commission depends for funds on what they contribute.[24] It has no independent source of revenue. In short, representativeness is inconsistent with a radical shift in the locus of major functions.

The DRBC's difficulties in getting established are illustrated by what has happened to its most important activity, pollution control. In this field more than any other, the commission has sought to exercise the broad powers that the compact grants. Pollution control accounted for nearly half of the 1972 budget of $1.5 million.[25] However, the commission never fully succeeded in establishing its jurisdiction, and as of 1973 its activity was declining.

## Controlling Pollution

In the mid-1960s, pollution control seemed a promising activity for a fledgling regional organization to undertake. In this as in other matters, the compact gives the DRBC comprehensive powers.[26] Public interest in the subject was rising. Because water quality regulation was predominantly a state function, the DRBC, as a state-sponsored organization, appeared to have a good chance of performing it, and there was a history of interstate cooperation. In 1936 the four states had created by parallel legislation the Interstate Commission on the Delaware Basin (INCODEL) and had cooperated through it to set standards and clean up the main stem of the river. One of the DRBC's first acts was to adopt INCODEL's standards. Moreover, a federal report on pollution of the Delaware

24. The United States, Pennsylvania, New York, and New Jersey each pay 23 percent of the operating budget; Delaware pays 8 percent.

25. The DRBC's appropriations, by program, were as follows in 1972: water supply, $56,000; water demand, $37,000; recreation, $72,000; power, $30,000; project review, $156,000; water quality, $713,000; comprehensive plan, $207,000; flood loss, $77,000; basin operation, $134,000; small watersheds, $38,000; capital program, $2,000.

26. Article 5 says: "The commission may undertake investigations and surveys, and acquire, construct, operate and maintain projects and facilities to control potential pollution and abate or dilute existing pollution. . . . The commission may assume jurisdiction to control future pollution and abate existing pollution in the waters of the basin. . . . The commission . . . may classify the waters of the basin and establish standards of treatment of sewage, industrial or other waste. . . . the commission may adopt . . . rules, regulations and standards to control such future pollution and abate existing pollution."

estuary gave the DRBC a specific opportunity to act. The Public Health Service began the study in 1961, when the DRBC was still being formed. In anticipation of the report, the DRBC resolved early in 1965 to translate the conclusions into appropriate water quality standards.

Having committed itself to set standards, the DRBC had to decide what standards to set. The federal survey, released in the summer of 1966, set the terms of debate. The survey covered the most industrialized and hence the most polluted portion of the river, an eighty-six-mile stretch of the estuary that begins at Trenton. It found that deterioration occurred rapidly below Trenton and became extreme below Philadelphia. The survey cited no hazard to health, but it said that recreational uses of the estuary were "severely restricted."[27]

The survey defined five different levels of water use and quality, called "objective sets," and estimated the monetary costs and benefits associated with each. Just to maintain the present quality of the river (Objective Set V), without realizing any additional benefits, would cost an estimated $30 million through the period 1975–80. To achieve water safe for swimming in the upper and lower reaches of the estuary and a high level of sport and commercial fishing (Objective Set I) would require an estimated expenditure of $460 million and would yield benefits estimated at $160 million to $350 million. The costs and benefits of the intermediate objective sets were estimated as follows:

| Set | Cost (millions of dollars) | Benefits (millions of dollars) |
|-----|---------------------------|-------------------------------|
| II  | 200–300                   | 140–320                       |
| III | 100–150                   | 130–310                       |
| IV  | 70–120                    | 120–280                       |

A reasonable and disinterested man, if he had based his evaluation on information in the federal survey only, would probably

27. U.S. Department of the Interior, Federal Water Pollution Control Administration, *Delaware Estuary Comprehensive Study: Summary of the Preliminary Report and Findings* (July 1966), pp. 1–4. For a technical analysis of this report and an account of action on it within the basin, see Allen V. Kneese and Blair T. Bower, *Managing Water Quality: Economics, Technology, Institutions* (Washington: Resources for the Future, 1968), pp. 224–35; and Bruce Ackerman and James Sawyer, "The Uncertain Search for Environmental Policy: Scientific Factfinding and Rational Decisionmaking along the Delaware River," *University of Pennsylvania Law Review*, vol. 120 (January 1972), pp. 419–503.

have chosen Set III, which promised substantial improvement in river quality at a favorable benefit–cost ratio (though no more favorable than that estimated for Set IV). As the middle course, Set III would constitute the compromise between contending interests. Nevertheless, the DRBC voted in 1967 to adopt Set II. The federal member and three states (New York, New Jersey, Pennsylvania) favored the higher standard. Only Delaware favored Set III.

Perhaps surprisingly, the commission's action on water quality standards did not divide the federal government and the states. State governments are reputed to be relatively responsive to material interests—industries, in this case—which could be expected to oppose both strict pollution regulations and higher taxes for waste treatment works. As Grant McConnell has written, "Material values are much more characteristic of narrow than of broad constituencies; 'altruistic,' 'sentimental,' or 'public' interests are more readily given expression and support in large constituencies."[28] Thus the federal government might have been expected to favor the "altruistic" interest in clean water and the states to prefer a lower standard of quality. Moreover, interstate organizations for pollution control are reputed to arrive at "lowest common denominator" positions. It might have been predicted that a joint organization, the DRBC, would yield a compromise between a (high) federal position and a (lower) state position. Decentralization within the DRBC might be measured by the states' ability to influence the federal position. But this was not the pattern, and at the level of commission action the effects of jointness within the DRBC were not apparent.

The staff took the lead in arguing for a very high standard of quality. "We were the first environmentalists," one later recalled.[29] The staff conceded that, if economic criteria alone were used, Set III would be preferable to Set II, but it argued that the decision should be based on intangible values: "a clean stream, similar to a beautiful park, reflects the conscience of a community and is an attribute far beyond monetary benefits that may be assigned."[30] In large part, this position reflected the preference of professional specialists for

28. *Private Power and American Democracy* (Knopf, 1966), p. 117.

29. Whitall interview, March 26, 1973.

30. James F. Wright, "Evaluation of Estuary Report," statement delivered at Water Quality Conference of the Delaware River Basin Commission, Philadelphia, July 27, 1966; DRBC files, Washington.

high standards of public service and amenity, but tactical considerations were also at work. The staff deliberately tried to overcome the unfavorable reputation of interstate compact organizations and to show that a state-created agency could take the relatively "progressive" position, serving nonmaterial values and a large, diffuse public, rather than a position that responded to parochial, material interests. The commission's executive director said at a public hearing that "[our decision] will influence national attitudes toward interstate river basin agencies."[31] Indirectly, then, the jointness of the organization may have encouraged the staff's choice of a high standard. It had an incentive to show the federal member and a larger national audience just how progressive the states could be.

In urging a high standard, the staff was assured in advance of backing from New York, whose governor was promoting a massive antipollution program, and from New Jersey. A newly elected governor in Pennsylvania, under intense and conflicting pressures within his state, decided in favor of the higher standard shortly before the vote. The only important opposition within the commission came from Delaware and from the city of Philadelphia, whose water commissioner, Samuel S. Baxter, served as adviser to the Pennsylvania member.[32]

Baxter argued that the commission should make a decision on economic grounds, and that the additional cost of Set II was not worth the benefits. He said that there was no point in making water in the port of Philadelphia pure enough for swimming, he doubted the technical feasibility of the standards, and he questioned whether knowledge of probable results was sufficient to justify large expenditures. He estimated that to meet the commission's standards would add $8,445,000 a year to Philadelphia's budget and raise the sewer rental charge for city residents by 33 to 44 percent, depending on the availability of federal aid. If Philadelphians could choose,

31. James F. Wright, "Delaware Estuary Pollution Control: The Problems, Issues, and Alternatives," staff presentation for DRBC water quality standards public hearing, Trenton, Jan. 26, 1967; DRBC files, Washington.

32. The cities of New York and Philadelphia, which were members of the DRBAC, had hoped for membership on the compact commission. The inferior legal status of the municipal corporation precluded this, but city officials—the water commissioners, usually—have had a connection to the commission as advisers to the New York and Pennsylvania members. Similarly, the Philadelphia district engineer of the Corps of Engineers serves as adviser to the federal member, partially offsetting the presumed advantage that the federal membership gives the Department of the Interior.

he said, they would rather spend the money for better schools than to make swimming, water skiing, and the passage of additional shad possible in the Delaware.[33] McConnell's proposition about constituency size may be confirmed in this case, but it took a constituency as small as a city (Philadelphia) or the smallest of the four states (Delaware) to reject the "altruistic" position in favor of the more realistic, or materially oriented, one.

The "constituency" of the staff in this case extended to the whole basin and beyond. Local newspapers were urging the commission to take a national lead. "From all directions," the commission's annual report had declared in 1966, "eyes were on the Delaware in search of evidence that a basin community could respond locally to the increasing public demands for cleaner streams."[34] In trying to broaden its support, the DRBC's position was just the reverse of the TVA's. Created by a national coalition without substantial support from the region, TVA had developed an ideology and strategy of local and regional accommodation. The DRBC had been created with regional but no national support, and it accommodated at the national level.

The dissenting state, Delaware, accepted the commission's decision. The Federal Water Pollution Control Agency would sooner or later have compelled Delaware to meet the higher standard anyway. Under the Water Quality Control Act of 1965, Congress had ordered that states set standards for interstate rivers and had given the FWPCA authority to approve the standards. The DRBC served as a medium for interstate coordination of standards for the Delaware and probably facilitated the definition of a common position, but without the commission standards would have been set by federal-state action. In fact, the federal and state governments proceeded as if the commission did not exist.

The commission did not replace the states in the conduct of pollution control. It has acted jointly with them in adopting water quality standards and regulations, making allotments of the river's

33. "Testimony of Samuel S. Baxter at Public Hearing of Delaware River Basin Commission, Trenton, N.J., January 27, 1967"; Baxter to DRBC, Feb. 3, 1967; Baxter to Norman M. Lack, Alternate Chairman, DRBC, Feb. 23, 1967; all in DRBC files, Washington. This account of the DRBC's action on water quality standards is drawn mainly from documents in those files, supplemented by interviews with James F. Wright and Samuel S. Baxter.

34. DRBC, *Annual Report, 1966,* p. 7.

assimilative capacity to dischargers, and issuing abatement schedules. It has relied on them for enforcement, although enforcement actions undertaken jointly with Pennsylvania in 1973 may set a precedent for more such activity. Under federal legislation, each of the states has continued to submit standards for federal approval. If the FWPCA had chosen to treat the commission's submission as the only legitimate one for the Delaware, the states would have had to defer to the DRBC, but this did not happen. The FWPCA's regional office delayed action on the DRBC's standards for several months, electing to treat the states' individual submissions as legitimate. It took the position that until the governors designated the commission as the agency to set standards it must deal directly with the states, and the governors had done no more than designate the commission as the basin's planning agency. Not until the commission's executive director appealed to Secretary of the Interior Udall did the FWPCA approve the commission's standards too. Where there were discrepancies, the FWPCA approved whichever standard was higher.

Nor did the federal government make concessions to the commission's jurisdiction. The DRBC failed to secure special recognition in the 1965 act, to which it proposed an amendment that would have prohibited the federal administration from directly promulgating standards "within a river basin which is under jurisdiction of a Federal-interstate agency created by a compact to which the United States is a signatory party and vested with the authority to set and enforce water quality standards for such basin."[35] When as a member of the commission the secretary of the interior voted for water quality standards, he said that this did not commit the department to approving them under the 1965 act. The normal review would still have to occur.

The headlong expansion of federal activity in the field of pollution control eventually brought the commission into conflict with both the Corps of Engineers, which began to require permits for discharge into navigable waters under the Rivers and Harbors Act of 1899, and the Environmental Protection Agency, created in 1970 to administer federal pollution control programs. The commission

---

35. *Water Quality Act of 1965*, Hearing before a Special Subcommittee on Air and Water Pollution of the Senate Committee on Public Works, 89 Cong. 1 sess. (1965), p. 90.

complained in 1971 that a series of new federal regulations failed
to acknowledge its existence as a federal-interstate agency, jeopardized its pollution control program, and threatened to displace the
states entirely. The federal agencies rejected or ignored the DRBC's
complaints. As new claimants entered the field of pollution control
and as old ones took new initiatives, the DRBC struggled to protect
its own newly asserted claim. As of 1973, it appeared to be losing
the struggle. The Water Pollution Control Amendments of 1972
authorized as a national policy the prohibition of discharges into
streams—which jeopardizes the DRBC's unique policy of allocating
shares of a river's assimilative capacity to dischargers—and gave the
Environmental Protection Agency broad powers to set standards
and issue regulations. Also, by imposing new obligations on state
governments the act further diminished the willingness of basin
states to cooperate with the commission; they have declined to
designate the commission as the planning agency for the basin under section 303(e) of the act, which requires that each state have
a continuing planning process for pollution control. This time,
in contrast to 1965, the commission did not seek a protective
amendment. Instead it began making plans to deploy staff to other
activities.[36]

The commission's best chance for affecting pollution control may
lie at the municipal level. It has a policy of promoting regional
solutions to pollution problems, which means that it tries to get
local governments to consolidate their waste treatment plants. This
policy was put to its first serious test in 1970–71 in the case of the
Darby Creek Joint Authority, a sewage treatment agency for twelve
residential boroughs in Delaware County, Pennsylvania. The DCJA

36. DRBC, *Annual Report, 1972*, p. 4. Pennsylvania's Governor Shapp informed
the acting administrator of EPA in 1973 that he wished to designate the DRBC to
"participate with our state in carrying out the continuing planning process in those
parts of our state located in the Delaware River Basin." Milton J. Shapp to Robert
W. Fri, Aug. 9, 1973; in files of the Pennsylvania Department of Environmental Resources, Harrisburg. Other states had agreed to send similar statements to EPA. However, far from agreeing to designate the commission as the planning agency in the
basin area, Pennsylvania proceeded in 1973 to let nearly $2 million in contracts to
a consulting firm for studies of the basin. Pennsylvania informed the DRBC that it
would have "a voice in our effort," but that to designate the commission as the 303(e)
agency would delay the state's planning program. James F. Wright to Maurice K.
Goddard, April 18, 1973, and Goddard to Wright, May 22, 1973; in files of the Pennsylvania Department of Environmental Resources, Bureau of Water Quality Management.

sought to double its treatment capacity. The DRBC, jointly with the Pennsylvania Department of Environmental Resources, refused a permit, arguing that the best course would be for the DCJA to connect with Philadelphia's southwest treatment plant via an interceptor. Despite opposition from the area's congressman, who supported the DCJA, the DRBC voted to compel the regional solution, which was much more efficient than the alternative. A similar effort that would have required cooperation between two counties and a number of industries in southern New Jersey failed for lack of economic justification. The commission has also worked on plans for a regional sewerage system for the Brandywine Creek watershed, an effort that will require interstate as well as interlocal cooperation. More important, the commission has adopted a wastewater treatment plan for the Tocks Island and Delaware Water Gap National Recreation Area. Worked out by the staff with the aid of a private consultant and other public agencies, this plan covers a three-state area above the Tocks Island dam site. Adoption should improve prospects for development at Tocks Island.

## Federal Coordination through the DRBC

Founders of the DRBC attached considerable importance to the single federal agent as a coordinator of federal action within the basin. The federal government must belong because "the Federal Government can be controlled only by itself. Having the Federal Government [in the compact] is the best way to . . . coordinate and integrate the programs of the Federal agencies."[37] The governor of New Jersey, Robert B. Meyner, put it more bluntly in an appeal to federal officials in the spring of 1961: "If you leave us as four states in a Compact, you are leaving us chasing around from agency to agency to get the job done. We think . . . that if you adopt this Compact, there will be one person appointed by the President who can coordinate these agencies, and at least get them to take a position."[38] Planners of the commission hoped that this one person would be able to speak authoritatively for the federal government; if he could

37. *Delaware River Basin Compact*, H. Rept. 310, 87 Cong. 1 sess. (1961), p. 7.
38. "Official Report," pp. 19–20.

not, the commission could not fulfill its functions of comprehensive planning and policy making for the basin. The dominant aim of federal agencies, however, has been to avoid making commitments through the DRBC. The federal commissioner has been in an anomalous position. He is supposed to represent within the commission the interests of a government that has never been convinced that its interests are served by his being there.[39]

If the federal commissioner were to find an ally anywhere in the executive branch, it would probably have been the Bureau of the Budget, now the Office of Management and Budget (OMB), because of that agency's interest in interagency coordination. In the spring of 1961, when regional proponents and federal agency opponents of the compact met on Capitol Hill, the Budget Bureau's deputy director, Elmer B. Staats, listened sympathetically to the complaint of Governor Meyner about having too many federal agencies to deal with. "I think a great deal can be done in this area," he remarked, implicitly acknowledging that the Bureau too was concerned about coordinating federal agencies.[40] But as the organization took shape with federal participation, Budget Bureau officials seemed more concerned that the commission *not* be a program operator than that it become a coordinator. The job of the federal member, Staats suggested to the White House in the fall of 1961, was to keep the commission pointed in the direction of planning rather than program action. The Bureau's invariable concern in dealing with the DRBC has been to ensure that it not be a medium for making federal commitments, not make jurisdictional claims that conflict with the duties of federal agencies, and not bypass or anticipate normal processes of authorization and appropriation. The Bureau has regarded the DRBC as a constitutional anomaly to be treated with caution rather than as an opportunity to be seized.

The resistance of federal operating and regulatory agencies to working through the DRBC is best illustrated by the use of the federal veto in 1968. The DRBC voted on an amendment to its comprehensive plan that would have authorized the development

---

39. The federal "member" of the DRBC is the secretary of the interior, but for most purposes the federal representative is the "commissioner," a presidential appointee who serves full time, holds the rank of GS-18, and has an office in Washington in the Department of the Interior.

40. "Official Report," p. 68.

of pumped storage at Tocks Island. The resolution was designed in large part to settle an environmental protection issue that had been raging over a placid, pretty place called Sunfish Pond and causing political problems for the governor of New Jersey. The Federal Power Commission (FPC) and the Corps of Engineers feared that the resolution would commit them to a particular development proposal, although the resolution was worded in very general terms. Because of their objections, Secretary of the Interior Udall decided that the federal commissioner should abstain from the vote. The Water Resources Council then agreed that the secretary should invoke the federal veto by filing a formal notice of nonconcurrence.[41] The council concluded that this was the only way to preserve the federal government's freedom of action. (Later, Congress did authorize construction of pumped storage at Tocks Island.)

The federal agencies are not uniformly hostile to the federal-interstate compact form, as internal debate in 1967 on a proposed compact for the Susquehanna basin showed. Discussing the proposal within the Water Resources Council, representatives of the FPC and the Department of the Army opposed another compact, whereas the secretary of the interior defended the form in general and the DRBC in particular. Being the federal member of the commission had influenced his view. Membership of the secretary of the interior was one sign of the President's intention to give that department a leading role in federal natural-resources development, and the experience of membership fostered loyalty to the organization and approbation of its actions, particularly in the field of pollution control. Below the level of the secretary's office, however, and when its own program interests are at stake, Interior has been no more willing than other agencies to make concessions to the DRBC. When it had charge of pollution control, it carefully refrained from making binding commitments within the DRBC, and it firmly resisted an attempt by the DRBC in the 1960s to realize revenue from the development of pumped-storage power at Tocks Island. This was an important issue for the commission inasmuch as the hydroelectric

41. The compact provides that federal agencies shall be bound by provisions of the DRBC's comprehensive plan if the federal member has concurred in them, but abstention from voting, which had occurred in this case, does not constitute nonconcurrence. Concurrence is presumed unless the federal member files a formal notice within sixty days of the vote.

power potential at Tocks Island was the commission's one hope of securing a sizable, stable supply of independent revenue. In cooperation with a combine of private New Jersey utility companies, the DRBC worked out a proposal whereby the utilities would have built a large pumped-storage plant, paid the commission a fee of $500,000 a year, and made available to the commission at cost an amount of power equivalent to what would have been produced by a conventional project at the site, such as the Corps of Engineers had proposed and Congress had authorized in the Flood Control Act of 1962.[42] By this arrangement with the DRBC, the utilities hoped to forestall federal development of hydroelectric power and introduction into the basin of the controversial federal policy of giving preference in the sale of power to municipal and cooperative distributors. The interests of Interior were much at stake in this proposal, since it markets the power generated at federal dams. The assistant secretary for water and power development challenged the legality of the utilities' plan and charged that it would permit the DRBC "to derive a windfall benefit from a Federal project."[43] He also feared that it would set a precedent for other river basins covered by interstate commissions. Interior's position was that the utilities should make their payment to the federal government, not the DRBC, and that they should make available to the federal government's preferred customers, of whom the DRBC should be treated merely as one, a block of power equivalent to what would have been produced by a conventional project at the site. This was

42. The legal basis for the utilities' proposed payment to the DRBC was complex. Because the utilities would use water from the Tocks Island reservoir for the pumped-storage process, and because the DRBC had agreed to pay the federal government the cost of creating the water supply, the DRBC was entitled—its staff reasoned and the utilities agreed—to realize benefits from the utilities' use of the water. Yet the figure of $500,000 was a flat fee; the utilities were not promising simply to reimburse the commission for water used. The amount of the payment was based on several assumptions: that, if the DRBC did not assume the costs of water supply, there would be no public development at Tocks Island; that without such development the utilities would have to meet their needs for power independently, at some other site at much greater expense; and that the benefits they would realize from participating in the Tocks Island development, estimated to be $1 million a year after their obligations to the federal government had been met, should be divided equally with the DRBC.

43. Kenneth Holum, assistant secretary, water and power development, to the undersecretary, Department of the Interior, March 15, 1967; DRBC files, Washington. The account of the dispute between Interior and the DRBC is drawn from documents in these files.

a prolonged, complex issue which pitted the DRBC staff against program officials in the Department of the Interior, and Interior won.

The DRBC would have made more headway in its jurisdictional struggles with federal executive agencies if it had had support in Congress. Once the commission was established, the basin's congressional delegation ceased to show much interest in it. Its existence does not enlarge the flow of federal benefits to their constituencies, and the committees with which the DRBC deals are more responsive to federal line agencies than to a regional commission. The Public Works committees declined in 1965 to grant the commission's requests for special recognition in the Water Quality Control Act of 1965, and later they took the federal agencies' side in jurisdictional disputes over developing the hydroelectric power potential at Tocks Island. Congress declined even to grant the DRBC status as a most preferred customer for the public power to be marketed at Tocks Island, although the DRBC staff lobbied hard for such a provision and the governor of New Jersey, Richard J. Hughes, appealed to the chairman of the Senate Public Works Committee.

Federal unwillingness to make commitments through the DRBC is one major limitation on the federal commissioner (and of course on the organization as a whole). Another is the federal inability to arrive at unified positions. Including in the commission a single federal representative was supposed to make it an instrument for resolving interagency differences, but neither the federal commissioner nor the DRBC staff is able to intervene successfully. For example, they were not involved in the 1960s in settling a major difference between the Fish and Wildlife Service and the Corps of Engineers over prospective losses to the New Jersey oyster industry as a result of the Tocks Island project. The Fish and Wildlife Service claimed that the damage would amount to $6 million a year; the Corps's estimate was $513,000. The benefit–cost ratio of the project depended critically on whose estimate was accepted. In 1968 Congress questioned both the Corps and the DRBC on this issue. The answers are worth quoting at length for what they show both about the DRBC's lack of involvement and, more generally, about the way such interagency disputes are handled.

MR. MORRIS [congressman from New Mexico]. Isn't it customary when you have an agency that does disagree, to take it to the Bureau of the Budget? Are they not the refereeing agency in the administration?

GENERAL KOISCH [division engineer of the Corps of Engineers]. Not in my experience, sir.

MR. MORRIS. Who is?

MR. WHITTEN [congressman from Mississippi]. Mr. Wright, would you care to answer that?

MR. WRIGHT [executive director of the DRBC]. I would like to comment on this alleged loss in a slightly different vein.

The oyster crop in the Delaware, and we have records that run back to 1880 . . .

MR. MORRIS. Mr. Chairman, I appreciate the witness' testifying; but what bearing does this have on the question that I asked?

MR. WRIGHT. Only this: Any allegation that Tocks Island would radically reduce the value of the oyster crop is highly questionable . . .

MR. MORRIS. Mr. Chairman, I appreciate the witness' speech. My question perhaps was misunderstood.

MR. WHITTEN. You might direct it to the General.

MR. MORRIS. My question was, what is the usual procedure when you have disagreements between the agencies . . . ? I thought the procedure was to refer the dispute to the Bureau of the Budget.

GENERAL KOISCH. Generally, sir, you are more or less on your own when you have an authorization from Congress to produce a project or to do a study. When we go to the other agencies of Government for advice or assistance, as we did in this case, and we have reason to question what they tell us or we think they may have followed the wrong guidelines, we consider it only appropriate then to utilize our own judgment. . . .

The next questions come from a congressional committee.

MR. MORRIS. I suggest, Mr. Chairman, that our staff review this wide difference of opinion between the Corps and the Fish and Wildlife Service . . .

MR. WHITTEN. Unless there is objection, we will ask the staff to make such a review and advise the committee of its findings.[44]

Intrafederal differences that affect the commission do not necessarily take the form of interagency differences. Another possibility

44. *Public Works Appropriations for 1969 for Water and Power Resources Development and the Atomic Energy Commission*, Hearings before the House Appropriations Committee, 90 Cong. 2 sess. (1968), pt. 1, pp. 1155–56.

is interregional differences within the same agency. In 1973 the Environmental Protection Agency requested the basin states to revise their quality standards for interstate rivers, but different regional offices sought different standards for the Delaware. (The basin is divided between the federal government's New York and Philadelphia regions.) State pollution control officials met with EPA regional officials under commission auspices, but it was not possible to resolve the differences in that forum. Ultimately, the issue was referred to the EPA administrator.

Unable to deliver commitments from the federal government or to state a unified position, the federal commissioner of the DRBC typically reports the positions of federal agencies. He is an "ambassador" rather than a "commissioner," according to a DRBC staff member. The routine, formalized means by which he secures agency clearances is a federal field committee which he chairs and which meets a week before the commission to review the forthcoming agenda. These meetings tend to be perfunctory because most agenda items are narrow and technical and the commission staff has usually worked out coordination with federal agencies in advance. The federal commissioner solicits policy guidance from agencies in Washington, either from the secretary of the interior and the Water Resources Council, as when the federal government cast the veto in 1968, or from the examiner in the OMB's Natural Resources Division who is in charge of reviewing the DRBC's budget. The OMB has tried to keep track of what the DRBC does. "Small bucks, potentially big issues," the examiner explained in an interview. The federal commissioner as of the early 1970s was regularly in touch with OMB for guidance and to provide information.

Whether OMB or the Water Resources Council should supply guidance has been an issue. In the late 1960s the council sought an executive order that would have given it the right to guide the federal vote. The DRBC prefers to avoid getting mixed up with an interagency coordinating council which acts slowly and speaks obscurely. By contrast, reporting to an examiner in OMB means "one-stop shopping," as the examiner put it. When the executive order was proposed, the four basin governors protested to the President, and the commission followed this up with a memorandum to the Bureau of the Budget, which refused to issue the order. Having supported the DRBC's claim that the federal member is responsible to the President and to him alone, the OMB is in a good position to exercise supervision itself.

## Appraisal of the Commission

Because the commission embodies a major attempt at innovation and because it depends so heavily on support from member governments, its evolution is bound to be slow. Still, it seems clear after more than ten years that the commission will not develop into the powerful organization that the compact authorizes, and it may atrophy. It might have done so before now if it had not had a competent, committed staff, who have been drawn to the organization because it is something new and different.

Predictably, the DRBC has been most successful in pursuing the purpose for which the states came together in the first place: settling their disputes over water allocation. Thus the lesson of the DRBC is a familiar, elemental one. A coordinating organization will work only to the extent that the participants share an interest in making it work. The shared interest of the states in avoiding resort to the Supreme Court helped them reach agreement through the medium of the commission, as it had led them to create the commission. But the states rarely launch initiatives of any kind through the commission; initiatives originate with the staff, which must cajole the states into cooperating. The states' contributions to the budget have occasionally been in doubt; their limited capacity to contribute is an important constraint on the commission.[45]

The lack of a federal commitment to the organization has been a handicap too, and the commission's uniqueness compounds this handicap. The DRBC needs federal cooperation, but as long as there is only one such organization (or two), federal agencies can ignore it (or them). If the form were more common, it would be harder to withhold acknowledgment that it exists.

The DRBC was formed ad hoc, as a result of fortuitous political opportunities and in response to particular needs that happened to

45. Interview with Harold Jacobs, former alternate member of DRBC from Delaware, May 24, 1973. State officials in Pennsylvania and New Jersey were also interviewed.

be strongly felt at the time. What has emerged over the course of more than a decade is a small, technically oriented organization that oversees the development and use of water resources in the region and tries to make improvements whenever the staff sees the chance. Though the commission does not begin to exercise the sweeping authority granted it by the compact, the existence of such authority enables it to do a variety of things that a mere planning and coordinating organization, such as a Title II commission, cannot do.

## Duplicating the DRBC

In the decade following the creation of the DRBC, federal-interstate compacts were proposed for several more basins—the Hudson, the Potomac, the Great Lakes, and the Susquehanna—but as of 1973 only the compact for the Susquehanna had been approved, and that despite the continuing reluctance of the executive branch.

Like the Delaware compact, that for the Susquehanna originated with the state governments, in this case New York, Pennsylvania, and Maryland. For both strategy and substance, the Susquehanna planners took the Delaware experience as a model. They did not invite federal participation in the drafting, and they built support in Congress and the state capitols in order to circumscribe federal executive opposition. Having a precedent to rely on—and the DRBC *was* a precedent, despite the federal agencies' denial that it should be—was a great tactical asset.[46]

Introduction of the Susquehanna compact in Congress early in 1969 compelled the federal agencies to prepare a position on it. A Water Resources Council task force on river basin management institutions considered the issues posed by federal-interstate compacts more systematically than either Congress or the executive branch had done before. The report noted that the problems arising from such compacts had not been adequately discussed in public, with the result "that most of the Congressional leaders have not officially learned that the Susquehanna and Delaware compacts

46. For a detailed history of the compact, see William Voigt, Jr., *The Susquehanna Compact* (Rutgers University Press, 1972).

present difficult questions of government organization and a serious threat to the ability of the Federal government to carry out nation-wide policies established by Acts of Congress because of the carving out of a growing series of regional river basin exemptions."[47]

The report found that the federal government should become a signatory only when a river basin compact authorized a commission to perform "certain necessary and appropriate functions," including consultation among executive branches of the member governments, coordination of development plans and operations, and undertaking projects and activities "which the signatory parties agree can best be conducted through a regional commission—rather than through any existing Federal, State or local agency." A commission should fill gaps and administer activities that would benefit from regional administration. It was emphatically not appropriate, the report declared, for a compact commission to duplicate the functional responsibilities of federal, state, or local governments or "to become a non-elected super-government over a river basin" in lieu of constitutional governments. The task force report argued that superseding the functional pattern of federal administrative organization with a geographic pattern would produce chaos:

all the . . . Cabinet Departments and independent agencies perform certain functional responsibilities over the whole of the nation. It would create intolerable duplication and confusion if the nation were now to establish a series of river basin commissions throughout the United States, with management and operating responsibilities, to conduct and operate regional projects and activities in the very same areas in which the national functional departments are now operating.[48]

The Susquehanna compact, like that for the Delaware, gave the regional commission functions far beyond what the task force thought appropriate, but opposition was impractical. The states' action had begun too long ago, had proceeded too far, and had too much support in Congress and too firm a claim to a precedent (the

47. "The Position of the Federal Government on the Consent Bill for the Susquehanna Basin Compact," Report of the Task Force on River Basin Management Institutions, April 17, 1969; Water Resources Council files. The public position of the Water Resources Council on federal-interstate compacts and other types of river basin organizations may be found in Water Resources Council, "Alternative Institutional Arrangements for Managing River Basin Operations" (Washington, August 1967; processed).

48. "The Position of the Federal Government."

DRBC) for the executive branch to stop it in 1969. The task force concluded that Congress should consent to the compact if reservations requested by the Water Resources Council were included. Again the pattern of the DRBC was being repeated.

Action on the Susquehanna compact was completed late in 1970. In 1973, with about half the staff and one-third the budget of the DRBC, the new commission had yet to undertake any major activity. It was reviewing for possible revision a plan for the basin completed by the Corps of Engineers in 1970. Other activities have included coordinating aerial photography of the flooding caused by Hurricane Agnes in 1972, preparing guidelines for stream clearance, and mapping flood-prone communities under a contract with the Department of Housing and Urban Development and New York and Pennsylvania.

Whether more such compacts will follow depends on whether states and their congressional delegations can unite in proposing them. The Delaware and Susquehanna cases suggest that where proponents are united, the executive agencies will find opposition impractical, but the failure of any state to consent destroys the possibility of a compact. In the cases of the Hudson, the Potomac, and the Great Lakes, and before them New England, the states have fallen short of consensus.

# ⌈4⌉

# The Appalachian Regional Commission

WHEREAS the founders of the Delaware River Basin Commission (DRBC) set out to create an organization, the founders of the Appalachian Regional Commission (ARC) set out to create a program of federal spending for a depressed region. The organization was more or less incidental to the program. Nevertheless, as organizations will, it has come to be valued for its own sake, and in 1972 a Senate subcommittee held hearings on a bill that would have authorized such commissions for the whole country.

## The Founding

A few weeks before the presidential election of 1960, the Conference of Appalachian Governors (CAG) called on presidential and congressional candidates to "recognize the pressing needs of the Appalachian Region."[1] The winning presidential candidate was highly susceptible to the region's appeal. John F. Kennedy brought to office a sharp memory of his campaign encounter with Appalachian poverty and a heavy debt to West Virginia, where a primary victory had boosted him toward the Democratic nomination. The Kennedy administration at first sought to give Appalachia special

1. CAG, "A Resolution Subscribing to and Supporting a Declaration for Action Regarding the Appalachian Region," Oct. 18, 1960. This and other documents relating to the CAG's drive for Appalachian aid are in files in the office of John D. Whisman, states' regional representative (SRR), ARC, Washington.

treatment within the Area Redevelopment Administration, which was created in 1961 to administer a new national program for depressed areas, but this limited commitment produced no results in two years. The CAG continued to press the administration for something more. In April 1963, after a meeting with the Appalachian governors, President Kennedy announced the formation of a committee to plan a comprehensive development program for the region. The committee would include representatives of the federal agencies and the states, with the undersecretary of commerce as chairman. Nature had done its part to precipitate the President's action. In March severe floods struck the Cumberland valley of Kentucky and brought state officials to Washington to ask for disaster aid. While there they renewed requests for a regional development program.[2]

Federal agency participants in the committee promptly concluded that they could do nothing more for Appalachia within the limits of their existing authority and budgets, but they responded to the opportunity to present new requests. Study teams with federal and state members (though the majority had federal chairmen) prepared proposals, most of which called for enlarging federal programs in Appalachia. The committee—which had named itself PARC, the President's Appalachian Regional Commission—was assembling these proposals late in 1963 when President Kennedy was killed.

Despite initial doubt about this legacy from the Kennedy administration, after the Bureau of the Budget had trimmed PARC's multi-billion-dollar requests to a more manageable sum President Johnson embraced the program as his own and transmitted it to Congress in the spring of 1964. However, it did not immediately come to a vote in the House because the President and House leaders were not sure that the Democratic party could produce a majority for it. After the election, the party surely could, and promptly did. The Appalachian Regional Development Act (ARDA) passed in the spring of 1965 by a vote of 62–22 in the Senate and 257–165 in the House, even though it benefited less than a fourth of the states and less than 10 percent of the population. A majority of Democrats in both houses voted for the bill,

2. James L. Sundquist, *Politics and Policy: The Eisenhower, Kennedy, and Johnson Years* (Brookings Institution, 1968), pp. 97–105.

while a majority of Republicans were against it. It authorized highway expenditures of $840 million over a six-year period and $252.4
million for two years for other purposes, including health, land
stabilization and conservation, erosion control, timber development, mining area restoration, and construction of vocational education facilities and sewage treatment works.[3]

It would have been possible to increase federal aid to Appalachia
without creating any new organization, especially if the additional
money were for established programs. This possibility occurred to
management officials in the Bureau of the Budget, but planners in
PARC took for granted that a new regional program would require
a new organization. One member of PARC, Deputy Undersecretary of Agriculture James L. Sundquist, wrote at the time:

> From the outset, it has been apparent to everybody participating in
> PARC that some permanent body would need to be established, to serve
> as a planning organization, a lobbying group to obtain Federal funds,
> a promoter and stimulator of local activities, and, to the extent appro-
> priate an action agency. Appalachia cannot be brought up to the level
> of the country as a whole without a disproportionate share of Federal
> expenditures and these will not be obtained if the program is left to a
> series of independent Federal agencies each of which is equally con-
> cerned with all parts of the country.[4]

PARC sought an organizational form that could be established
quickly, would combine federal and state participation, and would
be independent of other agencies without encroaching upon them.
It would not, as one PARC memorandum put it, have "authority to
make any existing agency do anything it doesn't want to do," but it
would have "funds of its own to supplement other agencies' programs."[5] The proposed solution was a corporation chartered by
Congress whose shares would be bought by both the federal and
state governments. Such shares would cost very little, so that the
states' purchases could be paid for from the governors' contingency
funds. PARC planners reasoned that this technique would be much
quicker than creating a federal-state compact on the model of the
DRBC. Like the DRBC, the new organization would combine fed-

3. 79 Stat. 5.
4. Memorandum to the secretary of agriculture, Dec. 18, 1963; Department of
Agriculture files.
5. Richard H. Kraft to Comprehensive Program Development Team, Sept. 20,
1963; PARC files, SRR office, ARC.

eral and state membership. The corporation would be run by a board of directors consisting of governors of the participating states and, on the federal side, heads of those agencies determined by the President to have a substantial interest in the corporation's work. The governors would elect a state cochairman, and the President would appoint a federal cochairman, not himself an agency representative. If votes were required, the federal cochairman would cast one on behalf of the federal members, and the state cochairman, one on behalf of the state members. No action could be taken unless the two voted the same way.

The corporation was to have a mixture of functions. It was to plan a development program for the region and recommend modifications of federal, state, local, and private programs that would make them more consistent with its own comprehensive plan. It was to encourage formation of local development districts by granting part of their administrative expenses, and it could guarantee the bonds that such districts might issue to finance development projects. It could issue bonds itself, with a federal guarantee, and it could receive appropriations from Congress. With these funds, it would be authorized to undertake a wide variety of welfare, public works, and natural resources programs, typically "in cooperation with" federal agencies.[6]

When Harold Seidman, the Budget Bureau's assistant director for management and organization, saw this proposal, he was aghast. His first reaction was that much of it was completely unintelligible. He believed that it raised serious constitutional questions and would produce chaos both in federal-state relations and in relations among federal agencies. He said he could hardly imagine a worse proposal. In November he set forth objections at length in a memorandum to Budget Director Kermit Gordon. His principal objection was that, although the new corporation would be in law and in fact a federal agency, because the governors would sit on the board of directors it would not be under federal control. He also argued that the proposed organization would be unworkable. The voting procedure, by giving a veto to each cochairman, federal and state, was likely to result in stalemate. Superimposing the corporation on federal activities might slow down help to Appalachia rather than

6. PARC staff, "A Proposal for an Appalachian Development Organization," Oct. 17, 1963; PARC files, SRR office, ARC.

speed it up. Budgetary and administrative responsibilities would be unclear in fields the corporation would share with conventional federal agencies.[7] As an alternative, Seidman suggested a joint federal-state body whose functions would be limited to planning and coordination, rather like the river basin planning commissions for which a proposal approved by the Budget Bureau was before Congress.[8] This alternative was presented to PARC at a meeting in mid-December. Bureau officials proposed then that the new organization be limited to planning and stripped of grant, loan, or loan-guarantee functions.

As a result of the Bureau's objections, PARC's proposal was revised to call for two organizations—one a joint federal-state commission with responsibility for planning and coordinating a development program in Appalachia; the other, a federally chartered corporation with authority to make loans to and purchase the bonds of local development districts. Seidman had no objection to such a corporation as long as state officials did not share in its governing.

Congress killed the federal development corporation—the only significant change it made in the administration's bill. Republican members of the Public Works committees charged that the corporation would be a case of "back door" financing, and Democratic members, similarly suspicious of the corporation device, preferred aiding the states directly with grants. Unable to get the corporation through Congress, the Bureau of the Budget eliminated it and agreed to enlarge direct grants. The joint federal-state commission remained in the bill, a product of the Bureau's revision of PARC's bold proposal. It was to be composed of one federal member, called the "federal cochairman," to be appointed by the President and paid the same as an assistant secretary, and one member from each participating state, either the governor or the governor's designee or "such other person as may be provided by the law of the State." The state members were to elect their own cochairman.

The Appalachian Regional Development Act states that the ARC "shall develop . . . comprehensive and coordinated plans and programs and establish priorities" to carry out the purposes of the act. The ARC was to make recommendations for program and project

---

7. Harold Seidman to Kermit Gordon, Nov. 12, 1963; Office of Management and Budget files.

8. The Title II commissions. See chapter 6.

expenditures and to develop spending criteria, but it was not authorized to make expenditures. This authorization remained with federal line agencies, which would get extra funds for Appalachia. The commission also had a general mandate to promote the economic development of Appalachia and to coordinate public and private expenditures for that purpose. It was to "review and study . . . Federal, State, and local public and private programs and . . . recommend modifications or additions which will increase their effectiveness in the region," and it was to "serve as a focal point and coordinating unit for Appalachian programs." However, it was given no means with which to induce other organizations to support its objectives. The PARC report had remarked disingenuously that the commission's "coordinating role will not be backed by any sanctions, for none are needed."[9] A report of the Senate Public Works Committee declared flatly that the commission should "have no authority over any other agency of Government at any level."[10]

In sum, the commission began life with a broad and vague mandate, very limited authority, and no program money of its own; but before long, it overcame these handicaps.

## What the Commission Does

The commission performs two principal functions. First, it makes policy for and to a considerable extent administers the federal government's special program of aid to Appalachia. This program has proved to have strong support in Congress, and it seems likely to continue indefinitely. As of 1973, authorization for highway construction stands at $2.09 billion and extends through fiscal 1978; net cumulative authorizations for other purposes (authorizations less lapsed amounts) were $788.2 million at the end of fiscal 1973. Second, the commission carries out what it calls a "brokerage" function on behalf of the region, which might more accurately be called skilled lobbying in a legally sanctioned cause—the provision of benefits for Appalachia. As the commission's first executive direc-

9. *Appalachia: A Report by the President's Appalachian Regional Commission, 1964* (1964), p. 57.

10. *Appalachian Regional Development Act of 1965*, S. Rept. 13, 89 Cong. 1 sess. (1965), p. 6.

tor, Ralph Widner, explained to Congress in 1972, "We came to think of the staff really as a brokerage operation in the broadest sense of the word. Highly skilled people who knew how to take advantage of the grant-in-aid system on behalf of poor communities, and that has worked extremely well. . . . In a poor region of the country, it gives them the opportunity to take maximum advantage of the system."[11]

The commission's role as grant-in-aid administrator began in 1967, when it won amendments to the ARDA that enabled it to consolidate control over Appalachian expenditures. Sundquist had been right in saying that federal agencies would resist giving special treatment to one section of the country. When Appalachian funds were their responsibility, they offered Appalachian items up for sacrifice to the Bureau of the Budget. Also, the commission depended on federal agencies to approve project expenditures, and although conflict did not develop with all agencies, it was severe in the case of the Department of Commerce, which controlled the expenditures that were most important to the commission.[12] To remedy these problems, the commission proposed to Congress that Appalachian appropriations be made directly to it and that it be given authority to approve projects if federal officials found them to be consistent with federal law. Again the Budget Bureau's assistant director for organization and management objected, on the grounds that the change would convert the ARC from an advisory and plan-

11. *Public Works Development Act of 1972*, Hearings before the Subcommittee on Economic Development of the Senate Committee on Public Works, 92 Cong. 2 sess. (1972), p. 241.

12. Until the Department of Transportation was created in 1966, Commerce had authority over highway construction, which accounted for nearly 80 percent of the Appalachian authorization. Commerce also had authority to administer funds under section 214 of the ARDA, which supplements the federal share of a wide variety of projects, and section 302, which provides funds for state and local administration and for research and development. Section 214 money was important to the commission because a little of it would influence the location of a lot of projects; and section 302 money was important because it created state and local client organizations and otherwise could be used in discretionary ways. Commerce had authority over these parts of the act by default. Because they did not obviously belong to any other department and because the Bureau of the Budget had been unwilling to give spending authority to the commission, they went to the federal department with the most plausible claim to responsibility for economic development. This in itself irritated the commission.

ning body to an operating agency, precisely what he had opposed in the first place. He continued to argue that a joint federal-state agency could not receive federal appropriations or make program decisions. This would encroach upon the President's appointment powers; at worst, it was unconstitutional. He also feared that what Congress did for the ARC it would eventually do for other regional commissions that were developing as imitators of the ARC. The result would be a series of autonomous regional agencies with functions that cut across those of the federal domestic agencies. Such agencies, in his view, would be new subgovernments that could not be held fully accountable to either the federal government or the states. Existing agency programs would be further fragmented and coordinating problems would grow worse.[13] Congress enacted the commission's proposal with one concession to the Budget Bureau: funds were appropriated to the President, not the commission, although with the understanding that the President would transfer them to the federal cochairman, who would transfer them to federal agencies as projects were approved.

As of 1973, the commission is carrying out a varied program of spending in the thirteen states of the region (Alabama, Georgia, Kentucky, Maryland, Mississippi, New York, North Carolina, Ohio, Pennsylvania, South Carolina, Tennessee, Virginia, and West Virginia). The biggest single item in its budget—$180 million out of an appropriations request of $302 million for fiscal year 1973—always is highway construction, but it also spends a sizable amount ($48 million in the budget request) for health and child development programs. Construction of vocational schools has been a highly popular program since the commission's founding; in 1973 it accounted for $25.5 million of the budget. Another leading item ($37 million) was for activities under section 214 of the act, which enables the commission to pay all or part of the federal share of any grant-in-aid project authorized under federal law.[14] Minor amounts go for mine area restoration, housing, administrative expenditures for local development districts (multicounty units formed in

13. Harold Seidman to Sam Broadbent, Nov. 29, 1966; OMB files.
14. Until 1971, section 214 applied only to supplements to the federal share. Amendments then enabled the commission to pay the whole federal share. More and more, it is doing so.

response to initiatives of the ARC), and research and technical assistance.[15]

The commission, which meets in Washington monthly, is occupied mainly with policy for this program, such as changes in its composition, adoption of spending guidelines, and allocation of funds among the states. The staff is occupied mainly with preparing proposals for the commission's consideration and reviewing the spending plans and project proposals submitted by the states. In function, then, the commission is similar to any federal agency that administers grants-in-aid, except that its responsibility for grant-in-aid administration is partial: it covers the beginning of the process (preparation of guidelines and funding decisions) but not the end (expenditures and monitoring expenditures). Because technically it still has no operating functions, the commission shares responsibility for the process as a whole with whatever federal line agency is in charge of the particular categorical grant. This sharing has worked fairly well when the grant is established in federal law and administrative practice, but it has caused serious problems when the ARC has undertaken a new program, such as health care demonstration or child development. Disputes arise with line agencies over who is responsible for what, and supervision of expenditure tends to be lax since neither the ARC nor the federal agency is adequately staffed, and the line agency is likely to lack commitment.[16] Either way, the ARC's involvement makes the grant-in-aid process more complicated. Whether this slows expenditures down significantly is hard to say. Except for vocational school construction, most Appalachian programs have moved slowly, with expenditures lagging way behind appropriations and authorizations, but it is not clear that the existence of the commission contributes substantially to the delay, since it is only one decision point among many.

In addition to administering the aid program, the headquarters

15. *Public Works for Water and Power Development and Atomic Energy Commission Appropriation Bill, 1973*, Hearings before a subcommittee of the House Appropriations Committee, 92 Cong. 2 sess. (1972), pt. 3, pp. 1353–60.

16. David A. Danielson, "The First Years of the Appalachian Health Program," Evaluation Study Paper 15 (Appalachian Regional Commission, October 1970; processed). In preparation for this book, Joy Silver, a research assistant at Brookings, made a detailed study of the ARC's child development program. Her findings are reported in an unpublished manuscript, "The Appalachian Regional Commission and the Grant-in-Aid System: The Case of Child Development," March 1973.

organization serves as an advocate for the region in Washington, helping the Appalachian states "to take maximum advantage of the system," as the executive director put it. The education staff, for example, has pressed the Office of Education to prepare grant-in-aid guidelines that would benefit the Appalachian region, has held seminars in the region to help institutions prepare grant requests, and then has urged the Office of Education to fund the applications.[17] On the initiative of the commission's housing specialist, Congress in 1967 created an Appalachian Housing Fund from which the secretary of housing and urban development may make grants and loans for the construction of housing for low- and moderate-income people. This has increased the capacity of the Appalachian states to use HUD's housing programs. The same staff member took the initiative in urging Appalachian states to create housing development corporations. By 1973 nine of the thirteen had done so, although only West Virginia's corporation, among those fostered by the commission, has been active. In 1969, partly on the initiative of the commission's health staff, Congress authorized a child development program that broadened the scope and volume of the commission's activity and increased the ability of Appalachian states to take advantage of social services funds newly available to state governments under Title IV-A of the Social Security Act. From the standpoint of the states, having a highly skilled staff in Washington to serve their interests is one of the principal benefits of the commission.[18] Nor are the benefits confined to Washington and to the brokerage (or lobbying) function. Available at the request of state and local officials, the staff also serves as a source of advice and technical assistance for a variety of government activities in the region.

For the staff of the ARC, the chief rewards have been the opportunities for innovation and individual enterprise that are available in a relatively small, nonhierarchical organization that has access to many governments but is controlled by none. These rewards have tended to come in devising new programs and getting them authorized by Congress and the states. For this function, the joint

17. Monroe Newman, *The Political Economy of Appalachia: A Case Study in Regional Integration* (Lexington Books, 1972), pp. 134–35. This book, by an economist who has advised the commission, is the most comprehensive published account of the commission's activity.

18. Interview with Blue Barber, Alabama state representative, Dec. 19, 1972.

character of the organization has been important and useful because it assures the organization's members a duality of access. A single locus of initiative and advocacy, the commission in Washington can seek action at two levels of government simultaneously without being constrained by obligations to any particular government. "We can move into a state situation with a white hat," a staff member observed. Coming from the commission, "you're not a Fed." For this staff member, the commission had "provided enormous opportunities for satisfaction." Here more than in a federal department (he had worked in HUD) it had been possible to experience the satisfaction of using government to make good things happen, things that would improve the quality of life for people in need.[19]

In practice, the commission's two basic functions, as a channel of extra public works expenditures and as a source of skilled staff assistance, complement each other. A good example is the case of Pikeville, a town of 5,000 in eastern Kentucky that is benefiting from massive and varied federal assistance for redevelopment and social services. (Among other things, the Corps of Engineers is relocating a river that frequently floods the town.) Funds from the commission's highway program are financing reconstruction of highways in and around Pikeville, which is crucial to the redevelopment; and a commission staff member was largely responsible for preparing Pikeville's model cities application to HUD, funds from which have also been important in executing the renewal plan.

## How Regional Is It?

The proponents of the Appalachian program began by emphasizing its regionalism. Assistant Director of the Bureau of the Budget Charles L. Schultze, who had taken responsibility for the program within the Executive Office of the President, told Congress that "while [the program] is a joint Federal-State effort, it differs in one major aspect from other such efforts. This is a regional program to attack a regional problem. . . . the whole concept we are getting at here is not county-by-county or State-by-State develop-

19. Interview with Francis Moravitz, June 12, 1973.

ment alone."[20] However, even before the act was passed regionalism had yielded to state-by-state development. And by 1967 the federal cochairman was arguing that the peculiar merit of the commission was that its "policy and procedures . . . are designed to honor the particular conditions found in each State."[21] What was briefly an effort to transcend the states turned very quickly into an organizational device that rationalized a larger role for them.

The strategy of relying on the states was incorporated in the act and then confirmed by early decisions of the commission. The preamble to the ARDA says that the states "will be responsible for recommending local and State projects, within their borders." Programs cannot be implemented unless the commission has consulted with state officials. Only a state or one of its subdivisions can apply for assistance, and applications must be made through the state member of the commission. Finally, among the criteria to be followed by the commission in financing projects is location in an area determined by a state to have potential for economic growth. The commission has not sought to prepare a regionwide plan for investments. Instead it requires each state to prepare a plan and to set its own priorities for locations and types of investment. The fund allocation procedures of the commission have assumed that each state would get a fair, or at least a politically defensible, share of the funds. Thus the state has been the basic unit for planning and fund allocation.

It took no particular ingenuity or enterprise on the part of state officials to secure a large role for their governments in administration of the program. Unlike the region, the states existed: they were real political communities and governments. As such, they were represented in the planning effort and, more or less as a consequence, in the commission itself.[22] To work through them was the

20. *Appalachian Regional Development Act of 1964*, Hearings before the House Committee on Public Works, 88 Cong. 2 sess. (1964), pp. 376, 389.

21. *Appalachian Regional Development Act Amendments of 1967*, Hearings before the Senate Committee on Public Works, 90 Cong. 1 sess. (1967), p. 52.

22. In 1964 the Bureau of the Budget received a plea from within the Kentucky government to halt the move away from regionalism. The state's budget director, Robert M. Cornett, forwarded to Harold Seidman the analysis of a staff member, Roger E. Buchanan, who argued that the states should not be represented individually on the commission. Rather, he recommended, they should jointly name a number of representatives lower than the number of states in the region. Buchanan wrote, "My fear is that, under the present proposal, we will merely effect another instrument for

most expedient way of getting the program under way promptly.
To attempt to transcend them in planning or fund allocation would
invite controversy, slow the program, and jeopardize support for
it, as the experience of the Title V commissions would later show.
Nor did John L. Sweeney, at that time PARC's executive director
and dominant figure, wish to transcend them. Sweeney had begun
his career in state government and, he later said, had been "ap-
palled at the number of federal officials (at all levels) who came to
our state to tell us how to do things that were absurd on their
face."[23] He did not shrink from entrusting powers to the state governments. Later, as the first federal cochairman of the commission,
he would vigorously uphold the wisdom of doing so. Anyway, "the
region" was an artifact whose boundaries expanded as the program
evolved. Beginning from the base of nationally publicized poverty
in eastern Kentucky and West Virginia, the planning effort drew
in more states, and then the states decided what counties to include.
Except that it was relatively mountainous and poor, the region was
quite varied and had no sense of identity.[24]

While the commission has not sought to define a broad range of
distinctively regional goals or compel the states to conform to a
regional plan, it nevertheless depends critically on achieving interstate cooperation, at least in the matter of dividing funds. Congress
did not stipulate how funds were to be allocated among the states.
The commission must make that decision, avoiding if possible
both the paralysis of prolonged conflict and a crude process of logrolling, which would harm its reputation. As the commission began
meeting, Sweeney as federal cochairman took several steps to com-
bat these dangers.

For one, he discouraged the governors from sitting on the com-

---

representing these several Appalachian states in Washington, instead of giving the
Region itself a measure of representation. It would seem unfortunate that, at last,
this opportunity may not be utilized for the singular purpose of getting the Region
represented, as opposed simply to intensifying the representation of the several Appalachian states. Even if the governors (or other individual state members) *consciously*
attempt to represent the Region instead of their state, their mere presence and inherent interests will result in their being dealt with *unconsciously* by the Washington
power structure as representatives of a state rather than as a representative of the
Region's people." This was in July 1964. Seidman replied in December that it was too
late to develop a new organizational approach. OMB files.

23. Personal communication, 1972.
24. Newman, *Political Economy of Appalachia*, p. 28.

mission. The law said that the state member might be the governor or his designee. Immediately after the bill-signing ceremony at the White House, the Appalachian governors decided that they would attend commission meetings. Sweeney promptly objected on several grounds, among them that governors could not isolate themselves from political pressures. Lower-ranking, less visible representatives of the states would find it easier to make the compromises that a limited supply of funds would require.[25] Formally, the governors are the state members of the commission, and they have occasionally come to the meetings, but more often the governor's appointed state representative or a lower-ranking alternate comes.

Second, Sweeney put before the commission a series of formulas, one for nearly every program, that had been devised by an economist on the staff. These included factors for equality, a state's percentage of the Appalachian population, and its per capita income. Factors applicable to the particular function were also introduced—the number of low-income farms for the land conservation program, the percentage of Appalachian mines for the mine restoration program, the percentage of Appalachian 14–17 year olds not in school for the vocational educational program. The result recognized the states' special interests in certain programs. For example, Pennsylvania got nearly all of the mine restoration funds but in all other programs the lowest per capita allocation of any state. Accepting the equity of the total allocation and no doubt aware of the hazards of conflict over this question, the state representatives approved the formulas at the commission's second meeting. According to the staff member who prepared them, the formulas "satisfied the congressional desire that every member state be able (if it wished) to participate under every section of the act."[26]

Finally, at Sweeney's suggestion the commission delegated authority to approve projects to its executive committee, consisting of the federal cochairman, the states' regional representative (a full-time official who represents the states at the Washington headquarters although his office is not authorized by the ARDA), and the executive director. The ostensible reason for the delegation was to

25. Memorandum, John L. Sweeney to Buford Ellington, March 19, 1965; federal cochairman (FC) files, ARC, Washington.

26. Newman, *Political Economy of Appalachia*, p. 91. For a detailed account of the formulas in operation, see Donald M. Rothblatt, *Regional Planning: The Appalachian Experience* (Lexington Books, 1971).

expedite project approval, but it also had the merit of preventing logrolling within the commission. Projects approved by the committee come before the commission, but it merely ratifies the committee's decision. The commission has approved projects en bloc and usually without discussion.

The three measures together reduced the scope of the commission's decision making and limited conflict and favor-trading among the states. Interstate conflict has been serious only in the programs that were not initially covered by an allocation formula, notably health care demonstrations and child development. The health program began selectively, with projects in seven states, but it had to be extended until every state was eligible. Where allocation formulas have been in effect, they are all but untouchable. The staff would have liked to revise them after five years, and occasionally a state asks for reconsideration, but the commission has avoided reopening that most basic of issues.

Besides arriving at a stable, mutually acceptable set of allocation formulas, the commission has been a medium for mutual adjustment of differing state needs. It has developed a procedure for interstate trading of categorical funds—an example of the flexibility the commission form is said to provide, in contrast to conventional administration of categorical grants. This practice has both enabled the states to satisfy their program preferences and helped to ensure that no funds lie idle. Such trades began on a voluntary basis, through a series of special resolutions. Later, the commission authorized its executive committee to revise allocations at the request of participants in a trade. Finally, the commission authorized the committee to make reallocations at its own discretion. The executive director and federal cochairman argued that this change was necessary to keep spending on schedule and assure a continuing supply of funds from Congress.

In sum, the commission has generally been able to arrive at adjustments of the states' separate interests, especially when its executives could argue that such adjustments were essential to maintenance of the commission's program. It has not sought to achieve subordination of the states' interests to the common good of the region.

In giving the states broad responsibility to plan public works spending, the ARC was perpetuating the tradition of American government.[27] The innovation that might have been expected—some organizational breakthrough that would transcend the states—did not occur. Yet there was innovation here, when the form of the commission was combined with the function of spending federal funds. Although there was nothing new in having the states plan how to spend federal grants, there was something new in having the guidelines determined by a federal-state commission.

## The Consequences of Being a Joint Body

In the ARC as in the DRBC, the underlying theory of joint organization seems to be that the two levels of government can meet as equals in a common organizational setting and jointly make policy for the region. This theory is not borne out in practice, if only because none of the member governments has a policy for economic development that the commission can discuss meaningfully. What it does is consider the policies that should guide the special program of federal expenditure for the thirteen states in the Appalachian region. In doing this, the state members are not quite equal to the federal member, since he represents the government that gives grants whereas they represent the governments that get them.

Within the commission, the role of the grant-givers (the headquarters organization in Washington) and that of the grant recipients (the state governments) differ sharply. The headquarters organization initiates policy proposals and reviews state plans and project applications; the states defer to the initiatives of headquarters and await its decisions on plans and project applications.

The principal restriction the commission has imposed on the states is locational criteria. Under the law, a state is supposed to make investments in "areas where there is a significant potential for future growth, and where the expected return on public dollars invested will be the greatest." This is potentially a controversial criterion because it implies selecting relatively prosperous places

27. Although in the mid-1960s it was possible to portray this as something new. See Jerald Ter Horst, "No More Pork Barrel: The Appalachia Approach," *The Reporter*, vol. 32 (March 11, 1965), pp. 27–29; and Max Ways, " 'Creative Federalism' and the Great Society," *Fortune*, vol. 73 (January 1966), pp. 121 ff.

for investment. As director of PARC, Sweeney had won support for the Appalachian program in the Bureau of the Budget by adopting this strategy, and he had successfully proposed it to Congress. In the early years of the commission, it seemed imperative to induce the states to conform.

For a time Sweeney sought to enforce the strategy with the implied threat of the federal veto. As justification for his choices, he had the report of a consultant, Litton Industries, hired during the planning period to identify growth areas for Appalachian investment. Ready in tentative form by early summer 1965, the Litton report named forty-four such places and ranked them in order of growth potential. Only one of the forty-four was even partially in Kentucky, and it was near the bottom of the list. West Virginia and eastern Kentucky, whose plight had inspired the program, were not to get the benefits, if Litton's maps were to be believed. Sweeney began by acting as if he meant to take Litton's maps seriously. Among the quick-start highway projects proposed for approval at the commission's second meeting, he did *not* include Highway 119 in the Pikeville-Harlan area of eastern Kentucky. But the Litton report would not work as commission policy, as Sweeney well knew and as reaction from the Kentucky and West Virginia representatives showed.[28] The report helped Sweeney to establish the principle of investment in growth centers and to improve his bargaining position with the states. He had managed very quickly to demonstrate the potential power of his veto and to make clear the objectives for which it might be used. (In the end he did not actually veto Kentucky's highway; he delayed the project until state officials had justified it on grounds that it would promote economic growth.)

By the spring of 1966, both Sweeney and the executive director, Ralph Widner, sensed the need for a statement of commission policy on concentration of investments. At a commission meeting in April,

28. In August 1965 Sweeney wrote a Litton official that the company could not expect actually to develop the strategy of public investment for the commission. "I will not waste your time explaining why I believe such a role would be inappropriate for any consultant, including Litton. This is no reflection on the wisdom and knowledge which Litton might offer nor is it intended to be a reflection on any other consulting firm. It is only the result of my own personal belief that development of a strategy of public investment is only partly scientific; the remainder of input is primarily political and must be made by those who exercise political responsibility." Sweeney to John Rubel, Aug. 26, 1965; FC files, ARC.

Sweeney observed that the projects "being filed by the States are not yet clearly enough related to growth potential" and that the commission "could not demonstrate that it has found a way to satisfactorily fulfill the mandate that its investments be in the areas of greatest potential growth."[29] In July, Widner presented a staff paper with draft guidelines for planning. It called for the states to submit a development plan to the commission every year. The plan should identify growth areas and list investment priorities within each area. After approving the plan, the commission could use it as a guide to investments in the state. Although the commission's proposed criteria for identifying growth areas were quite broad, some state members objected that the policies were "too rigid." Action was postponed until September to allow more time for consideration by the states.[30]

The commission adopted the staff proposal with no important changes, and it also approved a comprehensive resolution embodying guidelines for location of projects for each of seven programs. In general, these resolutions called for concentrating projects in growth areas, but several exceptions were provided. Some state members continued to object to the commission's adopting any criteria for a growth area, maintaining that this should be a function exclusively of the states. Sweeney and Widner countered that commission action was essential. Sweeney said that the commission's future support in Congress depended on a demonstration that state planning was of high quality. The state representatives agreed that inasmuch as the policy was flexible, it should be approved.[31]

Although the states had had a chance to comment and vote on the policy, it had originated with the staff; and the state representatives sensed that the staff was aligned with the other, federal side of the commission rather than with the states' side. A subtle distinction seems to have been developing between "the commission," which in practice was coming to mean the staff at headquarters, and "the states." There was a feeling among the states that "the commission" was not neutral.

In its duration (more than a year) and initial intensity (the Litton report had provoked a sharp reaction), the debate over applying

29. ARC conference minutes, April 12, 1966.
30. ARC conference minutes, July 12, 1966.
31. ARC conference minutes, Sept. 13, 1966.

the growth strategy remains unusual in the commission's experience, but in other important respects it proved to be characteristic. Proposals for new programs or new guidelines originate at the commission offices in Washington. It is officials at headquarters who state what the organization's interests require and who, having stated it, win a high degree of acquiescence from most of the states. The state members are prepared to do what they are told must be done to preserve the commission and keep federal funds flowing.[32]

Although in defining what must be done the commission's executives usually refer to what federal officeholders expect, the expectations of the staff are also important. The staff has preferred welfare and social service programs to public works or law enforcement. It prefers the innovative to the routine. It prefers concentration of funds to dispersion of funds, to attain programmatic purposes rather than the politician's presumed purpose of rewarding followers on the widest possible scale. While the staff serves the states, it tends also to view them as an object of reform.

Because they belong to the commission, the states are able to influence the content of policy directly, and often they modify proposals that come from the staff. For example, the staff argued unsuccessfully in 1971 for restricting child development expenditures to demonstration areas. The executive director declared: "Congress didn't really tell us to put a day care center here, and something here, and something there, and just run a regular project by project grants [program]. They said, 'Demonstrate that a comprehensive approach to child development is possible.'" The Alabama state representative argued for the states: "Don't restrict any of us with a code requirement as long as we can produce good programs and good situations comprehensive in design, adequate in their delivery, etc. Don't tie us into areas."[33] The staff proposal failed.

Another example of this staff-state relation is the guidelines adopted in the fall of 1971 for vocational education expenditure. Amendments to the ARDA had authorized expenditure for operations and demonstrations, an addition to the authorization for construction that had been in the original act and proved highly popu-

32. This analysis is based on a complete reading of the minutes of the commission's conferences (executive sessions) and of the conference transcripts for a year, as well as on interviews with commission officials.

33. ARC conference transcript, Sept. 22, 1971, pp. 394, 396.

lar in the states and Congress. The staff characteristically wanted to ensure that the new money would be used for innovation. Of $27.5 million available for vocational education, it proposed to reserve $3.5 million for demonstration projects approved by the staff, and it sought to state a rank order of priorities for the use of operating funds. The states succeeded in reducing the amount reserved for demonstrations to $1 million, with a ceiling of $150,000 on any state's share. They also succeeded in removing the rank order of priorities for operating expenditures and in broadening the categories of acceptable use.

The presence of the states in the commission and the commitment of the staff to flexible, responsive administration mean that the commission guidelines give wide discretion to the states, probably more discretion than would be provided by a conventional federal line agency administering grants.[34] But reviews of project applications continue to be made by line agencies, in conjunction with the ARC. The usual federal regulations apply, along with whatever policies and regulations have been adopted by the ARC. As long as the joint commission shares grant administration with a federal agency, the states do not really gain much freedom. Moreover, the difference between the conduct of the ARC headquarters organization and a conventional line agency is slight and subtle, as the staff recognizes. According to the commission's evaluation of itself:

One continuing concern in the administration of the Appalachian program is how to keep the Commission program from becoming federalized. With the federal cochairman as a full-time officer in Washington, Washington as a center of staff operations, and administration of federal grants-in-aid as the Commission's major business, the staff and the entire Commission operation could fall into a pattern of operating essentially as a federal agency.[35]

Probably the most important manifestation of jointness occurs

34. While simple guidelines give more discretion to the states, they also give discretion to ARC staff members, who review plans and project proposals. States frequently complain that the ARC staff makes policy. "God, I've heard that a million times in the last year, that the staff makes policy," the executive director told the commission in 1971. "It's because you guys haven't made it that it makes the policy."

35. ARC, *The Appalachian Experiment, 1965–1970* (Washington, no date), p. 13. This is the published version of the self-evaluation conducted by the commission in 1970.

in the headquarters structure of the organization rather than in the fourteen-member commission. A full-time "states' regional representative" is located in Washington and is coequal with the federal member in the executive committee, which makes all the important executive decisions for the commission. He has a veto that neutralizes the veto of the federal member, access to Congress, and as much access to the staff as the federal member.[36] This structure has assured him of a major role in the conduct of the organization. From this position, he seeks benefits for the states, such as authorizations of expenditure that are larger than or different in kind from what has received approval from the Office of Management and Budget. The structure obviously has advantages for the states, but it has disadvantages for the organization. Responsibility for executive functions—including direction of the staff, preparation of policy proposals for the commission, and the conduct of relations with OMB—is chronically in dispute. The logic of jointness supports the claim of the states' regional representative to an equal share of these functions, but his efforts to claim this share are divisive and raise serious questions about accountability for the conduct of a federally financed program. As the ARC has evolved into an operating agency, with its own federal appropriation (even if, technically, the appropriation is made to the President), it has become a "bureau" with two heads (not counting the executive director), of whom one is formally responsible to the President and the other is not even employed by the federal government. The presence of the states' regional representative at headquarters does not, however, alter the orientation of the commission toward the states. He has been no less inclined than other elements of the headquarters organization to view the states as objects of influence, in need of reform in their own interest. He has sometimes argued for stricter planning requirements than were favored by the staff.

Ultimately, what matters is whether government action is made more effective within the region by the decentralization, through jointness, of federal decision making. This is an elusive question, if only because effectiveness is so hard to define. The ARC has mea-

36. Under the law, the counterpart of the federal cochairman is the states' cochairman, elected by the state members, but since this office is held by a governor for a term of six months, it is largely symbolic. The functional counterpart of the federal cochairman is the states' regional representative.

sured its own effectiveness principally by the degree to which Appalachian investments have been concentrated in areas designated by the states as having potential for economic growth.

All states have designated numerous and inclusive growth areas, which together account for more than 80 percent of the region's population. Nevertheless, the commission's guidelines and staff reviews of state plans and project proposals appear to have produced some concentration of investments. A staff analysis made in 1971 showed that 5 percent of Appalachian counties (20 counties out of 397) had received 31.5 percent of Appalachian funds. More than half the funds were concentrated in 15 percent of the counties, and 64 counties had received no funds at all. Of approximately $250 million that had been approved for projects, about half had been channeled to areas designated by the states as being of "first-level growth potential" and 19 percent to areas of lower growth potential. The rest had gone to nongrowth areas (11 percent) or had been approved in the quick-start phase of the program before growth areas had been defined (21 percent).[37]

The scope of state discretion is shown by interstate variations in concentration of investments. The proportion of investment in areas with first-level growth potential ranges from 2.2 percent for Kentucky to 87.2 percent for Ohio. (Interstate variations in terminology make comparisons of limited significance, however. States have used widely varying methods for defining growth areas.) Nevertheless, in most states more than half of the investments have been concentrated in areas of first-level growth potential.[38]

From all this, it is fair to infer that decentralization through jointness does not preclude imposition of very general, centrally inspired constraints on state spending of federal funds. However, it is not possible to infer that state investment decisions are "better" than they would be, or even very different than they would be, if the spending guidelines were prepared by a federal grant-in-aid agency. There is no way of telling how the states would have spent

37. ARC, *Appalachian Experiment*, pp. 33–40. For a more detailed analysis, see John L. Preston, Jr., "An Analysis of the Growth Center Strategy of the Appalachian Regional Commission," Evaluation Study Paper 13 (ARC, March 1971; processed).

38. Failure to qualify for investments has not meant that an Appalachian county is deprived of federal development aid. It might still get funds from the Economic Development Administration. The existence of this other program for depressed areas has enabled the ARC to be selective.

the funds if there had been no guidelines at all but only a federal statement of purpose ("economic development"); nor is it possible to say how they would have spent the funds if a federal executive agency had been in charge of administration. The apparent outcome—very general conformance to guidelines grounded in federal law but wide interstate variations in practice—is what one would predict in a conventional grant program.

## The Federal Cochairman as Federal Coordinator

The law does not prescribe the functions of the federal cochairman, nor did the planners of the ARC give much thought to his role. The ARC was loosely patterned after the DRBC, though without the same deliberate commitment of the founders to creating an agent of federal coordination. Nor did management officials in the Bureau of the Budget conceive of the federal member as an active central coordinator of a wide range of federal activities in the region. In their eyes, coordination was the innocuous residual function left to this new federal-state agency after it had been denied the right to spend federal funds.

To a considerable extent, the office evolved out of the experience of PARC and was shaped by the man (John Sweeney) who directed PARC and then became the first federal cochairman. Yet the functions of the office did need a formal definition as the commission got started, and this was set forth in an executive order that Sweeney worked out with the Bureau of the Budget. Agency heads were authorized to approve projects. The federal cochairman was to conduct liaison with the federal government and solicit the agencies' reaction to plans and projects. For a "coordinated review" of commission proposals, he was to rely on an interagency committee, the Federal Development Committee for Appalachia, which he would chair. The principal purpose of this executive order was to ensure that the federal cochairman would act on behalf of the federal administration when he cast a vote in the commission. His vote would bind the federal government, but no agency was to be bound without its consent. The interagency committee was soon moribund, and in 1967 amendments to the ARDA gave the commission authority to approve projects. However, the federal cochairman continues to clear projects with the interested federal line agency, which must find that they are not inconsistent with federal law.

Although nothing in the law or executive order prescribed an active coordinating role for the federal cochairman, Sweeney essayed one. He made a major attempt in 1965–66 to influence both the Office of Economic Opportunity and the Economic Development Administration, agencies that were in direct competition with the ARC. The OEO had been created in 1964 to administer the antipoverty program; the EDA, lineal successor of the Area Redevelopment Administration, was created in 1965 to administer a program of grants and loans to depressed areas. Sweeney tried to get an agreement with OEO to work through the same local organizations, but OEO preferred to set up community action agencies independently of the ARC-sponsored local development districts. Early in 1966 ARC officials in Washington gave up on meetings with OEO and announced that coordination of the two programs must occur at the state and local levels. The effort at coordination with EDA has a similar history. Throughout 1966 the ARC tried to get EDA to cooperate in defining development districts, accommodate to the commission's growth strategy, and acknowledge the responsibility of the states for planning public investments. Experience showed that the programs of the two agencies conflicted, and Sweeney feared that "some enterprising newsman or Congressman will raise cain and justifiably so."[39] They were independently financing the creation of development districts at the local level, with the result that districts sometimes duplicated or overlapped one another. The two agencies were unable to reach agreement, and again, it was up to state officials to cope with disagreements. After reviewing these and other cases, the commission's in-house evaluation concluded that the commission "has not been able to coordinate the investments of other agencies in the sense of making them consistent with Commission development plans and programs."[40] "I must confess," the federal cochairman, Donald W. Whitehead, told Congress in 1972, "that I cannot claim to have

39. John L. Sweeney to Eugene P. Foley, Jan. 3, 1966; FC files, ARC.
40. Thomas A. Cotton, "Coordination of the Commission Program with the Federal Government," Evaluation Study Paper 9 (ARC, March 1971; processed).

90358

much influence over the investment decisions made by my colleagues in the Cabinet departments."[41]

Rather than being the overseer of federal actions in Appalachia, the federal cochairman is the representative of the ARC in relations with the federal government. It is his function to maintain favorable relations with the executive departments, OMB, the White House, and Congress. He coordinates with elements of the executive branch—that is, submits his own actions for clearance—to the extent that the law obliges and the need for maintaining good relations dictates. This entails a delicate balancing of the organization's interests.

Theoretically, the federal cochairman is responsible to the President, which means that for most purposes he is responsible to no one or to a budget examiner in OMB. If he ignores or defies OMB, this increases the danger that it will try to subject the commission to the control of an executive department, presumably Commerce. In 1967 the Bureau of the Budget prepared legislation to subordinate the federal cochairman to the secretary of commerce and it decided that all Appalachian funds should be appropriated to the Department of Commerce. Defeated in this, it issued an executive order that charged the secretary of commerce with liaison between the regional commissions and the federal government. The secretary is supposed to obtain a coordinated review of regional commissions' plans, review their budgetary and legislative recommendations, and provide guidance and policy direction to the federal cochairmen. He is assisted by a cabinet-level interagency committee, the Federal Advisory Council on Regional Economic Development, of which he is chairman.[42]

However, executive supervision does not restrict the federal cochairman very much. The Federal Advisory Council is wholly ineffective, as the federal cochairman (Sweeney's successor, Joe W. Fleming) foresaw in 1968. Fleming reported to the commission that the new executive order was "quite palatable" and that "there would be virtually no impairment of the Federal Cochairman's ability to deal freely with issues presented to the commission."[43]

41. *Public Works for Water and Power Department . . . 1973*, Hearings, pt. 3, p. 1381.

42. Executive Order 11386, *Federal Register*, vol. 33 (Jan. 3, 1968), pp. 5–8.

43. ARC conference minutes, Jan. 9, 1968.

What supervision there is comes from OMB, whose main concern is to prevent the commission's expenditure, particularly the big program for highways, from going on interminably, at unlimited cost. Caught between the states' steady pressure for more highway funds and OMB's resistance, the federal cochairman must either retreat from this issue or seek a compromise.

The organization as a whole, and to a degree its federal member, is freed from dependence on the executive branch by the generous, uncritical support of Congress, particularly the Senate Public Works Committee, which is chaired by a member (Jennings Randolph of West Virginia) whose state is the principal beneficiary of the program. Because high-ranking members of the Senate Public Works Committee value the program and because other members of the Senate value favors from the Public Works Committee, the Senate supports the commission overwhelmingly. The OMB must appeal to the House, where support for the commission is less, if it wants to revise the commission's legislative initiatives. The Senate will give the commission virtually anything it wants, and occasionally has pressed upon it something it did not ask for, such as an airport safety program that Senator Robert C. Byrd of West Virginia managed to add to the act in 1971.

Just how much the federal member yields to central supervision varies with circumstances and personality. Some have been more inclined than others to use influence in the commission to protect federal executive interests. But no matter what the circumstances or the style of the incumbent, the federal cochairman is not himself a central coordinator in the sense of inducing federal agencies to conform to the commission's investment strategies for the region.

## The Role of the Governor

According to commission doctrine, coordination of federal programs is not a function of the commission as a whole or of the federal cochairman, and it need not occur at the Washington level. Rather, it is a function primarily of state governments, whose development plans, submitted annually to the commission, are supposed to encompass and coordinate all public investments. Specifically, it is a function of the chief executives of the state governments, who recommend projects to the commission and receive Appalachian funds. The commission has emphasized the importance of enhancing the governor's power, consistent with theories of governmental reform that have prevailed in Washington in the 1960s and early 1970s, finding expression in reports of the Advisory Commission on Intergovernmental Relations and management activities of OMB. Elected chief executives are widely believed to need strengthening in relation to functional specialists; proponents of the commission form offer it as a means to that end within the states.[44]

So far, the link with the commission seems not to have made much difference in the governors' conduct of executive functions. The commission's own evaluation found in 1971 that "with notable exceptions, the Governors have not fully capitalized on the general management potential of the program. In fact, because of limited staff resources and the physical and geographic limitations of the program, there has been a tendency toward a refunctionalization in its actual administration." Apart from the short time the commission had been in operation, one reason given for this was that Appalachian funds account for a very small proportion of a state's budget. The program is just one of many federal programs, and in all states except West Virginia it applies to only a fraction of the state's area.[45] This legacy of the short-lived initial emphasis on

44. Federal cochairman John Sweeney explained to Congress in 1967 that reliance on the governors was one of the commission's important innovations (*Appalachian Regional Development Act Amendments of 1967*, Hearings, pp. 46–47):

"most [Federal-state] programs are accomplished within a relationship between a Federal agency and its counterpart at the State level. There is little opportunity given the Governor to participate in decisions that obviously has [sic] a profound impact on the welfare of the people of his State. And yet, the Governor is the only State official who is accountable to all the people of his State.

"The Appalachian program does vest the responsibility for whatever decisions are made at the State level with the Governor. It is he who makes the primary determination whether funds should be spent, what priorities should be given to the expenditures of those funds, and he is responsible for bringing projects to the Appalachian Commission and hence any Federal agency. . . . I do not believe it is possible to conduct a sound public investment program without the full involvement of the Governors."

45. The portion of the state population included in the region ranges from 5.3 percent for Maryland to 100 percent for West Virginia, with a median of 20.4 percent (North Carolina). The portion of the state land area ranges from 13.1 percent for South Carolina to 100 percent for West Virginia, with a median of 24.7 percent (New York). Even in West Virginia, ARC funds typically have amounted to no more than 5 percent of the total budget of the state, and if highway funds are excluded, the

regionalism has proved anomalous in a program that came to emphasize federal reliance on the states. Governors, who in theory were to exploit the program to control their own governments, in some cases have not shown much interest in it. (One sign of this within the commission is that the rank of state representation at meetings has steadily declined.) "The Governors themselves have frequently not made a strong enough commitment or become involved enough to bring their authority to bear effectively," according to the commission study. The evaluation also found that the states are poorly organized for central planning and management. Management staff and agencies were fragmented in most state executive branches, and state planning was not focused on program coordination.[46] Finally, commission sources cite rapid turnover of governors as an explanation for their limited involvement in the commission—they no sooner discover its existence than they are out of office.

The commission might try to correct the presumed defects in state government with requirements covering the administration of Appalachian funds, but except for specifying that the state development plan should be the governor's official policy and that the state representative should have a major, continuing role in preparation and application of the plan, the commission has not done this. Its restraint probably reflects the joint character of the program and the enhanced opportunity for the exercise of state influence. Conventional grant-in-aid programs, by contrast, very often impose conditions covering administrative organization. However, in 1973 the commission began to provide management grants to the states, and these give the staff an opportunity to encourage the

---

percentage is even lower. In other states, most of which have larger budgets than West Virginia and are only partially included in the region, the proportion is usually less than 1 percent. For detailed information, see ARC, *Appalachian Experiment*, p. 88.

46. Page L. Ingraham, "Administration of the Appalachian Regional Program in the States," Evaluation Study Paper 12 (ARC, March 1971; processed). The updated published version of the evaluation (ARC, *Appalachian Experiment*) is more optimistic, however. It finds "an encouraging trend toward placing the program in a broad administrative framework," and reports that "almost three-fourths of the Appalachian states have now housed responsibility for administration of the Appalachian program in a central management agency close to the governor, either an office of federal-state relations, a program development office, or a department of administration in the office of the governor or the state planning agency" (p. 95).

kinds of improvements in the staffing and structure of the governor's offices to which the commission is committed.

Commission officials have been disappointed by the seeming failure of state officials to regard investment plans as anything but a requirement for the receipt of federal funds. Following the commission's self-evaluation in 1971, its director of planning wrote, "Typically among the states there is a feeling that the plan is a fifth wheel, something they have to prepare in order to qualify for Appalachian assistance, but not something they would have done to fill their own needs. . . . The plans prepared for the Appalachian Regional Commission are really not used in actual program management decisions." They represent "planning for planning's sake."[47] More accurately, they represent planning for the sake of federal money. Planning requirements have no more originated with the states or grown out of their felt needs than in any other grant program. They were proposed by the federal cochairman and staff and more or less passively accepted by the states as an inevitable burden of receiving federal aid.

## The Impact of Commission Programs

Because commission programs have moved slowly and constitute only a very small fraction of public expenditures in the region, it is difficult to show that they have promoted the region's economic development.[48] Even with simple statistics, the progress of Appalachian programs cannot easily be summarized. Commission staff members, hoping in 1971 to make at least crude guesses about the program's effects, were frustrated by lack of data. The commission did not know, and could not satisfactorily find out from federal agencies, which of the projects it had approved were operational and what use was being made of them. In the highway program, where physical progress can readily be measured, only 664 miles

47. Ken Rainey, "An Assessment of Development Planning in Appalachia," ARC staff discussion paper, Oct. 27, 1971.

48. Federal outlays in Appalachia in fiscal year 1969 were estimated to be over $11 billion. Douglas N. Jones and Paul W. Kolp, *Federal Agency Planning Policies and Regional Economic Development*, Report RAC-R-103 (McLean, Va.: Research Analysis Corp., March 1970), p. 151. The ARC's appropriations in that year were about $174 million, or less than 2 percent of the total.

out of a planned 2,600 had been completed by June 1, 1972. The commission's self-evaluations, done with competence and a candor rare in official documents, do not claim that the commission's programs have had much effect on the region's economic performance.[49]

In any case, the impact of program funds must be distinguished from the impact of the commission as an organizational form. For the analyst of regional organizations, the essential question is not what the effect of Appalachian expenditures has been, but whether the effects are different than they would have been without the new regional organization.

The commission's decision to rely so heavily on the states for planning and program administration has meant that Appalachian program activities rarely transcend state boundaries.[50] While mutual adjustments among the states in fund allocation are routine (though time-consuming), active interstate collaboration in the execution of programs is exceptional. Of thirteen health care demonstration areas, only one crosses state boundaries (in the Chattanooga metropolitan area, which extends into Georgia as well as Tennessee). Of sixty-five local development districts, only two do so. The commission's principal impact on interjurisdictional relations occurs at the substate level. Throughout the region, it has fostered formation of multicounty local development districts that play a part in planning Appalachian expenditures. More selectively, it has fostered multicounty organizations to plan health programs. However, in inducing collaboration among local units, it is not doing anything different in kind from what federal line agencies have been able to do with comparable monetary incentives.

The commission's evaluation of itself concedes that anyone who expected "a regional solution" to the area's problems will doubtless be disappointed, but argues that the failure of "bureaucratic solutions" to Appalachia's problems justifies an organization that gives

49. For example, see the ARC's *1971 Annual Report*, p. 12.

50. For official criticism of the commission on this score, see a report of May 12, 1971, by the Comptroller General to Congress, "Highway Program Shows Limited Progress Toward Increasing Accessibility To and Through Appalachia," which found that the ARC had allowed states to set their own priorities for use of Appalachian highway funds "regardless of the extent to which they might further regional accessibility." The report concluded that "the organization directing any future regional development program will need to exercise strong leadership to ensure that State actions provide the greatest benefit to the region as a whole."

states and their governors "a policy voice in the management of the federal system."[51] This remains commission doctrine; the staff continues to hope that in time it will be possible to demonstrate the practical merits.

## Duplicating the ARC

Predictably, creation of the Appalachian program and commission fostered demands for comparable treatment from other coalitions of state interests, which formed mainly in the Senate. In response, the Johnson administration in 1965 acceded to legislation that authorized regional commissions for other parts of the country. The resulting organizations, the "Title V" commissions, are the subject of the next chapter; they differ from the ARC in being far less well financed and less independent of federal executive supervision.

Being a special case has exposed the ARC and its program to the charge that they are inequitable. Not only does this invite efforts at duplication by other states, it also invites efforts from federal management experts to extinguish the commission or revise it drastically, as when the Johnson administration tried to bring it under the control of the secretary of commerce.

Authorizations for the commission and all of its programs except highway construction were to expire in 1971. The Nixon administration recommended that the Appalachian program be ended in favor of a proposal for rural development revenue sharing, after the President's Advisory Council on Executive Organization (the Ash Council) found that regional commissions had "not produced a regional approach to economic development," were "an unnecessary additional administrative layer," and tended "to further fragment Federal program responsibility."[52]

Congress chose to renew the commission and its program. A bill for that purpose passed the Senate in 1971 by a vote of 77–3; the

51. *Appalachian Experiment*, p. 94. For an appraisal of the commission by a journalist in the region, see the series by Bill Peterson in the Louisville *Courier-Journal and Times*, April 8–11, 1973.

52. The President's Advisory Council on Executive Organization, *Memoranda for the President of the United States: Establishment of a Department of Natural Resources; Organization for Social and Economic Programs* (1971), p. 153.

vote in the House, where the Appalachian extension was combined with certain other public works authorizations, was 320–67. While members of Congress not from Appalachia would like equal treatment for their states, they seek to achieve parity not by depriving Appalachia of a well-established program, but by winning executive consent for more such programs elsewhere.

Because extinction of the ARC and its program is politically impossible and because politicians in other states are unwilling to acquiesce silently to special treatment for Appalachia, extension of the commission form and associated programs has remained an issue. Backers of the Title V commissions have continued to ask large appropriations for them. Appalachian officials, especially the states' regional representative, have argued for more commissions on the model of their own, and in 1972 secured introduction of a bill for that purpose in the Senate. This bill would have declared Congress's intention to establish federal-state development commissions for the whole country and authorized such commissions to make public works and other grants.[53] For some, including the Appalachian governors, this was a political tactic: one way of defending their anomalous organization has been to urge its duplication elsewhere. But for others, including especially the incumbent states' regional representative, the commitment to duplicating the Appalachian form arises out of a belief that it is the best of all forms for conducting intergovernmental relations.

53. *Public Works Development Act of 1972*, Hearings before the Subcommittee on Economic Development of the Senate Committee on Public Works, 92 Cong. 2 sess. (1972).

# [5]

# The Title V Commissions for Regional Economic Development

TITLE V of the Public Works and Economic Development Act of 1965 was a result of logrolling in the Senate at the time the Appalachian Regional Development Act (ARDA) was passed. Members from outside of Appalachia sought comparable benefits for their states. To protect the Appalachian act from amendments yet assure its passage, the Johnson administration promised to introduce legislation to create regional commissions for other parts of the country. This legislation passed in August 1965 as one part of a comprehensive revision of laws for the aid of depressed areas.

In the next seven years seven commissions were created with twenty-nine states as members, yet none of them really duplicated the Appalachian Regional Commission (ARC).[1] Whereas in Appalachia's case the regional organization resulted from a major spending program, in the Title V case the organizations came first—and then the spending programs failed to follow. Lacking presidential support, the commissions have lacked funds, and they may have no future. The Nixon administration has proposed to end federal participation in them altogether.

1. In 1966–67 commissions were created for New England (Maine, New Hampshire, Vermont, Massachusetts, Connecticut, Rhode Island); the Ozarks (Kansas, Missouri, Arkansas, Oklahoma); Upper Great Lakes (Michigan, Minnesota, Wisconsin); Coastal Plains (North Carolina, South Carolina, Georgia); and Four Corners (Utah, New Mexico, Arizona, and Colorado). In 1972 Louisiana joined the Ozarks commission, and two new commissions were established, for the Old West (North Dakota, South Dakota, Nebraska, Montana, and Wyoming) and the Pacific Northwest (Idaho, Oregon, Washington).

## Origin

In January 1965 the chairman of the Senate Public Works Committee, with thirty-two cosponsors, introduced S. 812, which authorized federal-state commissions for depressed regions in language lifted wholesale from the Appalachian bill, then pending. Senate bill 812 authorized the President to establish commissions, required him to provide liaison between the federal government and the commissions, and stipulated that he appoint a federal member who would receive pay equivalent to that of an assistant secretary. The bill stated that the commissions should formulate "for the Congress" a development program with proposals for federal funding.

The Bureau of the Budget, which opposed more such organizations, proposed a much weakened version of the Appalachian commission, in which federal participation would be tentative and qualified. Except for the President's commitment to the Appalachian program, the Bureau would not have cooperated in the creation of the ARC, and even then it had sharply cut back the organizational design of the President's Appalachian Regional Commission (PARC). If it had not been for the President's promise to the Senate, the Bureau would certainly not have proposed regional commissions for the rest of the country. In both cases it bowed to political necessity, but in the second case at least it had a chance to design its own response. Its proposal for regional commissions, Title V of S. 1648, which the President sent to Congress in the spring, was very different from the Senate's.

Senate bill 1648 made regional commissions creations of and advisers to the secretary of commerce. It authorized him to initiate commissions with an invitation to the states, required him to provide liaison between the federal government and the commissions, and implied that he should have authority to define program development criteria for them. Thus it subordinated the commissions to a federal executive department. It did not guarantee federal participation; it stated that the President should appoint "the Federal member or members of such commissions, if any." Such members were to report to the President through the secretary of commerce and were to be compensated at a per diem rate. The Bureau apparently anticipated that they should serve part time, if they existed at all. The Bureau's bill called for the commissions to initiate and coordinate the preparation of economic development programs, a provision weaker than the Senate's language, which called for the commissions to "develop" plans. More significantly, whereas the Senate bill called for the plans to be submitted to Congress, the Bureau's called for them to be reviewed by the secretary of commerce, interested federal agencies, and then the President. In general, the Bureau's bill safeguarded federal prerogatives vis-à-vis the states and executive prerogatives vis-à-vis the Congress, and it refrained from creating organizations that would report directly to the President.

As enacted, Title V combined elements of S. 812 and S. 1648.[2] The Senate prevailed with the provisions for full-time, high-ranking federal cochairmen.[3] The Bureau of the Budget prevailed with the provisions for executive control over the commissions' plans and proposals. The commissions were to submit their plans to the secretary of commerce, who was to transmit them to federal agencies for review and then to the President "for such action as he may deem desirable." The secretary of commerce was to "provide effective and continuing liaison" between the federal government and each commission, and coordinate the federal cochairmen. The law's definition of the commissions' functions includes both the weak language of the Bureau of the Budget ("shall . . . initiate and coordinate the preparation of long-range overall economic development programs") and the stronger language of the Senate ("shall . . . develop . . . comprehensive and coordinated plans and programs and establish priorities").

The Senate also prevailed with language defining the criteria of a depressed region in such a way that even a highly developed, relatively prosperous area like the southern states of New England might be included. For example, among the criteria of eligibility are that "the economy of the area has traditionally been dominated

---

2. 79 Stat. 6-23.

3. Nevertheless, there is a slight but significant difference between the language of the ARDA and of Title V about the cochairman's rank. The ARDA states that the federal cochairman of the ARC shall be compensated *at* level 4 of the federal executive salary schedule, whereas Title V states that the federal cochairmen shall be compensated *up to* level 4. Like the ARDA, Title V stipulates that the state member be the governor or his designee or someone designated by state law. Formally, the governors serve, but they are often represented by alternates.

by only one or two industries, which are in a state of long-term decline," and that the area is adversely affected by "changing industrial technology" or "changes in national defense facilities or production."[4]

This compromise did not resolve the essential conflict between the senatorial sponsors of Title V and the administration. The leading proponents of Title V legislation have been members of the Senate Public Works Committee who anticipated benefits for their states: Patrick V. McNamara of Michigan until his death in 1966, Edmund S. Muskie of Maine, Joseph M. Montoya of New Mexico, and Fred R. Harris of Oklahoma. The Office of Management and Budget has sought to keep the commissions under executive control and prevent their becoming lobbies for large new public works programs. This conflict has continued since the commissions' initiation, making it hard for them to define their functions or to establish a distinct identity. They have more often been an object of this executive-legislative struggle than they have been independent actors.

## Competing Conceptions: Planning versus Spending

The five commissions created in 1966–67 have prepared comprehensive regional development plans and the secretary of commerce has forwarded them to the President, but the President has taken no action. All five have had responsibility for grant-in-aid pro-

4. Defining other depressed regions and creating other commissions is one way in which non-Appalachian members of Congress have tried to get Appalachia's benefits for their constituencies. Another way has been to argue for extending the statutory boundaries of Appalachia. Four members of the House Public Works Committee from New York and New Hampshire wrote in 1969: "We wish to point out that northern New England and northern New York are Appalachia. If you read the definition in Funk & Wagnall's Dictionary of the English language, you find 'Appalachian, *** a. 1. Of or pertaining to the mountain system of the eastern United States extending from eastern Quebec to northern Alabama and including the White and Green Mountains of New England, the Adirondacks and Catskills of New York, the Alleghenies, Blue Ridge, Black and Smoky ranges, etc.' . . . Since we are part of the Appalachian Mountain system and are suffering many of the same problems, we fail to see why all of the Appalachian Mountain system has not been included in the Appalachian Act, especially its crowning glory in northern New York and New England." *Appalachian and Regional Action Planning Commissions*, H. Rept. 336, 91 Cong. 1 sess. (1969), p. 22.

grams, but as of 1973 the average appropriation per commission in any one year had never exceeded the minor sum of $8 million. Because what they ought to do has been so much in dispute, the commissions have found it hard to do anything.

The Bureau of the Budget conceived of the Title V commissions as functionally analogous to PARC, the planning group that preceded the ARC, rather than to the ARC. The Bureau hoped for a prolonged period of planning. Title V contained no new program authorizations, but authorized the secretary of commerce to give the commissions technical assistance with planning and to pay their administrative expenses for two years. For these very limited purposes, the law authorized appropriations of $15 million.

Partly because the Bureau of the Budget emphasized regional planning, so did the original administrators of Title V in the Department of Commerce. Commerce established the Office of Regional Economic Development to oversee the Title V program, and in 1967 ORED issued guidelines instructing the commissions at length on the proper way to plan. Above all, ORED insisted that planning be regional and not just an aggregate of the plans of individual states. Guidelines called for the commissions "to view the region itself as a socio-economic entity" and to concentrate planning on those "dimensions of the region's economy that are primarily *regional*."[5] Both the assistant secretary for economic development, Eugene P. Foley, and the director of ORED, Jonathan Lindley, aspired to a high level of distinction and technical competence for the ORED staff and for the federal cochairmen of the commissions. Lindley argued that the President's appointees to the commissions should have experience in economics or public administration, should come from "federal agencies, universities and colleges, foundations, the World Bank and similar institutions," and "should not be the candidate of the Congressional delegation or the Governors."[6]

In contrast to this technical, apolitical conception of the commissions that prevailed in the executive branch were the expectations of Congress and the commissions, which consisted of the governors

5. U.S. Department of Commerce, Office of Regional Development Planning, "Guidelines for Program Formulation for Regional Action Planning Commissions," August 1967.

6. Information Memorandum, Oct. 10, 1966; special assistant for regional economic coordination (SAREC) files, Department of Commerce.

as representatives of the states. Whereas the Bureau of the Budget tried to make sure that the commissions would spend no money except on the basis of regional planning, the commissions wanted to do no planning without being assured of federal money. The commissions thought of themselves as analogous to ARC, not PARC.

Scarcely a year passed after 1965 without a major spending proposal that challenged the administration. In 1966 members of Congress from the Ozarks proposed a $681 million regional program to the President. In 1967 Ozark senators led by Harris of Oklahoma sponsored authorization of a supplemental grant program under Title V. Late in 1968, as the Johnson administration was leaving office, all the commissions submitted large spending programs to the secretary of commerce. In 1969 Muskie and twenty-seven other senators sponsored a bill that would have required the secretary of commerce to provide each of the federal cochairmen with funds to carry out activities included in the commissions' comprehensive plans. The activities were to include "programs and projects in the fields of natural resources, agriculture, training, health and welfare, transportation, and other fields related to the purposes of this Act," without regard to whether the programs were authorized in any other federal law.[7] It would have been an extraordinary grant of authority. In 1971, when the Nixon administration was trying to limit new authorizations under Title V to one year, the chairman of the House Public Works Committee, John Blatnik of Minnesota, who is a partisan of the Upper Great Lakes program, sponsored a two-year extension combined with a sizable increase in the authorization. In 1972 Blatnik sponsored a bill that authorized $100 million a year for every commission having an approved long-range plan.

Neither side in this dispute over the commissions' functions prevailed. For several years the commissions barely worked on regional plans. Meanwhile, the Bureau of the Budget conceded a critical point: the commissions received program funds and began spending before their comprehensive plans had been approved. The Bureau did not attempt to kill authorization of a small grant program in 1967 at a time when most of the commissions had not even begun

7. S. 1090, in *Regional Economic Development Legislation of 1969 (Part 1)*, Hearings before the Senate Committee on Public Works, 91 Cong. 1 sess. (1969), pp. 6–9.

TABLE 1. *Budget Requests for Title V Program, Selected Fiscal Years*

Thousands of dollars

| Fiscal year | Commissions' request to Commerce Department | Commerce Department's request to Budget Bureau or OMB | President's request to Congress | Appropriation |
|---|---|---|---|---|
| 1967 | 13,150 | 10,800 | 7,550 | 6,100 |
| 1969 | 60,000 | 45,000 | 21,000 | 12,500 |
| 1970 | 58,000 | 48,075 | 16,500[a] | 23,618 |
| 1971 | 216,475 | 138,194 | 45,000 | 39,000 |
| 1972 | 339,760 | 269,620 | 39,000 | 39,054 |

Sources: The data are drawn from House Appropriations Committee hearings except for the 1970 figures, which are from Senate hearings. For example, see *Departments of State, Justice, and Commerce, the Judiciary, and Related Agencies Appropriations for 1972*, Hearings before a Subcommittee of the House Appropriations Committee, 92 Cong. 1 sess. (1971), pt. 3, p. 18.

a. Nixon administration request. Johnson administration request was $21,613,000.

to meet, let alone to plan.[8] On the other hand the Bureau has succeeded in keeping the substantive terms of authorization restricted and the amount of appropriations low. The 1969 amendments to Title V authorized funds for the whole share of a grant-in-aid project otherwise authorized by federal law and for demonstration projects, language that considerably broadened the commissions' discretion but was still quite a different thing from authorizing whatever the commissions put in their plans.[9] Also, the Budget Bureau has regularly made severe cuts in the Title V appropriations requests that come from Commerce. Thus, even though Congress's authorizations have risen sharply (from $10 million for the fiscal year ending June 30, 1969, to $305 million for the two-year period ending June 30, 1973), appropriations, as shown in Table 1, have grown very slowly.

In the prolonged contest over the commissions' functions, neither side won because neither had the full support of the White House. The President did not appoint distinguished professionals from the field of economic development as federal cochairmen, as pro-

8. 81 Stat. 266-267. The 1967 amendments authorized the secretary of commerce to provide supplements to federal grant-in-aid programs to the federal cochairmen of commissions whose comprehensive plans were in effect. This condition was not enforced. Commissions without an approved regional plan received supplemental grants.

9. 83 Stat. 216-219.

gram officials in Commerce had hoped he would. Nor did the White House heed an appeal from the director of the Budget Bureau to choose men from outside the region. It chose instead to use the appointments for patronage. But while the White House offered up the high-paying jobs in the commissions to senatorial protégés, it never bowed to the congressional pressure for program funds.

## The Commissions' Spending Activity

Like the ARC though on a much smaller scale, the Title V commissions have been channels for additional federal grant-in-aid funds for the depressed regions they serve. Most of the funds have been used to supplement the federal share of a variety of construction projects, such as industrial parks, water and sewer facilities, access roads, airports, and vocational education schools. Under the so-called first-dollar authority they received in 1969, the commissions can pay 100 percent of the federal cost of such projects, but they usually choose to supplement federal agency funds rather than substitute for them altogether. By the end of fiscal year 1971, the commissions had spent a total of $64 million on 584 projects. The following list shows the volume of the commissions' supplemental grants for fiscal years 1971 and 1972, by federal agency:

|  | Number of projects | Grants (thousands of dollars) |
|---|---|---|
| Health, Education, and Welfare | 135 | 12,189 |
| Agriculture | 102 | 4,151 |
| Economic Development Administration | 83 | 9,267 |
| Transportation | 52 | 5,150 |
| Environmental Protection Agency | 49 | 4,705 |
| Interior | 26 | 1,095 |
| Housing and Urban Development | 19 | 1,934 |
| Justice | 1 | 5 |

Independently of federal agencies the commissions may also use their funds for planning, investigations, studies, demonstration projects, and training programs approved by the secretary of commerce, and by the end of fiscal 1971, they had spent $32 million for these purposes, half as much as for supplemental grants. For a Title V commission as for a federal agency, a demonstration project can demonstrate almost anything. The Coastal Plains commission has invested demonstration grants heavily in marine research facilities, including an ocean science center at Savannah, Georgia, and a marine resources center at Charleston, South Carolina. The New England commission, which has been more inclined than the others to undertake health and education programs, invested over $2 million of demonstration funds in fiscal 1971 in programs for teacher education ("spreading innovative educational techniques throughout the region") and in giving assistance (model curricula, for example) to vocational and technical schools. With their research funds, the commissions have financed dozens of studies on the widest imaginable variety of topics. The New England commission, for example, in 1971 listed eighteen publications ranging from "Algae Control by Mixing" to "New England: An Economic Analysis." A 1970 list of research and technical assistance projects for the Ozarks commission ranged from a study by the Corps of Engineers for economic development along the Arkansas-Verdigris Waterway to a "concept statement for the National Leisure Institute" prepared by Arkansas Polytechnic College. The Corps's study, if carried out, would identify "potential industrial, commercial, and residential sites to completely utilize the resources of the Waterway area." The proposed National Leisure Institute was to "define the challenges of man's leisure," investigate by "serious scientific inquiry" appropriate "solutions" for these challenges, and, after "thorough testing and evaluation of these solutions," disseminate them nationally through "demonstrations and informative programs." It was proposed that the institute occupy 2,200 acres on Dardanelle Reservoir near Russellville, Arkansas. Contractors for such studies have been other government agencies, universities, or private consulting firms.[10]

All the commissions have regularly given planning grants to state governments of from $19,500 to $65,000 per year per state. In addition to these routine planning grants, the commissions have

10. This summary is drawn from annual reports of the commissions and from appropriations hearings. The quotations are from *New England Regional Commission Annual Report Fiscal Year 1971*, pp. 13, 21, and *The Ozarks Regional Commission 1970 Annual Report*, pp. 16–17. For a summary of program data, see *Departments of State, Justice, and Commerce, the Judiciary, and Related Agencies Appropriations for 1973*, Hearings before a Subcommittee of the House Appropriations Committee, 92 Cong. 2 sess. (1972), pt. 3, pp. 264–65.

financed a variety of services to state and local governments, especially in New England. For example, grants from the New England commission established the New England Municipal Center to provide training, technical assistance, and information to the region's cities and towns, and, in cooperation with the New England River Basins Commission, helped the states plan their administration of grants under federal coastal zone management legislation.

With their low level of activity, their heavy investment in research and planning, and their dependence on the supplemental grant technique for public works projects, the commissions' own impact on economic development is invisible, and they are vulnerable to the charge of spending disproportionate amounts on administration. In 1972 a muckraking exposé of the New England commission in the Boston *Globe* began under the banner: " 'Do-nothing bureaucracy' squanders millions of tax dollars." "Although the Commission's mandate is to stop downhill trends in New England's economy," the *Globe* reported, "it has spent less than 1 percent of $23 million in Federal funds on business development. Most money has gone to on-going programs that are initiated by others. . . . While the Commission underwrites studies that usually recommend more study, and stacks of its reports collect dust, unemployment since 1967 has doubled in just about every New England state . . . and approximately 2800 businesses have failed in the region." The *Globe* also attacked the use of high-paying federal jobs in the commission as patronage. The New England commission may have been more vulnerable to criticism than the others because it has spent over half its funds, an exceptionally high proportion, on technical assistance, research, and demonstration grants rather than on supplemental grants for public works projects, and it has emphasized programs for developing human and natural resources rather than commercial and industrial development. The *Globe* series singled out the teacher training program as a waste of money.[11] Commissions that concentrated on subsidizing industrial parks, sewage treatment works, and vocational education schools, as the Upper Great Lakes commission has done, were less open to this kind of attack. Whereas New England spent about six of every eight dollars in 1971 for research, training, or demonstrations, Upper Great Lakes spent about six of every eight for public works. The

11. Boston *Globe*, Oct. 8–13, 1972.

Upper Great Lakes commission has also taken pride in its efficiency. In 1971 it had a staff of only nineteen, while the New England commission had thirty-three, although their program budgets were comparable.

The commissions have had nearly equal amounts of money to spend. Dubious about an even split, the Budget Bureau has pressed Title V administrators in the Department of Commerce to develop a rational method for allocating funds among commissions. In 1969 they devised a formula that was based on equality (30 percent), quality of plan (25 percent), need as measured by employment and income (25 percent), and the preferences of the Senate (20 percent), which had sought to stipulate a dollar allocation to each commission. Commerce officials judged the quality of the commissions' plans to be the same though conceding that this could be a variable item. The formula produced near-equality in allocations.

Small as the commissions' program expenditures are, they have occupied most of the commissions' time and attention. Commission members spend relatively little time in their meetings discussing the contents of comprehensive plans.

## The Commissions' Planning Activity

The commissions' plans are lengthy documents that include a description of the economy of the region, the commission's goals (usually stated as closing the "income gap" or the "job gap" between the region and the nation), development strategies, and recommendations. The plans usually call for at least several hundred million dollars of additional federal expenditure, but the proposals vary greatly. For example, the plan of the Upper Great Lakes commission, which has jurisdiction over an area of 116,000 square miles and a population of 2.9 million, calls for a $382 million federal investment in natural resources, public works, and manpower training over five years. The federal expenditure is expected to generate $1.2 billion in private investment and 100,000 new jobs. Coupled with the public investment plan is a proposal for incentives, through tax credits, to private investors. The plan of the Coastal Plains commission, which has jurisdiction over a smaller area (80,000 square miles) but a larger population (5 million), calls for an increase in federal expenditure of $12 billion in an eight-year period, of which $10 billion would be for human resources programs, principally manpower training.

By the summer of 1973, the President had taken no action on these plans. The secretary of commerce has asked little action of him. In memorandums in 1971, Secretary Maurice H. Stans asked only that the President urge the federal agencies "within the constraints of law and available funds to give the Plan full consideration in the development of [their] programs in [the region]."[12] Because the Nixon administration attempted in 1971 and again in 1973 to end the Title V program, the secretary is constrained from advocating the program. His reaction to plan submissions is equivocal: enough action, in the form of qualified, tentative approvals, to respond to congressional and commission pressure but not so much as to invite a rebuff from OMB or the White House. Secretary Stans's letters to the commissions said flatly that approval does not commit federal funds to implementation of the plans.[13]

Throughout the program, lack of executive support has diminished the incentive to prepare regional plans. The commissions have not supposed that their efforts would be rewarded with executive approval and funds. When Secretary Stans asked for revision of New England's plan early in 1970, the commission's executive director wrote the federal cochairman that the staff had decided to make "a major effort," but that this was "not an easy decision to make" in light of "the seven months it took Commerce to conduct an inconclusive review of the first plan" and "a very low FY '71 budget request by the Administration, suggesting a pointlessness to a major regional development plan."[14] When an alternate member of the Ozarks commission asked the executive director to justify the plan, the director replied that "regardless of our thoughts on the Plan, it does put something into the hands of the secretary of

12. Memorandum for the President, Sept. 20, 1971, and Memorandum for the President, Nov. 15, 1971; SAREC files, Department of Commerce.

13. Secretary of Commerce Stans to Thomas F. Schweigert and Patrick J. Lucey, Sept. 20, 1971, and to G. Fred Steele, Jr., and Robert Scott, Nov. 15, 1971; SAREC files, Department of Commerce.

14. Richard Wright to Stewart Lamprey and New England Regional Commission Alternates, March 16, 1970; NERC files, Washington.

commerce and complies with the Law. Therefore, it should be done." [15] If it had not been for the insistence of Secretary Stans after 1969 that the commissions prepare plans, they might not have done so.

As regional planners the commissions were handicapped by a problem still more fundamental than the lack of presidential support, a handicap inherent in the "catalyst" as a coordinating type. Introduced into a milieu of hitherto uncoordinated or poorly coordinated organizations, the catalyst is supposed to induce changes in their conduct. It does not have the resources to achieve its goals independently; it works by affecting others or it does not work at all. Although this is a relatively new type of coordinating organization, it has become fairly common in American government in recent years. On the local level, model cities and community action agencies are catalysts. [16] Among the six cases analyzed in this book, the ARC and the Title V commissions are examples of catalysts. Both are charged with planning and coordinating a wide range of public actions in support of regional economic development, but neither has found a way to induce the cooperation of federal agencies in carrying out regional development strategies.

In an early theoretical paper, the Office of Regional Economic Development tried to develop the rationale for the commissions as coordinators. The paper distinguished five possible roles for a regional commission: lobbying, industrial development, research, legislative planning, and public investment planning and coordination. The paper concluded that the last of these, though "the most difficult," would be "the most effective" in the long run.

This role would focus the Commission's attention on the existing structure of public investment programs at the Federal, State, and local levels. The Commission would seek to develop better ways of using these programs to achieve economic development. It would attempt to formulate a consistent development strategy aimed at enhancing economic growth and then relate specific projects to that strategy. It would work

---

15. Minutes, Ozarks Regional Commission Meeting, June 2, 1971.

16. On community action and model cities agencies as local coordinators, see James L. Sundquist, *Making Federalism Work: A Study of Program Coordination at the Community Level* (Brookings Institution, 1969), and on model cities, Lawrence D. Brown, "Coordination of Federal Urban Policy: Organizational Politics in Three Model Cities" (Ph.D. dissertation, Harvard University, 1973).

with the Federal, State, and local governments on implementing this strategy.[17]

The ORED paper argued that as a planner and coordinator the commission had a unique advantage in that "it has no special bureaucratic interest to protect. It will be independent of the State agencies and the numerous bureaus and agencies in Washington. It can question all public investment programs from a consistent and comprehensive viewpoint—namely how does it affect the development of this region?" But this independence was also a defect: if a commission was independent of existing agencies, how was it to influence their conduct? There never was a plausible answer. "Because of its close relationship to the Governors and Federal establishment in Washington, it will also be in a unique position to see that its approved recommendations are put into effect."[18] But Title V, like the ARDA, did not give the commissions any authority over federal agencies. It stated only that each federal agency should, "consonant with law and within the limits of available funds," assist the commissions in carrying out their functions. After the commissions prepared regional plans, interested federal agencies were to review them but were under no obligation whatever to carry them out.

As the Title V program was beginning, ORED recognized the need to engage federal agencies in planning. Director Jonathan Lindley wrote that "the success of the regional program rests substantially upon the active involvement of many federal agencies." He proposed a high-ranking interagency council, to be chaired by the secretary of commerce, and functional subcommittees (for instance, a natural resources subcommittee with representatives from Interior, Agriculture, and the Corps of Engineers; a human resources subcommittee with representatives from HEW, OEO, and Labor), which would review the commissions' proposals. After confirmation by the parent council, "subcommittee recommendations would reflect appropriate Federal policy."[19]

The Bureau of the Budget declined at first to approve Lindley's

17. "The Role of a Regional Commission," unsigned, no date (about 1966); SAREC files, Department of Commerce.

18. Ibid.

19. Action Memorandum, June 30, 1966; Eugene P. Foley to Charles L. Schultze, Sept. 20, 1966; SAREC files.

proposal. Later, in 1967, it did issue an executive order that spelled out the secretary of commerce's responsibility for guiding the federal cochairmen and created a cabinet-level committee—the Federal Advisory Council on Regional Economic Development (FACRED) —to review the commissions' plans. Thus an organization was set up that might serve Lindley's original purpose, but the Bureau's purpose was more to subject the commissions to the secretary's influence than to open federal agencies to the commissions' influence. In 1967 the commissions' supporters in the Senate had proposed legislation to free them from the Commerce Department's supervision altogether. The administration managed to kill this, and issued the executive order soon thereafter to make the secretary of commerce's responsibilities explicit.

Despite the existence of FACRED, the commissions and federal agencies have not cooperated in planning. A consultant to the Department of Commerce reported in 1970 that "the Commissions have generally failed to establish good working relationships with Federal agencies in the regions and to determine how the latter's programs and objectives mesh with their own." Interviews with major federal agencies confirmed "the absence of any significant degree of cooperation or even contact with the Commissions on major planning and programming issues." [20] At least one commission, the Upper Great Lakes, did send parts of its plan to federal regional officials for comment and arranged a meeting with them to discuss the plan, but, according to a commission consultant who participated, this was "a lacklustre session," "a lukewarm venture." "You need some bait," he added, noting that the commission had none to offer. [21] No structure of working subcommittees such as Lindley proposed developed, and without working-level participation, any hope of coordination through FACRED can only be vacuous. The secretary of commerce sends draft plans to the federal agencies, which respond with brief, usually noncommittal letters. To discuss the comments FACRED meets infrequently and typically with lower-ranking officials substituting for the department heads. [22] Nothing in this process commits the agencies to carrying

20. "Regional Action Planning Commissions: An Evaluation," Report to the U.S. Department of Commerce by Arthur D. Little, Inc., 1970, pp. 27–28.

21. Interview with Victor Roterus, Nov. 11, 1972.

22. The Department of Commerce has published reports of FACRED's meetings, beginning with the first meeting in October 1968.

out the commissions' plans or induces them to alter their behavior in the slightest. The departments do not want the commissions to determine their spending priorities, and the commissions do not seem to expect that the departments will be guided by their plans. "The federal agencies are going to read our plan?" one director asked rhetorically in an interview. "Of course not. One agency's long-range plan for another is not going to be followed." [23]

One might think that the regional commissions and the agencies have common interests that would lead to cooperation. Regional coalitions have formed to seek federal benefits. When this happened in Appalachia, federal agencies did join with the regional interests to produce a regional program. But there are important differences between the case of Appalachia and that of Title V. In the Appalachian case, the President endorsed the coalition's effort, giving federal agencies reason to expect that their own programs would be enlarged. The federal agencies dominated planning. Under their leadership the program took shape before a new regional organization had even been formed, and most of the components of the program expanded the agencies' own activities. In the case of Title V, new organizations distinct from the federal agencies, and with an obvious lack of support from the President, were created to do the planning. As a planning and coordinating organization, the ARC too faced the fundamental problem inherent in the organizational type: how was it to influence the conduct of others? But because a large Appalachian spending program already existed, the ARC was able to surmount the problem. Rather than struggle with how to influence federal agencies, the ARC asked how it could get control of Appalachian funds. It found the answer in the 1967 amendments to the ARDA, which provided for a single appropriation of Appalachian funds and authorized the commission to approve projects. As for influencing the states, the ARC does this as any federal grant-in-aid administrator does—by stating conditions of expenditure.

After the ARC and the Title V commissions were functioning, a post hoc theory of coordination developed that stressed supplemental grants as a way of influencing federal agency conduct. The ARC to a considerable extent and the Title V commissions to a greater extent operate by supplementing the federal share of the

23. Interview with Richard Wright, executive director of the NERC, April 4, 1972.

cost of a variety of public works projects, raising it to, say, 80 instead of 50 percent.[24] The Title V commissions, unlike the ARC, have only a very limited right to initiate and finance projects themselves; and the ARC, when it does this, must rely on federal agencies for help with administration. The theorists of the regional commissions as coordinators argue that the technique of supplementation gives the commissions access to a wide range of federal actions and enables them to induce federal agencies to finance projects that contribute to regional development. But the commissions hardly ever approach federal agencies with project proposals, and with good reason.[25] Projects are rarely initiated at the federal level; they begin with a state or local request for funds. If a commission seeks to influence the choice or location of projects, it must influence state and local planning. Interviews with state officials indicate that they do not perceive supplemental funds as an instrument of a commission's or a state's development strategy.[26] They view such funds quite pragmatically for what they are—a way of

24. The ARC's use of supplemental grants has been declining since 1971, when it received authorization to finance the entire federal share of any grant-in-aid project provided for in federal law.

25. Douglas N. Jones and Paul W. Kolp, *Federal Agency Planning Policies and Regional Economic Development* (McLean, Va.: Research Analysis Corp., 1970), and the Arthur D. Little report document the lack of contact between the commissions and federal agencies for any purpose, either comprehensive planning or the selection of particular projects. Of nineteen federal agencies surveyed for the Research Analysis report, only the Economic Development Administration reported significant contact with all the commissions and eleven agencies reported only slight contact or none at all. The Arthur D. Little study found: "The failure of the program to exert meaningful leverage on Federal plans and outlays is its most telling weakness. A major potential of the Title V approach lies in the opportunity to shape regional investment strategies which constitutes frameworks for planned Federal outlays designed to produce explicit development outcomes. Yet, there is no visible evidence that the program has begun to affect the allocation of Federal funds, and there are only faint and tenuous indications that regional commissions and regional offices of Federal line agencies have even approached the early stages of systematic communication" (p. 6).

26. David K. Hartley and Francis B. Mahoney, "Regional Commissions: A View from the States," Report to SAREC, July 1, 1970. This report by consultants to the Department of Commerce was based on nearly a hundred interviews with state officials and on other sources. It found that few state officials appeared to think of the commission "as a vehicle for focusing State (as contrasted with Federal) efforts and expenditures on lagging regions." Interviews with twelve state representatives or their alternates in four commissions, including the ARC, confirmed this. For an account of the commissions' impact on state planning by an official of the Department of Commerce, see Robert T. Murphy, "The Regional Commission System," *Public Administration Review*, vol. 33 (March–April 1973), pp. 179–84.

enabling a locality to get a federally aided project when it lacks funds for the matching share. The supplemental funds do not, however, induce a federal agency to sacrifice any of its own programmatic objectives or standards to those of an agency for economic development. The federal agency whose specialty is, say, construction of airports or hospitals or vocational schools must still spend its normal share of the project cost, and is under no legal or other obligation to choose locations preferred by regional development commissions or states purporting to pursue economic development objectives.

### The Federal Cochairmen as Federal Coordinators

Their lack of program funds is one major difference between the Title V commissions and the ARC; the other is their greater integration with the federal executive branch. The commissions are contained within the Department of Commerce, whose secretary receives appropriations for them and is responsible for coordinating the federal cochairmen. Federal executive officials saw this structure as a way of coordinating the commissions' actions with federal action. Officials in the Bureau of the Budget argued that it would serve the commissions' own interests because it would assure the support of a cabinet member and, ultimately, of federal executive agencies. According to this argument, the commissions can succeed only if their plans are accepted as federal policy, and the plans will be accepted as federal policy only if the federal cochairmen submit to federal executive direction.[27] The first administrators of the Title V program in the Department of Commerce shared this conception.

There was a touch of the disingenuous in the Budget Bureau's argument that the commissions should defer to Commerce's direction for their own good. The ARC was thriving on independence. The Bureau's aim was to keep the commissions under control and to forestall claims on the Treasury. Commerce, on the other hand,

27. Harold Seidman, assistant director for management and organization, Bureau of the Budget, to Roger Adkins, May 22, 1967, and Adkins to Messrs. Bast, Broadbent, Frey, and the Director, with enclosure, "Direction and Coordination of Federal Cochairmen and Regional Development Programs," May 24, 1967; Office of Management and Budget files.

in trying to assert control was pursuing programmatic purposes. Officials there hoped to lead the commissions in an important new program of regional economic development. Lindley, as the first and only director of ORED, wanted ORED to recommend federal policy for regional economic development, supervise the commissions and control their spending, control the votes of the cochairmen, and actually do a large part of regional planning itself. ORED was to have a staff of sixty persons, of whom half or more were to be GS-14s and above. Foley, the assistant secretary for economic development, scouted the country for talent.

To officials in both the Budget Bureau and the Commerce Department, the key to controlling the commissions was to control the federal cochairmen. Initially, they hoped to influence the President's appointments so that the offices would be filled by men who shared their apolitical approach to the program.[28] But this failed, and by the fall of 1966, Lindley had grown pessimistic about making the cochairmen agents of federal executive policy. He wrote:

in the absence of effective leadership by the Secretary of Commerce the Federal Cochairmen naturally are going to gravitate towards the Governors and the Congressional delegations. . . . In fact, the Federal Cochairmen now are primarily preoccupied about their popularity rating with the Congressional Delegations and the Governors and regard themselves as lobbyists for their interests. They seem to be primarily concerned about "getting projects" and project money even though they have hardly begun to hire a commission staff and have not yet started their planning process. In short, there is no indication that they have any concept of their job as a *Federal* Cochairman loyal to the Department of Commerce and the Executive Branch. As far as I can tell, the Federal Cochairmen regard their job as being that of a passive broker reconciling the interest of the Congressional Delegations and the Governors of the states.[29]

Subsequently, Lindley tried to regulate the cochairmen. Commerce's first rules, issued at the end of 1966, required them to submit to close departmental supervision: they should "actively endeavor to speak for the President and the Secretary of Commerce

28. Harold Seidman to the Director, July 20, 1965; Commerce and Housing (Adkins) to the Director, Feb. 4, 1966; Memorandum for Mr. Califano from Charles L. Schultze, Feb. 23, 1966; OMB files.

29. Information Memorandum, Nov. 2, 1966; SAREC files, Department of Commerce.

in all matters of Federal concern" and "before casting a vote on any specific proposal, obtain guidance from the Secretary with respect to Federal policy."[30] These regulations pointedly omitted any provision for making cash grants for technical assistance to the commissions even though Title V provided for them. Instead, the rules said that the commissions would get technical assistance from the Department of Commerce, other federal agencies, or private consultants whose contracts Commerce had approved. The regulations were issued without having been cleared with the cochairmen, and they reacted sharply.

Soon thereafter, the Department of Commerce ended the effort to control the cochairmen. ORED was abolished and Lindley was appointed to another job. New regulations, acceptable to the federal cochairmen, were issued, which softened earlier assertions of supervisory authority and provided for technical assistance grants to the commissions. The ORED staff was merged with another part of the department; soon it became demoralized and began to dwindle. In short, the centrifugal tendency of American politics had prevailed. The cochairmen would henceforth be oriented to the senatorial delegations or the statehouses, not to the federal executive branch.

Having failed to assert control over the cochairmen, the Department of Commerce tried to ignore them. There followed a period (1967 to mid-1968) of utter indifference toward the commissions, but the Budget Bureau put an end to that, fearing that indifference would end in their getting free of executive control altogether. After 1969 a new secretary of commerce sought a modus vivendi with the cochairmen. He made a sweeping delegation of spending authority to them, but urged his special assistant for regional economic coordination (SAREC) to prepare guidelines for planning and spending that would give priority to developing industry and jobs. The special assistant never issued these guidelines because "no single definition [of economic development] appeared adequate to meet the needs of the regions."[31] The country was too varied and the federal cochairmen were too independent of the secretary's

30. *Federal Register*, vol. 31 (Dec. 30, 1966), pp. 16679–82.
31. George J. Pantos, "Report on the Activities of the Office of the Special Assistant for Regional Economic Coordination," June 30, 1969–Aug. 1, 1970, p. 14; SAREC files, Department of Commerce.

supervision to make a common policy feasible. The great variation in their regional plans and their spending practices shows how much discretion the commissions have had.

The Bureau of the Budget continued to hope for regional planning to justify the spending. After enactment of supplemental grants in 1967, the Bureau said it would apportion no money until Commerce had stated planning requirements for the commissions' use of the funds and the commissions had developed a specific strategy of expenditure. This delayed the initial apportionment but did not result in detailed planning of annual expenditures. A commission's annual financial plan, which the secretary of commerce must approve, is a list of broad categories and projected amounts of quarterly expenditure with little supporting rationale.

Within the commissions, the federal cochairmen have occasionally invoked their vetoes in defense of what they took to be the federal interest, but such actions are infrequent and are not occasioned by systematic guidance from Commerce. The federal member of the Ozarks commission once vetoed a project on the grounds that federal guidelines applying to the case, which would have been the commission's first use of its first-dollar authority, had not been issued. In the Coastal Plains commission, the federal member vetoed a resolution that would have committed $100,000 a year to each of the member states for an indefinite time, arguing that he could not make such a commitment without approval from Congress and the Bureau of the Budget. In the New England commission, the federal member vetoed an increase in funds for building a treatment center for drug users, apparently because the secretary of commerce was then (1969–70) urging the commissions to confine themselves to more conventional projects of economic development. The secretary's special assistant for coordinating the commissions, the man chiefly responsible for liaison with the federal cochairmen, told Congress in 1971 that he did not know of the vetoes.[32] Speaking of the federal cochairmen, the executive director

32. *Public Works Acceleration Act Amendments of 1971 and Public Works and Economic Development Act Amendments of 1971*, Hearings before the House Committee on Public Works, 92 Cong. 1 sess. (1971), p. 410. The veto has not been an important issue in federal-state relations. Representative Ed Edmondson of Oklahoma, upon learning of the vetoes, remarked: "Let us get this nailed down closer because I have talked to a lot of Governors about these regional commissions and I have yet to hear of a Governor complaining of a Federal veto being exercised" (ibid.).

of one commission commented, "They call their own shots on their own welfare functions."[33]

The functions of the federal cochairmen have remained ill defined because the functions of the commissions have been in dispute. Throughout the history of the commissions, the federal cochairmen have been preoccupied with establishing their organizations, securing federal funds, and increasing their independence from the secretary of commerce. The Appalachian commission remains the model to which they aspire. Lacking support from the President, they have failed. Whether as advocates for the region in relations with the federal government or as spokesmen for federal policy within the commissions, they are undermined by the indifference of the executive branch.

## Regionalism

Because there was greater federal control over the Title V program than over the ARC, originally there was greater emphasis on regionalism. The Budget Bureau urged that regional commissions develop programs that would be more than mere aggregations of state programs. Again, Commerce officials initially shared this conception. "Regional planning should be coordinated with State planning," an early Commerce document says, "but should not be delegated to the States."[34] Early guidelines reiterated this theme, as did Commerce's comments on the commissions' first attempts at planning. This was the opposite of the ARC's approach, which delegated planning to the states and advertised the merits of decentralization for the states' benefit.

It is not clear how the states were to be induced to subordinate their interests to those of the region. Apparently, ORED was to secure a regional approach by supervising the commissions closely and doing some planning itself. However, Commerce officials found it hard to define what problems or activities should be regarded as regional. Regional planning also encountered technical problems such as lack of data. Except for New England and to a degree the

33. Interview with Richard Wright, NERC.

34. Office of Regional Development Planning, Economic Development Administration, to the federal cochairman, Upper Great Lakes Regional Commission, Sept. 14, 1967; UGLRC files, Washington.

Upper Great Lakes, where some interstate cooperation had preceded the Title V program, the regions in question were artifacts of congressional politics, "little more than slices of poverty thrown together from several States, with little else in common in terms of economic, social or political structures."[35] Because no one had conceived of them as socioeconomic entities before, it was hard to do so now.

As the effort at federal executive direction of the commission subsided, the commitment of Commerce officials to regionalism waned. In 1970 a consultant recommended abandoning the ideal of regional planning in favor of aggregating state plans.[36] Guidelines to the commissions in 1970 failed to stress the regional principle. Draft language requiring that funds be invested in programs "which are primarily regional in scope and beyond the effective range of solution by local and State governments" was dropped.[37] Increasingly, the Title V commissions were justified as mechanisms for improving state planning. It had proved impossible to transcend the states.

Like the ARC, the commissions treat the state as the basic unit for allocating funds. They usually arrive at a more or less even split, after allowing for differences in the portion of the state's territory included in the region. The New England commission experimented briefly with an allocation formula copied from the ARC, but concluded that a formula would not work when applied to much smaller amounts of money; allotments would have to be tailored more closely to individual proposals. The Four Corners commission decided one year on an even split: $648,750 for each of the four states. The commissions describe some projects as regional. Usually these are projects, like the Coastal Plains' marine research centers or New England's teacher training program, that are financed with demonstration funds and seem likely to distribute services or knowledge without regard to jurisdictional boundaries. As another example, the Upper Great Lakes commission finances several mobile units to bring a career guidance program to school districts that otherwise could not afford one, and some of

35. Arthur D. Little report, p. 20.
36. Ibid., pp. 11–12.
37. SAREC, Memorandum for the federal cochairmen, Jan. 30, 1970; NERC files, Washington; and U.S. Department of Commerce, "Guidelines to Federal Cochairmen and Regional Commissions," March 17, 1970.

these units operate across state lines. However, designating projects as regional does not necessarily preclude equal distribution among the states. It is understood in New England that each state will be the locus of a "regional" project. Despite the decreased emphasis on regionalism, efforts at interstate cooperation do occur within the commissions. Through the Upper Great Lakes commission, the three states have planned jointly for highway development and have been working on reciprocal education agreements. They have agreed to waive out-of-state tuition in vocational schools.

## Jointness

Their functions have been so much in dispute and their expenditures so limited that the Title V commissions are a poor test of the practice of joint decision making. In general, they have been organizations of limited accomplishment and low morale, but the contrasting case of the ARC indicates that these are not the inevitable consequences of jointness. The ARC, with a large program budget and competent executives and staff members, has been distinguished during much of its history by high morale. On the other hand, jointness accounts in part, at least indirectly, for the Title V commissions' crippling lack of federal executive support. The Office of Management and Budget has feared that the commissions would be nothing more than regional lobbies pursuing federal funds for their own sake and allocating them among the states and within the states on essentially political grounds, all the while taking advantage of their jointness to escape federal executive discipline. By reducing the organizations' responsiveness to the secretary of commerce, jointness also undermines his interest in them and his willingness to serve as their advocate. Various secretaries, finding that they could not control the commissions, elected to leave them alone. As joint organizations lodged within a federal executive agency, the Title V commissions are a structural anomaly that has frustrated all participants.[38]

38. Early in 1970 Secretary of Commerce Stans proposed to the administration's Rural Affairs Council a wholly new Title V which would have eliminated the commissions as independent planning bodies and made regional development planning an exclusively federal function. This plan called for the secretary of commerce to designate administrative regions for economic development, presumably encompassing

Within the commissions, jointness also proved divisive. Not that there was a pattern of federal-state conflict over policy (federal vetoes were infrequent), but there has been conflict between the federal cochairmen and the executive directors over who will exercise the executive functions of the commissions. The executive director often solicits support from the state members in these struggles, with the result that he is sometimes perceived as a partisan of the states. Except for the Coastal Plains commission, the state members of the Title V commissions have not followed the ARC's example and created an office of states' regional representatives to speak for them in the daily conduct of commission business. The separation of the commission offices, which are in the regions, from the federal cochairmen's offices, which are in Washington, probably exacerbates internal conflict. The Upper Great Lakes commission alone has avoided these internal problems by the simple expedient of having the same man serve as federal cochairman and executive director, an arrangement that also has the merit of saving money.

Because federal funding has been so low, state governments have not felt much impact from the commissions' activity. A pair of Department of Commerce consultants, after nearly a hundred interviews with state officials and others, concluded in 1970 that state officials perceived the commissions as "interesting mechanisms in intergovernmental relations" which "probably take more time than they are worth now in financial returns from the Federal Treasury."[39]

Largely because they have had less money but also because they have been less committed to a spending strategy that responds to the governors' interests, the Title V commissions have not been as successful as the ARC in engaging the governors' support. "Eight million dollars [the commission's budget] isn't enough for the governor to worry about," the Massachusetts representative to the New

---

the whole country; to appoint a federal regional economic development director for each; to invite other federal agencies to join regional advisory councils for economic development, which the secretary's appointee would chair; and to invite the states in each region to establish a development commission, of which the federal regional development, which the secretary's appointee would chair; and to invite the states in ity to approve plans submitted to them by the federal member. This plan had no support outside the Department of Commerce.

39. Hartley and Mahoney, "Regional Commissions."

England commission said in an interview.[40] Whereas ARC doctrine stipulates that all project proposals should be routed through the governor's office, this is not invariably the practice in the Title V commissions. In the New England commission, at least, governors have sometimes been surprised by projects on the commission's agenda for their own states. Nor have the staffs of the Title V commissions been imbued with a commitment to serving the states such as that of the ARC staff. A member of North Carolina's Department of Administration familiar with both the Appalachian and the Coastal Plains commissions compared the Title V commission to the ARC unfavorably, saying that it sometimes imposed projects on the state.[41] Lacking money, the commissions have been unable to evoke the governors' strong support; lacking such support, the commissions have found it difficult to get money.

## The Future of the Title V Commissions

As of 1973 the Nixon administration has not succeeded in ending federal support for the commissions, but in eight years no administration of either party has been willing to make a major commitment of funds to them. Substantial expenditure is at stake. If all the commissions were funded on the scale of the ARC, over $2 billion would be added to the federal budget.

The Nixon administration has denied that it seeks to end the commissions, maintaining that the states would be free to create commissions on their own initiative. The administration's budget for fiscal year 1974, though it contained nothing for the commissions, did propose $110 million in planning grants for the states, some portion of which they might use to finance participation in regional planning. However, it seems unlikely that the states will maintain regional development commissions without direct federal participation and incentives.

40. Interview with Robert Marden, Feb. 12, 1973.
41. Interview with J. D. Foust, March 20, 1973.

# [6]

# The Title II Commissions for River Basin Planning

THE TITLE II commissions for river basin planning are not a major new departure in regional organization; rather they are an elaboration and codification of what went before. They and their predecessors, a series of interagency coordinating committees, are the form of river basin organization most acceptable to the federal executive departments. Because they have no operating or management authority, they do not threaten to supersede the federal agencies. They are forums within which agency representatives meet with state representatives to coordinate planning for river basin development.[1]

The initiative for creating the Title II commissions as a standard form came principally from the Bureau of the Budget, whose deputy director in the late 1950s took a personal interest in problems of water resources coordination, but the Bureau's interest diminished as a result of amendments in Congress. As of the early 1970s, the Office of Management and Budget is considering other forms for regional coordination of federal natural resources agencies.

1. Typically, the following federal agencies are represented: the departments of Agriculture, the Army, Commerce, Health, Education, and Welfare, Housing and Urban Development, the Interior, and Transportation, the Federal Power Commission, the Atomic Energy Commission, and the Environmental Protection Agency. The number of state members ranges from five to eleven.

## Origin and Conception

If it was up to them, the federal development agencies would probably choose not to have any regional organizations for coordination, preferring to resolve their differences through direct negotiation or competitive appeals to Congress and to the Executive Office of the President. But it has not been left to them. For decades, their conduct and organization have been subjected to an almost continuous stream of criticism from study commissions and the Executive Office, which have struggled to bring coherence, consistency, and a comprehensive conception of purpose to federal water resources policy.[2] Congress has also instructed that plans should encompass many purposes and accommodate a variety of organized interests, including those of state governments. In addition to these pressures for reform, the federal development agencies have occasionally been challenged by the appearance of rival forms—a federal corporation, the Tennessee Valley Authority (TVA), in 1933, and a federal-interstate compact commission, the Delaware River Basin Commission (DRBC), in 1961. The development agencies have thus been impelled to cooperate in creating coordinating committees at the basin level.

Several major interagency committees were set up between 1945 and 1950. The first three, for the Missouri (1945), Columbia (1946), and Pacific Southwest (1948), were created through a Washington-level coordinator, the Federal Inter-Agency River Basin Committee, which the development agencies had established in 1943. The next two, for the Arkansas-White-Red basin (1950) and the New England–New York area (1950), were created by a presidential di-

2. For a summary of these efforts to 1960, see *Water Resources Activities in the United States: Reviews of National Water Resources During the Past Fifty Years*, printed for the use of the Senate Select Committee on National Water Resources, 86 Cong. 1 sess. (1959). Leading examples are the report of the first Hoover Commission, *Reorganization of the Department of the Interior: A Report to the Congress by the Commission on Organization of the Executive Branch of the Government*, March 1949, and especially the report of the commission's task force on natural resources, *Organization and Policy in the Field of Natural Resources*, January 1949. For analysis, see James W. Fesler, "National Water Resources Administration," in Stephen C. Smith and Emery N. Castle, eds., *Economics and Public Policy in Water Resources Development* (Iowa State University Press, 1965), pp. 368–402.

rective after Congress had authorized in each case a basin survey by the Corps of Engineers. Although these committees were principally federal, representatives of state governments participated at federal invitation.

These river basin coordinating committees were very weak organizations. They had no statutory authority, no executive leadership, and no staff other than what the member agencies assigned to them. The operating agencies continued to do the planning. The coordinating committees assembled a common stock of information about the basin, assembled agency development proposals, and sometimes tried to reconcile differences when these proposals were incompatible. They operated by consensus, which inhibited decision.

The committees quickly came under attack. A lengthy staff analysis within the Bureau of the Budget in the late 1940s concluded that "the regional inter-agency committees have probably prevented certain gross errors by encouraging exchanges of information and by their attempts to keep conflict from breaking into the open," but "merely arranging so that agencies do not get in each other's way too often" was not enough.[3] A presidential commission found in 1953 that the Missouri Basin Inter-Agency Committee had "failed to design a comprehensive basin program" and had not "proved competent to settle basic and major conflicts between agencies."[4] A case study for the second Hoover Commission in 1954 found a number of weaknesses in the Arkansas-White-Red Basin Inter-Agency Committee, including "a great amount of indecision," "delaying tactics," and the lack of anyone "to arbitrate honest differences."[5] Among the executive agencies themselves, the departments of Agriculture and Interior were increasingly dissatis-

3. "Organizing for the Development of the Columbia River Valley," undated, unsigned memorandum in Bureau of the Budget files, National Archives. See also *Organization and Policy in the Field of Natural Resources*, especially pp. 25–26.

4. Missouri Basin Survey Commission, *Missouri: Land and Water* (Washington: Government Printing Office, 1953), pp. 241–42.

5. Wallace R. Vawter, "Case Study of the Arkansas-White-Red Basin Inter-Agency Committee," in Commission on Organization of the Executive Branch of the Government, *Task Force Report on Water Resources and Power*, vol. 3 (June 1955), p. 1446. See also Irving K. Fox and Isabel Picken, *The Upstream-Downstream Controversy in the Arkansas-White-Red Basins Survey*, Inter-University Case Program, no. 55 (University of Alabama Press, 1960).

fied with coordinating committees because the Corps of Engineers was able to dominate them.[6]

A reform of the committees, which culminated eventually in the passage of Title II, began to develop in the mid-1950s through the work of President Eisenhower's Advisory Committee on Water Resources Policy. Composed of the secretaries of Agriculture, Defense, and Interior, the departments with responsibility for water resources development, this committee recommended that "regional or river basin water resources committees be formed with a permanent nonvoting chairman appointed by the President and with membership composed of representatives of all Federal departments and States involved."[7] This recommendation, though it did not propose legislation, was the beginning of a formal federal position favoring creation of river basin commissions as a standard form.

A proposal for legislative authorization of river basin commissions came in 1959 from the House Interior and Insular Affairs Committee, and was seized upon by the Bureau of the Budget as a means of realizing some of its own objectives. Throughout 1960, the deputy director of the Bureau worked with the committee and federal agencies to try to get agreement on a bill. There was no important disagreement about river basin commissions. Both the Bureau and the committee drew on the language of the Eisenhower advisory committee. However, the committee's bill also contained provisions concerning criteria for project planning and methods of cost-benefit analysis, to which the federal agencies objected. The Bureau's unsuccessful attempt to get agreement on this more comprehensive bill consumed much of two years. In January 1961 the Bureau formally transmitted a bill for river basin commissions to Congress as part of the outgoing President's program.

The Kennedy administration promptly incorporated the proposal in a larger bill, the "Water Resources Planning Act of 1961,"

6. Daniel H. Hoggan, *State Organizational Patterns for Comprehensive Planning of Water Resources Development* (Logan: Utah State University, Utah Water Research Laboratory, 1969), p. 140. Hoggan's study includes an interview in which Henry P. Caulfield, Jr., executive director of the Water Resources Council, recalls lessons from planning for the Arkansas-White-Red basin.

7. *A Report by the Presidential Advisory Committee on Water Resources Policy* (1955), p. xi.

of which it became Title II. Title I created the Water Resources Council, which was authorized to set standards for river basin plans and evaluate water resources projects. Title III authorized federal grants to the states for water resources planning. No important controversy developed over these titles. Oddly, it was Title II, on which the most time had been spent, that proved most difficult to enact. The Interstate Conference on Water Problems (ICWP), an affiliate of the Council of State Governments, wanted major changes made.

Title II, which had been drafted within the executive branch, would have made the new commissions wholly federal instrumentalities. The President was authorized to create them. Although governors might nominate state members, the President would appoint them, thus giving them federal legal status. The commissions would report to a federal body, the Water Resources Council, which would have authority to modify their plans "in the national interest."[8] These provisions were consistent with the theories of constitutional law and intergovernmental relations that prevailed in the Department of Justice and the Bureau of the Budget, which insisted that none but a federal official might make plans or policies for the federal government. They were also consistent with the Bureau's purpose of enhancing the President's control of federal agencies and protecting his powers of appointment.

The states sought to make the commissions truly joint—for example, by providing that the state members be appointed by the governors rather than the President.[9] Federal executive officials

8. *Water Resources Planning Act of 1961*, Hearings before the Senate Committee on Interior and Insular Affairs and Senate Committee on Public Works, 87 Cong. 1 sess. (1961), pp. 1–7. On the origin of the legislation, see also *River Basin Planning Act of 1964*, Hearings before the Senate Committee on Interior and Insular Affairs, 88 Cong. 1 sess. (1963), and *Water Resources Planning Act*, Hearings before the House Committee on Interior and Insular Affairs, 88 Cong. 2 sess. (1964). The original bill that came from the House Interior and Insular Affairs Committee was H.R. 3704 of the Eighty-sixth Congress. For this history of the Title II commissions, the author has relied heavily on files of the Bureau of the Budget as well as on published sources.

9. Revisions proposed by the ICWP called for the President to "declare the establishment" of river basin commissions rather than to "create" them. He would have to have concurrence of at least half of the affected states. State members would be appointed by the governors or in accordance with state law. They would elect a vice chairman of the commission, who would be their chairman and coordinator. The commission chairman, an appointee of the President, would be chairman and coordinator of the federal members. Each side would cast one vote, and thus each would have a veto (although in a still later amendment, this language was changed to provide for decision making by "consensus"). The commissions would submit annual

gave in on the essential point. Since they had acceded to federal membership with the states in the Delaware River Basin Commission, which had comprehensive authority, they could not now prevent a joining of the federal government with the states in mere planning commissions. A federal-interstate compact compromised federal autonomy far more than Title II would. Moreover, Title II would give the federal government a statutory alternative to federal-interstate compacts and, even with amendments proposed by the ICWP, create a form far more acceptable to federal agencies. Nevertheless, officials in the Bureau of the Budget were sufficiently disturbed by the states' changes to seriously consider deleting Title II from the bill. In their view, much of its value as an instrument of federal coordination was being lost; instead it seemed likely that federal action would be impeded or excessively influenced by the states. What had appeared to be a way of facilitating central control of river basin planning was threatening to become an obstacle to such control.[10]

Although the issue of constitutional principle had been settled by the beginning of 1963, mainly through federal concessions, it took two more years to refine the language of Title II and overcome procedural delays in Congress. The Water Resources Planning Act did not become law until 1965.

Title II grew out of a decade of planning and negotiation, beginning with the work of President Eisenhower's advisory committee. More than the other acts of authorization described in this book, Title II was negotiated by the governments and government agencies whose interests would be primarily affected. Certain principles underlay their agreement and shaped the form and function of the commissions.

The commissions would bring together representatives of those governments and government agencies with an interest in river basin development. Members from federal departments would "be

reports to the governors as well as to the Water Resources Council. The council could recommend, but not actually make, revisions in commission plans. It could set standards and procedures for the federal participants in the commissions, but not for the commissions as a whole. In sum, under the states' amendments, the commissions ceased to be purely federal instrumentalities, formally responsible to the President.

10. Memorandum, Wesley K. Sasaki to Elmer B. Staats, Aug. 20, 1963, Bureau of the Budget files. This memorandum is also included in the Lee C. White papers, John F. Kennedy Library, Waltham, Mass.

appointed by the head of such department . . . and . . . serve as the representative of such department." Each state member was to be appointed according to the laws of the state "which he represents." No member could be compelled by others to sacrifice the goals or interests of his government or agency. The commissions would operate by consensus. Title II presumes that the commissions will be forums for adjusting government and agency interests rather than independent decision makers for their regions. It says that each commission should be an agency "for the coordination" of plans. Yet it also opens the way to planning, saying that each commission should "prepare and keep up to date . . . a comprehensive, coordinated, joint plan for . . . development of water and related resources."[11] No government would be committed to carrying out a commission plan. The legislatures would have to act, but because the commissions were representative, the drafters of Title II assumed their plans would prove politically acceptable.

In authorizing this kind of coordinating organization, Title II formalized the practice of two decades, yet it also incorporated changes. Hitherto, river basin coordinating committees had lacked independent resources of organizational maintenance. They had not had their own staffs or budgets or a full-time chief executive.[12] Title II created an independent—that is, presidentially appointed—chairman, who would appoint and supervise the commission's staff. Federal appropriations of up to $750,000 a year were authorized. The function of the chairman, Secretary of the Interior Stewart Udall testified, was "to see to it that the work gets done" and "to provide the necessary and impartial leadership." State representatives had participated in river basin coordinating committees before, but state participation now had a statutory foundation and the statute acknowledged the states' formal independence of federal direction. This meant that the coordinating organizations were now joint rather than federal, and the right of either the federal or the state governments to supervise them was limited. As Senator Clin-

11. 79 Stat. 244-254.

12. River basin planning commissions created by law in 1958 for Texas and the Southeast were more formal than the interagency coordinating committees and thus were precursors of the Title II commissions, but they differed from the Title II commissions in that they were designed to be temporary. See Robert H. Pealy, *Organization for Comprehensive River Basin Planning: The Texas and Southeast Experiences* (University of Michigan, Institute of Public Administration, 1964).

ton P. Anderson of New Mexico explained, "The commissions will be entities of themselves—not Federal commissions or State commissions, but Federal-State partnerships with individual identity much as Interstate Compact Commissions are entities in their own right." [13]

The new features of the commissions—their statutory foundation, the ambiguity of their legal status within the federal system, their right to a staff and appropriations, their authority to be planners as well as coordinators—meant that they had the potential, at least, of evolving into a different sort of organization than the coordinating committees they would replace.

## The Commissions' Activity

By 1972 seven Title II commissions had been created for regions that included thirty-two states. Four commissions—for the Pacific Northwest, Great Lakes, Souris-Red-Rainy, and New England—were formed in 1967. One for the Ohio was established in 1971, and two more, for the Upper Mississippi and the Missouri, in 1972.[14] Most of the northern part of the country is covered by Title II commissions. The Southwestern, Gulf, and South Atlantic states are not.

All five of the Title II commissions created between 1965 and 1971 have been responsible for either a framework (type 1) study or a river basin (type 2) study, or both.[15] By the end of 1971, ten such studies were under way, but in only half of these had the Title II commission benefited from the initial authorization. In the other

13. *Congressional Record*, vol. 109, pt. 4, 88 Cong. 1 sess. (1963), p. 4322.

14. The Souris-Red-Rainy commission was terminated in 1973 and its jurisdiction subsumed under that of the new Upper Mississippi commission. The executive order creating the Souris-Red-Rainy commission was unusual in that it provided for termination of the commission upon completion of the comprehensive plan. The other commissions are presumed to be permanent. Executive Order 11359, *Federal Register*, vol. 32 (June 22, 1967), pp. 8851–52.

15. A type 1 study covers a large area (e.g., Columbia–North Pacific, Great Lakes, North Atlantic, Pacific Southwest) and results in projections of economic development, water needs, and water supply. It does not propose projects, but sets the framework for such proposals. A type 2 study covers a smaller area, typically a major basin or tributary (Big Black, Big Muddy, Connecticut, Genessee, Grand). It identifies projects in sufficient detail to lay the basis for authorizations.

half, which were concentrated in the Pacific Northwest and the Ohio, the commissions were continuing studies that had been started by predecessor organizations.

The Title II commissions are similar in important respects to the interagency coordinating committees that preceded them. For one thing, they have been coordinators of agency planning rather than independent planners. This means that their staffs are small, averaging less than twelve in 1972, as is their share of the expenditures for the river basin studies for which they are responsible, amounting usually to less than 10 percent of the total and in no case to more than 20 percent. For another, most of the commissions are occupied with exchanges of general information about the member organizations' separate activities or with procedural matters such as definition of commission tasks, preparation of budgets, preparation of planning schedules, and progress reports. Matters of this sort are discussed by most commissions at their quarterly meetings; what they do not discuss is the contents of plans. Occasionally they consider the goals of development planning, but such discussions are brief, inconclusive, and unrelated to specific development choices. Finally, the commissions have found it hard to complete work expeditiously. The plans for which they are responsible compete with many other demands on the member agencies' planning capacities. Deadlines slip, despite the presence of the chairman to exhort the federal agencies. By the spring of 1973, only one major plan (for the Souris-Red-Rainy basin) had been wholly accomplished by a Title II commission, and it had not yet reached the Water Resources Council.[16]

16. Information about Title II commissions is drawn mainly from their annual reports, minutes, and other documents; hearings before the appropriations committees of Congress; the files of the Water Resources Council; and field trips to the New England and Great Lakes regions, which included interviews with the commission chairmen, representatives of the Corps of Engineers, one state member and the executive director of the Great Lakes commission and five state members of the New England commission; from the files of the New England commission; and attending a meeting of the Great Lakes commission. Also of benefit were notes and interview protocols belonging to Helen Ingram, now of the Department of Government at the University of Arizona, and an interview and correspondence with Guy J. Kelnhofer, who represented Minnesota on two Title II commissions. Both Dr. Ingram and Dr. Kelnhofer did research on the commissions for the National Water Commission. There is less literature on the Title II commissions, either scholarly work or official evaluations, than for any of the other organizations covered in this book.

In addition to serving as a forum for interagency and intergovernmental communication about planning, the commissions tried briefly to set project priorities. Title II says that each commission shall "recommend long-range schedules of priorities for the collection and analysis of basic data and for investigation, planning, and construction of projects." In 1968 Senator Allen Ellender of the Appropriations Committee challenged the director of the Water Resources Council to show that the commissions were carrying out this provision. The council then issued guidelines to the commissions covering the preparation of priority reports.

The results were disappointing to the Water Resources Council, which failed to urge the reports on the Budget Bureau or Congress. Although the contents varied widely, which is one reason for the council's not submitting them to Congress, none would have been much help to someone needing to decide among project requests. The New England commission explained in general terms what activities were most important for the region and projected aggregate costs for each category. The Pacific Northwest commission declined to set priorities; it listed projects for each state and closed each list with an indiscriminate endorsement. The Great Lakes commission went into extreme detail, listing several hundred activities and assigning numerical priorities (1, 2, 3) to them, but it gave most items top priority. For example, of the 191 studies it listed, it said 120 should be funded in the next fiscal year. Before long, priority reports were discontinued.

The problems encountered by the Title II commissions have long been recognized as characteristic of the coordinating type, the "forum of peers," which is less an organization than a meeting place of organizations. The dominant obligations of the members are to the organizations they represent. Coordination is voluntary. The forum is supposed to foster goodwill, facilitate communication in matters of shared interest, and provide a setting within which mutual adjustments may take place, but it lacks authority or other means for inducing mutual adjustments. Also, members have a very limited capacity to speak for their organizations, which in Title II commissions are whole federal departments or whole governments, the states. The represented units are large aggregates of diverse interests, and coordination within them is too ineffectual to sustain the functioning of a representative coordinating council at a higher level.

Recognizing the limitations of the forum of peers, the planners of Title II sought to overcome them by introducing an agent of central coordination, the presidentially appointed chairman, who would be supported by an independent staff. Thus the Title II commission represents a modification of the type, and looking at the consequences of the modification is desirable.

## The Chairman as Central Coordinator

In the spring of 1968, not long after the first commissions were established, the newly appointed chairmen met with officials of the Water Resources Council to discuss their functions. The council stressed that the commissions should be coordinators, and that for the chairmen coordination should mean resolving federal interagency conflict. The chairman's job was to settle disagreements in the field and, if he could not, to refer them to the Water Resources Council. What the council could not resolve, it would refer to the President. The council staff promised that the coordinating function would be spelled out in rules and regulations for Title II.

This definition of the chairman's function appears to have been derived from history. The major coordinating committees, beginning with that for the Missouri basin, had been a response to interagency conflict. Analysis of the committees, especially that for the Arkansas-White-Red basin, had revealed the need for a leader who could settle disputes. The definition was also born of necessity. The council could not ask the chairmen to coordinate affirmatively, by seeing that the council's principles and standards were applied to planning, because the council had not yet formulated any.

The council's limited definition of coordination and lack of guidance placed on the chairmen a considerable burden of initiative. It was up to them to look for issues to bring to the council's attention. Most have not done this. Federal agencies in the field have developed ways of resolving or obscuring their differences, and none of the chairmen has found intervention in federal interagency relations to be an attractive, necessary, or feasible function. The chairman of the Pacific Northwest commission specifically told his commission in 1968 that he was not ready to accept responsibility for coordination "until PL 89-80 had been suitably amended or interpreted."[17] A detailed analysis of that commission by two political scientists at the University of Washington found in 1970 that there had been no significant change in the coordination of planning as a result of the changes introduced by the Title II form. They found "a continued bias toward water project construction; a lack of innovation in water resources planning; and constraints upon the Commission's serving as a forum for important but controversial issues." They concluded that "the chairman and staff have not produced a counterforce to the influence of the major federal agencies."[18]

Since there have been few appeals from the chairmen for action in specific matters—appeals have come only from the New England commission, whose chairman has been much the most enterprising —the Water Resources Council has paid little attention to the Title II commissions. It has never issued rules and regulations to cover Title II, and thus has never interpreted the law in a way that might enhance the chairmen's authority.[19] The council's own power is so limited that it can do little to support or constrain the commission chairmen. Like the commissions, it is an interagency coordinating committee, stronger than its less formal predecessors but still without broad power or authority despite its statutory foundation, and handicapped by the inherent defects of the form, which inhibit decision. It is also without direct access to the President, for the Office of Management and Budget stands in its way. The lack of systematic support or restraint from Washington means that commission chairmen are free to define their own roles and to search for assets of power wherever they can. As most of the chairmen have not exploited their freedom, the commissions function much as predecessor organizations did without a chief executive.

17. Pacific Northwest River Basin Commission, *Minutes of the Eighth Meeting* (April 26, 1968), p. 4.

18. Geoffrey Wandesforde-Smith and Robert Warren, "A Comparative Analysis of American and Canadian Governmental Arrangements for the Development of Regional Water Policy in the Columbia River Basin" (Seattle, 1970; processed), pp. 187, 202.

19. The council published a preliminary version of Title II regulations in 1967, but never issued a final version. The preliminary version did no more than paraphrase the law. *Federal Register*, vol. 32 (April 13, 1967), pp. 5939-44.

*The Case of New England*

Although significant changes in water resources planning at the basin level have not in general been a result of Title II, the case of the New England River Basins Commission suggests that the addition of the independent chairman, along with a separate staff and budget, can make a difference. The NERBC has replaced the Corps of Engineers as the coordinator of multipurpose river basin studies in New England, and the chairman has conceived of coordination in broad, activist terms.

The chairman, R. Frank Gregg, began by asserting certain jurisdictional claims on the commission's behalf, in particular the right to direct type 2 studies. Floods struck Southern New England in the spring of 1968, not long after the NERBC was organized, and in response to requests from Rhode Island's senators, the Senate Public Works Committee promptly authorized the Corps of Engineers to undertake a coordinated study of flood control and other problems in the Narragansett Bay drainage area. Gregg responded with a resolution declaring the commission's intention to begin a study and to treat the Corps's study as one component. The Corps abstained from "consensus" on that resolution. Gregg successfully appealed to the Water Resources Council for support on the jurisdictional question, and despite disallowance by the Bureau of the Budget of the Water Resources Council's budget request for the study, Congress provided appropriations. The study was started in 1972 and is scheduled for completion in 1974 at a cost to the federal government of $3.5 million, of which 20 percent, an unusually high proportion, is allotted to the commission. It covers most of Rhode Island and all but a small part of the Massachusetts coast. The NERBC also has a major study under way for Long Island Sound, for which it will receive about 17 percent of a budget of $3.4 million. According to Gregg, the commission has a large enough technical staff to control the design of these studies, dominate the study apparatus, and monitor specific study elements. It has a full-time manager for each study. It has direct control of some study elements, including legal and institutional analyses, and it has the chairman's position in plan formulation, which enables it to trade off between conflicting single-purpose or limited-purpose plans advanced by individual agencies. The chairman and staff are also able to influence the allocation of planning funds to participating agencies.[20]

If the commission in New England can become something more than a passive assembler of agency plans, why have the other commissions not evolved in the same way? The explanation commonly given for the NERBC's relatively high level of activity is the personality and career orientation of its chief executive. The critical change introduced by Title II was the presidentially appointed chairman, and the consequences have depended greatly on who holds that office. Commission chairmen have usually been political appointees, without strong commitment to programmatic goals. Gregg's career has been in conservation, and he is an exceptionally determined, energetic, and articulate man. That he is special is indicated by the fact that in 1969 he was the only one of the four incumbent chairmen whom the new administration did not replace. Also, the political and organizational milieu of New England has favored Gregg's activity. A predecessor committee did not set a pattern, as in the Pacific Northwest, where the Title II commission evolved directly out of the long-established Columbia Basin Inter-Agency Committee and perpetuated its way of operating. Furthermore, development opportunities are relatively few in New England and political support for development is weak, which makes it relatively easy for the chairman to assert leadership within the commission. Traditionally the region has received only a tiny fraction of federal public works expenditures. This too contrasts sharply with the Pacific Northwest, where all three federal development agencies have big budgets and foresee many development opportunities, and where there is a shared regional interest in developing water resources in order to forestall the claims of drier parts of the West on the water of the Columbia. In the Northwest, the federal construction agencies have dominated Title II activity and the chairman has not been able to counter their influence.[21]

20. Interview with R. Frank Gregg, Aug. 11, 1972, and personal letter from Gregg, Nov. 17, 1972.

21. See Wandesforde-Smith and Warren, "Columbia River Basin," especially chapter 5, for an analysis of the NERBC's political role and the interests it serves; and Helen Ingram, *The New England River Basins Commission: A Case Study Looking into the Possibilities and Disabilities of a River Basin Commission Established under Title II of the Water Resources Planning Act of 1965* (National Technical Information Service for the National Water Commission, November 1971).

For Gregg to establish the commission as leader of river basin planning in New England has required both forbearance and active cooperation from the New England division of the Corps of Engineers. Asked why it had yielded its leading role to the commission, an official of the Corps responded by citing the law. "Frank's got the charter," he said. Since the President and the Congress had decided to create river basin commissions and the President had decided to establish one in New England and appoint his representative as the chairman of it, then, this official said, "the commission is a way of life, and we will make it work." He acknowledged that in New England Gregg's personality had added considerably to the force of the law, and that Gregg had had support from the Water Resources Council as well.[22]

### Relations with the OMB

Led by Gregg, the Title II commission chairmen have made suggestions to OMB for strengthening their organizations. In a letter to the Program Coordination Division in 1972, they raised the possibility of amending the Water Resources Planning Act to secure coverage of the whole country by Title II commissions; to broaden the commissions' jurisdiction to "natural resources" programs; to build "a system of incentives realistically rewarding Federal agencies and the States for joint efforts"; and to make clear that the commissions' coordinating functions would "relate to direct Federal activities, to the administration of grant programs, and to some process for review and comment on Federal program and budget proposals at field level."[23] The commission chairmen seemed particularly concerned about the need to provide incentives to participate in commission activities, and with good reason. Although federal agencies and representatives of state governments assented to the creation of Title II commissions, in general they have little interest in contributing to the commissions' work. If the chairmen's suggestions were followed, the Title II commissions would become much more than a medium for the preparation of comprehensive plans. They would review and presumably make recommendations about all federal spending for natural resources. The chairmen

22. Interview with John W. Leslie, Aug. 11, 1972.
23. Frederick O. Rouse et al. to Kenneth Kugel, Office of Management and Budget, Program Coordination Division, no date (1972); NERBC files, Boston.

have not pursued these suggestions, nor has OMB, which has been experimenting with natural resources coordination through regional councils, a rival approach.[24]

In view of the Budget Bureau's role in creating the Title II commissions, its subsequent indifference may seem puzzling, but what went into the law in 1965 was not what the Bureau's deputy director had proposed in 1960–61. State-sponsored revisions in Title II compromised the commissions as potential instruments of the President's purposes, as did the creation of the Water Resources Council as an intermediary between the President and the commissions.[25] The OMB's preferred way of coordinating federal water resources activity would be to consolidate in a single line agency functions that are now scattered and to obtain more staff for itself. Because neither was politically feasible in 1961, the Bureau of the Budget accepted the creation of a statutory interagency council as the least bad of the several alternatives that were being proposed.

In general, management officials in OMB perceive interagency committees as places in which agencies logroll to their collective advantage, and when the interagency committees are also intergovernmental, as in the case of Title II commissions, the presence of the states is presumed to reinforce the committees' tendency to generate and amalgamate spending proposals.[26]

## The Commissions as Agents of Decentralization: The Effects of Jointness

Title II is supposed to enhance the role of the states in planning for water resources development by giving statutory endorsement

24. See below, chapter 7.

25. On OMB as seen from the Water Resources Council, see the remarks in 1969 of Henry P. Caulfield, outgoing director of the council, in Norman A. Evans, ed., "Water and Western Destiny: From Conflict to Cooperation," Proceedings of the Third Western Interstate Water Conference, Colorado State University (1969; processed), p. 28.

26. It is explicit and enduring OMB doctrine that interagency committees not be given program responsibilities. Thus the Nixon administration has specifically rejected land-use planning legislation, sponsored by Senator Henry M. Jackson, that would have expanded the jurisdiction of the Title II commissions and the parent Water Resources Council by giving them a role in administering land-use planning grants to the states. The administration's land-use planning bills have specified that grants be administered by the Department of the Interior.

to their membership in river basin planning commissions. Title III of the Water Resources Planning Act complements this element of Title II by authorizing federal grants to the states for water resources planning. Commission membership is valuable to the states, however, only if the commissions make important decisions about water resources planning and if the states are able to influence those decisions.

Because the commissions do not plan but instead await production of plans by the member organizations, states can influence commission work substantially only if they can contribute to this planning. Membership in the commissions gives state governments the right to contribute to river basin plans, even creates an obligation to do so; but the states have not seized the opportunity, and state officials have occasionally seemed to resent the obligation, as if it had been forced upon them by the federal government. In a critique of Title II in 1970, Minnesota's director of water resources planning and its representative on both the Great Lakes and the Souris-Red-Rainy commissions, Guy J. Kelnhofer, argued that "the basin planning approach to water management is much more beneficial to the Federal interests than to the States."[27] In an interview, he described Title II commissions as "no more than interagency coordinating committees with a staff that the states have been coerced into supporting."[28] Of Minnesota, he wrote:

The water resources planning that is being promoted in Minnesota rests on no broad base of local approval. The Legislature did not demand it; the Governor did not order it; and no groups of State agencies have petitioned for it as a necessary adjunct to their own mandated water management responsibilities. The water planning program in Minnesota was born from Federal legislation and is supported largely with Federal grant funds. The Federal legislation is designed not to create independent state planning bodies to take over planning responsibilities which are too much for Federal agencies to carry. They are designed, instead, to supply a basis of state legitimation for the traditional construction activities of the Federal development agencies, i.e., the Corps of Engineers, the Soil Conservation Service, and the Bureau of Reclamation. . . . Our water planning then is not so much a citizen-serving

27. "Regional Water Resources Planning: A State View," in Souris-Red-Rainy Basins Commission minutes for July 23–24, 1970 (processed), pp. 4–15.

28. Interview, Aug. 14, 1972.

activity as it is an effort to comply with Federal program directives so as to secure the benefits of Federal grant resources.[29]

If the states lack interest in river basin planning, as Kelnhofer says, one wonders why they join Title II commissions at all. The law says that at least half the states in the basin must consent to formation. The Water Resources Council, which has actively promoted creation of commissions, seeks the concurrence of all. Most states appear to join for defensive purposes, on the chance that they may be able to veto federal actions that threaten them, such as diversions of water. They seek defenses against one another as well as against federal action. Collectively, they may seek a defense against another region. The Pacific Northwest states were quick to form a commission because they believed it would improve their chances of resisting claims from other states on their water supply.[30] Agreement by the states to form a commission depends more on the nature of interstate than federal-state relations. This is true especially in the West, where interstate conflicts over water allocation are intense. In the Pacific Southwest, California has resisted a commission for fear it would open discussion of the present allocation of Colorado River water, from which Southern California benefits. An attempt by the Water Resources Council staff in 1968–69 to create a commission in the Pacific Southwest foundered on California's objections. In New England, state governments agreed more or less by default on a Title II commission after a proposed federal-interstate compact had failed for want of federal and state support. An earlier regional organization, the Northeastern Resources Committee, formed in 1956 as the successor to an interagency committee led by the Corps of Engineers, had spent most of its time trying to find a way to augment its own limited authority and financial support.[31] Issues connected with development of the Connecticut River tend to engage the interests of most of the New England states in a regional organization. Maine, whose major rivers are wholly intrastate and which shares a border only with

29. Guy J. Kelnhofer to Joseph E. Sizer, Minnesota director of environmental quality planning, Oct. 7, 1971.

30. Wandesforde-Smith and Warren, "Columbia River Basin," p. 97.

31. Edwin A. Gere, *Rivers and Regionalism in New England* (University of Massachusetts, Bureau of Government Research, 1968).

New Hampshire, is a conspicuous exception, and its participation in the Title II commission is especially tenuous. For many states, the decision to join a Title II commission appears to be marginal; the anticipated benefits are barely worth the costs. But if the states have little to gain, they also have little to lose. It therefore takes only one or two governors with a reason to promote a commission for one to be formed. Other governors are likely to go along.

Once in Title II commissions, states are at a severe disadvantage in relation to federal agencies. Their water resources functions are slight by comparison; hence their interests in development are less well defined and their staff capacity is very much lower, often insignificant. Such interests as they perceive do not necessarily extend beyond their own boundaries. New Hampshire and Vermont, for example, do not care very much about development plans for southeastern New England. In sum, states lack both the incentives and the resources with which to contribute to planning, and the state members of the commissions find it hard to define a role for themselves within the commission. Paradoxically, the states with the largest water resources programs and thus the greatest capacity to participate in commissions seem to be the least interested in joining. These states, Texas and California in particular, are relatively well able to defend their interests themselves. Joining a commission, in which all states are formally equal, actually deprives them of an advantage in dealing with other states.

Unless the federal government pays the costs, state governments are unlikely to take part in regional planning for river basin development. Under Title III, most states receive $40,000 to $100,000 a year for water resources planning, but state members of Title II commissions argue that this is not enough to sustain participation in comprehensive studies and that it should be supplemented by allocations in the federal budget for such studies. Early in 1972 the New England commission adopted a formal policy statement to that effect. At a commission meeting in the spring of 1973 the staff of the Great Lakes commission formally proposed that $250,000 of a budget of $1.5 million for a type 2 study of the Maumee River be earmarked for state participation. This touched off sharp disagreement between federal and state members. The federal chairman voted for the proposal, but the representatives of Agriculture, Army, Interior, Commerce, and the Federal Power Commission voted against it, not wanting funds for state participation to come out of their budgets. The issue was referred to the Water Resources Council.

In the special case of New England, an active chairman has pursued strategies intended to elicit state participation. Each New England state is supposed to be preparing its own development plan. Gregg has argued that river basin planning has emphasized regionalism at the expense of the states, "the basic political subdivision of the United States," whose "natural resource planning agencies are in a position to be closely attuned to local interests, and more or less directly accountable to elected officials."[32] Planning in the NERBC deemphasizes regionalism in an attempt to respond to the states. Insofar as Gregg leads any governmental subgroup within the commission, it is the states, which are more in need of leadership than the federal agencies and more amenable to it. Gregg and the commission staff try to provide services for the states, such as technical reports that will help with legislation, seminars and reports about federal legislation, and skilled advocacy of the states' interests before federal agencies. For example, the Rhode Island state representative to the NERBC spoke of a commission staff member's weekly trips to Washington to consult with a federal department while it planned administration of a new grant-in-aid statute. "He tries to hold their pencils as they write the guidelines," he said. "I can't do this. I don't have the time or the contacts."[33] The existence of a staff that is independent of federal agencies and has an incentive to serve the states makes such activity possible. Yet even in the NERBC, whose chairman has made an effort to engage and serve the states, it has been difficult to elicit from them contributions of activity and funds. And as the states' obligations to the federal government under pollution control and coastal zone management programs have increased, their natural resources agencies have even less time and resources to devote to a regional planning and coordinating organization.

At least tactically, however, the presence of the states has been helpful to the NERBC. Because a Title II commission is not a purely federal agency, its chairman is probably even freer than

32. "Water and Relating Land Planning in New England" (speech, 1970; processed); NERBC files.
33. Interview with Donald Varin, Feb. 6, 1973.

other federal officials to challenge the President's budget privately (none of them are free to do so publicly, of course); and he can call upon the state members of his organization for help. When the Budget Bureau denied funds for the southeastern New England study, Gregg at first argued to the Water Resources Council and the Bureau that the federal government was breaking faith with the states and reneging on a commitment to joint planning. Invoking the states in this way, as other governments to which the federal government owed an obligation, did not work. What did work, with Gregg's encouragement, was direct appeals to congressmen from the governors of Rhode Island and Massachusetts.

## Impact of the Commissions

Because the commissions' activity is limited to planning and because their planning is still incomplete, it is hard to say what the consequences of the commissions' activity will be. Also, the plans they prepare—the "framework" or "river basin" plans—are antecedent to the plans on which development activity is actually based. It is not until a third level of planning is reached that it constitutes a design for construction. A great deal of comprehensive river basin planning has been done in the United States in the last two decades with few visible results. Many a multivolume study, the monumental work of a defunct coordinating committee, sits on government shelves. Of the Title II commissions, it can only be said that their plans have at least as good a chance of affecting the course of development as other such plans prepared by similar coordinating organizations.

The significance of the Title II commissions must be judged by whether the content of their plans is different than it would be if planning were done by some other type of coordinating organization, presumably a committee with the Corps of Engineers as lead agency, and that in turn depends on the goals and influence of the independent chairman and staff, the new elements introduced by the Title II form.

Title II alters the organizational setting within which federal agencies plan projects. By introducing a new set of actors, the chairman and staff, it may alter the values and interests that are taken into account in federal water resources planning. Whether this will happen generally remains to be seen. It seems not to have happened in the Pacific Northwest, but again, the special case of New England is suggestive. There, an activist chairman, a career conservationist, has had a strong commitment to certain programmatic goals. Office in the commission requires him to temper this commitment and to seek courses of action that will protect the interests of construction agencies as well as conservationists. In his view, asserted repeatedly in conversation, the commission exists to serve "the public interest." In practice, this gives the chairman a mediator's role. Usually he seeks to reconcile demands for economic development and flood protection with competing demands to preserve aesthetic values. If only because of Gregg's background, conservation interests in New England perceive the commission chairman and staff as their allies. On the other hand, because Gregg has the confidence of conservation interests, he can help the Corps of Engineers find the terms on which projects can be made publicly acceptable.

A good illustration of the commission's role in New England is its handling of the comprehensive report on the Connecticut River basin that a coordinating committee led by the Corps completed in the fall of 1970. The coordinating committee's development proposals had stirred controversy in western Massachusetts. The commission created a citizens' review committee which called for restudy of some construction projects and adoption of alternative flood control methods in other cases. The commission accepted the citizens' recommendations for restudy without, however, repudiating the coordinating committee's plan. As a mediator, the commission was more help to the opponents of development than to the proponents. The restudy, called the Connecticut River Supplemental Study, has begun under the aegis of the commission, which will receive $195,000 out of a budget of $700,000.

River basin plans in New England henceforth may be different (less likely to contain construction proposals) than they would have been without the commission. Some of the state members interviewed thought that the effect of the commission was to open a wider range of alternatives for consideration. On the other hand, Wandesforde-Smith and Warren found that environmental protection groups in the Pacific Northwest have little standing as part of

the commission's regional public and have gained more acceptance with other local, state, and federal units of government than
with the commission.[34]

## The Future of the Title II Commissions

Title II commissions now cover most of the country; eventually,
they may be extended. The existence of this centrally planned form,
which is offered to the states as a matter of policy, is certain to discourage creation of alternative forms. Where vacuums in river
basin organization exist, Title II commissions are likely to fill them.

Whether the form will evolve is an open question. In the 1950s,
a fairly wide consensus formed in favor of strengthening interagency coordinating committees by adding an independent chairman and staff. At present there is no consensus about next steps or
even whether next steps should be taken.

34. "Columbia River Basin," p. 197.

# [7]

# Federal Regional Councils

OF THESE SIX CASES, only the Federal Regional Councils are not authorized by law. They are interagency committees created by executive action. Started on an experimental basis in four places in 1968, they were soon extended by President Nixon to the rest of the country. As of 1973 there are ten of them, one for each of ten standard federal administrative regions.

The councils are composed of the top regional officials of the major domestic agencies of the federal government.[1] According to an executive order issued in February 1972, the councils are bodies "within which the participating agencies will . . . to the maximum extent feasible, conduct their grantmaking activities in concert."[2]

1. The original membership included the departments of Health, Education, and Welfare (HEW), Housing and Urban Development (HUD), and Labor, and the Office of Economic Opportunity (OEO). The Department of Transportation was added in 1970, and the Environmental Protection Agency and Law Enforcement Assistance Administration in 1972. In 1973 the departments of Agriculture and the Interior were added, and the councils' functions were broadened to include coordination of direct federal action as well as grants-in-aid. Executive Order 11731, July 23, 1973.

2. Executive Order 11647, Feb. 11, 1972. A more recent executive order states that each council shall "assist State and local government by the coordination of the Federal program grants and operations through: (1) the development of better ways to deliver the benefits of Federal programs over the short term; (2) the development of integrated program and funding plans with Governors and local chief executives; (3) the encouragement of joint and complementary Federal grant applications by local and State governments; (4) the expeditious resolution of conflicts and problems which may arise between Federal agencies; (5) the evaluation of programs in which two or more member agencies participate; (6) the development of more effective ways of allocating Federal resources to meet the long-range needs of State and local communities; (7) the supervision of regional interagency program coordination mechanisms; and (8) the development of administrative procedures to improve day-to-day cooperation on an interagency and intergovernmental basis." Executive Order 11731.

They have no authority to make operating decisions, to plan programs, or to spend funds. They are exclusively a forum for coordination and for developing coordination strategies.

The councils meet twice a month in the regional city that serves as the members' common headquarters.[3] Each of the member agencies assigns a staff member to work on council activities, but he continues to work in his agency since the councils as such do not have offices.

The Under Secretaries Group for Regional Operations (USG), composed of the undersecretaries of member agencies, chaired by the deputy director of the Office of Management and Budget, and supported by a staff secretariat called the Working Group, has supplied policy guidance to the councils. The Program Coordination Division (PCD) of the OMB has assigned a liaison man to each council and staff assistance to the USG.[4]

## Origin

Management officials in the Bureau of the Budget[5] sponsored creation of the councils, which are just one part of a major attempt by the Bureau to reform federal field administration. Begun in the late 1960s under President Johnson, this effort was carried forward in the Nixon administration.

The Bureau's effort arose out of a belief that "Federal field activities . . . have undergone a genuine transformation, both in their character and in their objectives." The Bureau's deputy director, Phillip S. Hughes, told Congress in 1966 that the federal government was filling "a role in many communities and most States which did not exist 10 or even 5 years ago: it acts as a catalyst for joint attacks on common problems—environmental pollution, rural

3. The headquarters are in Boston, New York, Philadelphia, Atlanta, Chicago, Dallas–Fort Worth, Kansas City, Denver, San Francisco, and Seattle.

4. In a major reorganization of the Office of Management and Budget in 1973, the Program Coordination Division was abolished and its functions transferred to a Field Activities Division, which will report to an assistant director for operations. The old name will be used in this chapter.

5. The name "Bureau of the Budget" is used in the discussion of the councils' origins, which is historical, and "the Office of Management and Budget" is used in discussion of events since 1970.

and urban development, and regional economic growth—and in many cases becomes an active partner in these cooperative programs, through the common effort of several Federal agencies on a specific project within an individual community."[6] This new role followed directly from the massive expansion of federal grant-in-aid programs in the early 1960s.

One of the Bureau's first reactions to what it saw as a new situation was to ask Congress for authority to establish small field offices. It had maintained four such offices for a decade beginning in 1943, although Congress had never permitted a nationwide system of them; in 1953 a new director in a Republican administration eliminated the offices on grounds of economy. In 1966, the Bureau declared that the changing nature of federal field operations made it imperative to reestablish a field staff. This staff "would collect and disseminate information for the President and the Bureau of the Budget; provide assistance to Federal agencies in the coordination of their local efforts; and serve as field-level representatives of the Executive Office of the President."[7] Appropriations committees in both the House and Senate turned the request down.

After the rejection of its request for field offices, the Bureau concluded that it was politically impossible to establish a central (that is, presidential) presence in the field. However, it remained convinced of the need for field coordinating machinery, and this conviction was buttressed first by findings from field surveys and task force reports on intergovernmental relations done by Bureau personnel in 1966 and then in 1967 by a self-study, which concluded that management officials in the Bureau should be less concerned with organization of the federal executive branch and more concerned with finding "solutions to current problems in intergovernmental and interagency program effectiveness."[8] Following the

6. *Departments of Treasury and Post Office and Executive Office Appropriations for 1967*, Hearings before the House Committee on Appropriations, 89 Cong. 2 sess. (1966), p. 730.

7. Ibid., pp. 730–31.

8. "The Work of the Steering Group on Evaluation of the Bureau of the Budget," February–July 1967 (3 vols., in OMB library, Washington; processed). See also Allen Schick, "The Budget Bureau that Was: Thoughts on the Rise, Decline, and Future of a Presidential Agency," *Law and Contemporary Problems*, vol. 35 (Summer 1970), pp. 519–39 (Brookings Reprint 213). For the Bureau's statement of the management problems, see the testimony of Director Charles L. Schultze in *Creative Federalism*, Hearings before the Senate Committee on Government Operations, 89 Cong. 2 sess. (1967),

self-study the Bureau redefined and reorganized its management functions so as to put more emphasis on operational coordination. The Office of Management and Organization was abolished and a new Office of Executive Management created in its place, consisting of an operational coordination staff to do ad hoc problem solving and a management systems staff to deal with recurrent management problems resulting from new grant programs.

As a way of promoting interagency coordination in the field, the new operational coordination staff decided on interagency committees to be composed of regional directors and loosely supervised and supported by Bureau staff. Because program officials within the federal social service and development agencies had little interest in such an arrangement, management officials in the Bureau had to time their proposals carefully and work through generalist officials, either the undersecretaries or the assistant secretaries for administration, who are traditionally the principal point of contact within the departments for the Bureau's management section.

The Bureau advanced its proposal at a meeting of the undersecretaries in July 1968 called to consider recommendations made by a federal interagency task force following a study of federal programs in Oakland, California.[9] This report (the Oakland Task Force Report) recommended creation of a permanent interagency committee of regional directors in the western region (San Francisco) to search for ways of coordinating federal human resources programs in urban areas.[10] Although the report had been prepared by a private consulting firm (Marshall Kaplan, Gans, and Kahn) with very limited participation from most of the regional directors in San Francisco, its origin with an interagency task force made it useful

pt. 1. For a scholarly analysis, see James L. Sundquist, *Making Federalism Work: A Study of Program Coordination at the Community Level* (Brookings Institution, 1969), pp. 1–31.

9. HUD took the lead in launching the study of Oakland. It appears to have been more interested than other departments in interagency coordinating mechanisms, perhaps because its model cities program depended on the cooperation of other agencies. However, HUD's undersecretary in 1968, Robert C. Wood, left government very skeptical about presidentially led efforts at operational coordination. See his testimony in *Regional Planning Issues*, Hearings before the Subcommittee on Urban Affairs of the Joint Economic Committee, 91 Cong. 2 sess. (1970), pt. 4, pp. 732 ff.

10. Oakland Task Force, San Francisco Federal Executive Board, *An Analysis of Federal Decision-Making and Impact: The Federal Government in Oakland*, 2 vols. (Oakland Task Force, 1968 and 1969). The recommendations are in vol. 1, pp. 179–216. The introduction to vol. 1 gives an account of the origin of the task force.

to the Bureau as a medium for broaching the subject of interagency coordination generally. The Bureau's short-term objective was to get the agencies to agree to creating councils of regional directors in Chicago, New York, and Atlanta as well as San Francisco, cities chosen because the major grant-in-aid agencies all had regional offices there.

Shortly before the undersecretaries were scheduled to meet, the director of the Bureau's operational coordination staff, Kenneth Kugel, wrote Deputy Director Hughes that the meeting "should provide the opportunity for launching our strategy for creating the brave new world of more effective field coordination of Federal urban human resource development programs." Hughes would have a chance to propose creation of regional councils in four cities and to get the undersecretaries to agree to the Bureau's acting as "the gadfly, counselor, and catalyst of the regional councils as well as the informal secretariat of whatever Washington level counterpart emerges." Meanwhile, Kugel had been discussing the regional council proposal with the assistant secretaries for administration in the affected agencies. He expected to continue this "mission work" and to be "home free with at least a general acceptance of the principles we have proposed." With agreement from subcabinet officials in Washington, the Bureau would have "a hunting license to go after the regional directors."[11] The meeting with the undersecretaries went much as Kugel foresaw. Hughes suggested that the Oakland Task Force recommendation was generally applicable. The undersecretaries approved in general the suggestion of regional councils and accepted Hughes's offer to have the Bureau circulate a statement of proposed next steps.

As it turned out, the next step was a two-day conference of Housing and Urban Development (HUD), Health, Education, and Welfare (HEW), Office of Economic Opportunity (OEO), and Labor regional directors from Atlanta, Chicago, New York, and San Francisco held near Washington in August 1968. Undersecretary Robert C. Wood of HUD and management officials from the Bureau introduced the proposal for regional councils. At the end of the conference, the directors agreed to set up the councils, but many were skeptical, and it was clear that their perception of the "coordi-

11. Kugel to Hughes, July 19, 1968; Office of Management and Budget, Program Coordination Division files (hereafter cited as OMB, PCD files).

nation problem" was different from that of Washington-based officials. The Bureau's report of the conference says, "It was clear from our discussions . . . that many of the regional directors did not feel that Washington has a perfect understanding of all the problems. The excitement, not to say hostility, was pretty apparent. . . . Significant improvement in interagency collaboration at the field level probably requires, first of all, better communication between Washington and the regions, including a lot more listening by Washington." "Perhaps the loudest message from all of the regional directors," the report concluded, "was that interagency coordination or collaboration requires first of all a considerable increase of the type of generalist staff to the regional directors which is capable of looking at problems of ghettos, the poor, the cities, rather than just health, education, jobs, housing, or any other specialized input." The regional directors seemed to be saying that they could not coordinate with one another unless they could first coordinate the functional specialists in their own agencies. This appeared to be a problem especially in HEW: "To a man the HEW regional directors agreed that the word 'director' in their title was something of a euphemism. They all felt that too often they stood in relation to the regional people from [the Office of Education and the Public Health Service], for example, as unwelcome intruders. Without staff and without specific authorities over program decisions, they have the capability for only limited and episodic coordination efforts within HEW."[12] Shortly after this conference, the undersecretaries met again, approved creation of the councils in the four cities, and sent letters of instruction to their respective regional directors.

Extension of regional councils to the whole country, which was what the Bureau hoped for, depended on the progress of a Bureau proposal for creating common regional headquarters and boundaries for the participating agencies. The Bureau had prepared this proposal in 1967, but President Johnson did not approve it. Lacking approval, the Bureau had not proceeded with yet a third proposal for administrative change, an effort to get the agencies to decentralize more, and equal amounts of, authority to their regional directors. Decentralization too was logically linked with the cre-

12. "Report to the Under Secretaries Group on Airlie House Conference on Regional Councils, August 13–15, 1968," Aug. 27, 1968; OMB, PCD files.

ation of regional councils. Regional directors could not make decisions collaboratively unless they had adequate and equivalent degrees of authority.

In 1969 a new president approved the Bureau's proposals. President Nixon announced the creation of uniform regional boundaries and common regional office locations for the five agencies covered in the Bureau's plan; the extension of Federal Regional Councils to all of the regions; and the initiation of an effort at decentralization, to be carried out by the director of the Bureau of the Budget and the heads of nine agencies (seven domestic departments, OEO, and the Small Business Administration). The President announced the creation of eight standard regions, but congressional pressure soon led to the definition of two more. The President described the regional councils as "an excellent means through which the various arms of the Federal government can work closely together in defining problems, devising strategies to meet them, eliminating frictions and duplications, and evaluating results. Such councils can make it possible for the Federal government to speak consistently and with a single voice in its dealings with states and localities, with private organizations, and with the public."[13] The Bureau's deputy director put the point in plainer language at a press conference: "The Federal Government has been organized categorically over the years and agency programs, I think, have tended to construct walls around themselves. We need, by these kinds of measures, to attempt to pierce these walls."[14]

## Conception

Because regional councils were a creation of the Office of Management and Budget rather than the regional directors' response to their own interests or felt needs, it was up to OMB to define the councils' purposes and functions. It did this in two concept papers, issued by the undersecretaries in January 1970 and January 1971, and in an executive order that the President issued early in 1972. The OMB has been reluctant to state purposes in any but the most

13. Office of the White House Press Secretary, "Statement by the President on Restructuring of Government Service Systems," March 27, 1969.

14. *Congressional Record*, vol. 115, pt. 7, 91 Cong. 1 sess. (1969), p. 9179.

general and permissive terms. Having induced the agencies to form councils, it took the position that it was up to the councils to find useful things to do, within the framework of a general mandate to coordinate.

A year before the first councils were formed, Budget Bureau Director Charles L. Schultze told Congress, in the course of a lengthy analysis of management problems:

I think my basic and fundamental point is that coordination is best done when it is done with respect to specific identifiable problems on a case-by-case basis. Now, for the moment this says nothing about what kind of machinery is best to do that. But what I would insist is that the formation of a council or a committee offers no hope per se.[15]

In creating the councils, OMB may have violated the spirit of its former director's statement, but it remained faithful to that spirit when it defined the councils' tasks. The concept papers stressed problem solving as the councils' function. "Councils," the first of these papers began, "provide a framework for participating agencies to work together in defining and solving shared problems."[16]

Very early in the councils' history, before they actually began to function and while the undersecretaries were still considering what they should do, it became clear that there were certain kinds of coordination problems the councils could not expect to solve. The undersecretaries agreed in the fall of 1968 that councils should not "intrude on or disrupt the lines of program authority and responsibility established by the lead agencies" for interagency program efforts such as model cities.[17] In other words, regional councils were not to supplant coordinating mechanisms that the agencies had worked out independently. Nor were they to make decisions about program operation. These prohibitions were stated in the first concept paper: the councils were "not to inject new operating and decisionmaking points into the system, nor assume authority or

15. *Creative Federalism*, Hearings, pt. 1, pp. 399–400.

16. "The Federal Regional Councils," Jan. 14, 1970; OMB, PCD files.

17. At a meeting only two months before, the undersecretaries had agreed that "the regional councils should be made supporting of the coordination required in the Model Cities program and that in fact making the Model Cities program viable should be considered to have top priority on the agenda of each of the regional councils." "Minutes of the Meeting of the Under Secretaries Group," Aug. 30, 1968; OMB, PCD files.

responsibility now lodged in individual agencies or existing co-ordinating mechanisms."[18]

What the councils should do, the undersecretaries agreed, was to solve management problems. They should look for ways to improve "interagency delivery systems" and to simplify procedures. The first concept paper said that they should identify "conflicting agency policy and program operating practices which limit the effectiveness of Federal assistance" and design "coordinated and consistent agency actions to improve the effectiveness of Federal programs."

Initially, OMB stressed the need to improve the effectiveness of federal action. The aim was better coordination of federal programs at the regional level. Later, OMB began to stress the need to respond to state and local governments. The second concept paper listed as one of the councils' major functions that they should "develop and strengthen a real partnership with State and local government, and especially with governors and mayors."[19] Early in 1971 President Nixon sent each of the governors a letter describing the councils as mediums through which the federal administration would respond to their problems and urging them to suggest to the councils ways of improving "the Federal-State partnership."[20] The President's 1972 executive order directed the councils to develop "integrated program and funding plans with Governors and local chief executives" and to develop "long-term regional interagency and intergovernmental strategies for resource allocations to better respond to the needs of State and local communities." Under the Nixon administration, the councils were increasingly being seen as a means of decentralizing federal authority, in the sense of making it more accessible and responsive to state and local executives.

## Activity of the Councils

Most of the councils organized slowly. It was mid-1970 before the last of them began functioning. Changes of regional directors

18. "The Federal Regional Councils"; and "Highlights of the Meeting of the Under Secretaries Group, October 31, 1968"; OMB, PCD files.

19. "The Regional Council Concept," Jan. 25, 1971; OMB, PCD files.

20. *Weekly Compilation of Presidential Documents*, vol. 7 (Jan. 25, 1971), p. 87.

were one cause of delay; the Nixon administration replaced many career holders of regional offices with political appointees. Another cause was the need for relocations. Also, agencies were slow to detail a member to council staff work. Staffing problems persisted long after the councils began meeting.

From so brief a history, it is hard to draw firm conclusions, but it is possible at least to characterize the councils' initial activity and to identify the most important obstacles to realizing OMB's conception. Like interagency coordinating committees before them, councils have avoided dealing with interagency conflicts, and in intergovernmental relations they have not found a way to be responsive to state and local governments without exceeding their mandate from OMB.

### The Councils as Interagency Coordinators

OMB's conception of the councils' coordinating function was relatively modest. Made up of administrators, the councils were charged with identifying administrative problems, such as conflicts in agency policies or programs that caused trouble at the point of execution. They were to resolve such conflicts or refer them to the USG in Washington.

So far, the councils have not functioned as resolvers of conflict. "Identification of interagency policy conflicts and elevation for Washington resolution has been nearly nonexistent," an OMB document says.[21] Most councils seem to have avoided such conflicts from the very beginning, and the only one that did not do so, Kansas City, soon followed the practice of the rest. Not long after the Kansas City council was established and before the Denver council was functioning, a representative from OEO referred to it a conflict with HUD over a legal services project in Denver. OEO had refused to grant more than $250,000 to the project in the belief that it could not absorb more, only to learn that HUD had made a grant of $380,000 to the same project through its model cities program. The Kansas City council created a task force which eventually recommended that coordinating responsibility rest with the Regional Interagency Coordinating Committee for Model Cities. Had that committee been working properly, the problem presum-

21. OMB, PCD, "Fact Sheet on Regional Councils," Jan. 3, 1971.

ably would not have arisen. Shortly thereafter, the mayor of St. Louis complained to the council about bureaucratic competition between the community action agency and the model cities agency in his city, saying that it stemmed "from the top," meaning OEO and HUD, the respective sources of federal funds and policy direction. OEO and HUD members of the council argued about the problem, thereby confirming its existence, but the council did nothing to resolve it.[22] No further consideration of interagency conflicts appears in the minutes of the Kansas City council.

A council may get caught up in interagency conflict by accident. The best example, from New York, shows the difficulty of achieving a solution even under pressure from OMB and with its help. Several councils, including that in New York, played a part in 1970 in evaluating and closing out the neighborhood service program, under which federal agencies had cooperated to create neighborhood multiservice centers. In New York, the regional council encountered the problem of what to do with the Hunts Point multiservice center in the South Bronx. An audit revealed serious deficiencies in financial and personnel practices. HUD was willing to keep the center temporarily alive with its own money, but only if HEW would agree to suspension of the executive director and chairman of the board. HEW opposed any punitive action, including forwarding the audit report to the state attorney general, for fear of antagonizing the Spanish-speaking community. On June 30, 1971, after having been involved with the issue for more than a year, the council voted to cease further consideration of Hunts Point. OMB immediately urged the council to continue working toward a solution. The council responded that a coordinated response was impossible at the regional level since the OEO representative did not have the authority to commit his agency to a solution. All the parties realized that this was an excuse to avoid further action, and ordinarily it would have disposed of the issue; but OMB was determined that the council should act and therefore applied pressure to the Washington headquarters of OEO to allow the regional director to act. OEO complied and this had the effect of returning the issue to the council; but no solution was forthcoming. HEW

22. Minutes of the meeting of the Kansas City Federal Regional Council, Aug. 26, Sept. 23, and Oct. 14, 1969, and March 5, 1970.

continued to fund Hunts Point while the other agencies refused to do so.[23]

Resolving specific, overt, and often intense conflicts between agencies is not the only test of the councils' capacity to coordinate, and perhaps is not the fairest test. Councils might be expected to do better at resolving inconsistencies in policy if they did not have to deal with live, specific issues. OMB's initial concept paper encouraged such effort with an instruction to design "coordinated and consistent agency actions."

One area that has seemed to offer promise for such activity is that of equal employment policy. Preventing discrimination in employment is an obligation of many federal agencies and a clear national policy, yet for most agencies it is a marginal activity. Equal employment officers in different agencies can probably cooperate more easily with one another than with program officers in their own agencies. Perhaps for these reasons, several councils have attempted coordination in this field, and one, Kansas City, made a serious and sustained effort at it in 1971, soon after the issuance of a new executive order on the subject. This time, the council met defeat in Washington. Over the course of several months, the council managed to work out a set of regional guidelines to cover minority hiring by contractors doing business with the federal government. After approving the guidelines, the council forwarded them to Washington with a request for approval by the USG. Meanwhile, the Office of Federal Contract Compliance (OFCC) of the Department of Labor was trying to arrange coordination on a national scale. The Labor member of the USG refused to approve the submission of the Kansas City council, although a Labor representative (the regional manpower administrator) had approved it at the regional level. OMB tried unsuccessfully to get Labor's approval of the regional council guidelines. OFCC did agree to consult with the Kansas City council in a pilot effort at coordination with regional councils, but this ended in disagreement after one meeting. The council then gave up on the subject.[24]

23. The minutes of the council throughout 1970 and 1971 are filled with references to Hunts Point, but see especially memorandums from David Weinman to Kenneth Kugel, May 7 and July 2; OMB, PCD files.

24. Stanley Doremus, deputy chief of the Field Coordination Branch, PCD, summarized these events in a memorandum to Working Group members, July 7, 1971; OMB, PCD files.

Kansas City's effort in this case actually to work out a common agency position was unusual. When they do not ignore policy or procedural differences among agencies, councils typically react by arranging exchanges of information. For example, the Atlanta council sponsored a series of seminars so that federal field officials of different agencies would be aware of the differences in requirements for citizen participation in their programs. The Boston council, noting that federal health grants in Boston often overlap, negotiated an informal agreement between HEW, HUD, and OEO that none would fund a project in Boston without giving advance notice and an opportunity for comment to the others.

What do councils do if they do not work at settling interagency conflicts? After all, they meet twice a month, and several GS-14s or -15s, one from each member agency, are supposedly at work for them all the time. The answer is that they work on "projects," or what OMB's second concept paper describes as solving "ad hoc special problems that involve more than one council agency." According to an observer in OMB, "the councils are doing more of [this] than everything else put together. It is visible, fun for the council members, and, as long as they stay away from deep issues or interagency efforts, apt to be successful. The wide variety of problems to choose from is a horn of plenty for an active council, but only as long as it doesn't include profound social or systemic issues."[25]

In 1969 the director of President Nixon's Urban Affairs Council, Daniel P. Moynihan, exhorted the councils to avoid special projects. "Creation of special projects to demonstrate the ability to coordinate should be avoided," the minutes of the USG say.[26] But the councils were drawn inexorably to projects, and OMB's second concept paper, with its reference to ad hoc problem solving, made that development legitimate. The more important projects involve concerting federal action to fill lacunae in national policy or administration. A number of them focus on the problems of minority groups, such as Indians, the Spanish-speaking, or migrants. Often they are a response to natural disaster or a social crisis. In 1972 the

25. Oliver Taylor, "What Do Councils Do Now? What Should They Do in the Future, and How Should They Be Equipped to Do It?" Dec. 14, 1971; OMB, PCD files (hereafter cited as Taylor memorandum).

26. Minutes of the meeting of the Under Secretaries Group, June 13, 1969.

Denver council helped Rapid City, South Dakota, cope with a flood. Less successfully, the Philadelphia council tried to help flooded Pennsylvania communities after Hurricane Agnes; when the council's effort proved ineffectual, a high-ranking OMB official went into the field for three months to coordinate federal activity. The San Francisco council became involved with the problems of urban Indians as a result of the seizure of Alcatraz by Indian demonstrators, and the Boston council became involved in New Bedford as a result of rioting there. Some projects originate in Washington. A cabinet committee requested the Dallas and Atlanta councils to help find jobs for black teachers displaced by desegregation. Each council was asked to hold a regional conference on problems of the aged in support of the White House Conference on the Aging. It is characteristic of projects that none of the agencies involved has an overriding responsibility for the activity or perceives that coordination will be harmful to it. In many cases, the projects entail giving support to nonmember federal agencies. Thus councils take part in disaster relief in support of the Office of Emergency Preparedness.

The OMB has appraised the councils' performance often and realistically. Its evaluations have repeatedly noted the councils' failure to confront conflicts, to develop new coordinating procedures, or to extend ad hoc problem solving beyond a few rather special and limited situations. OMB officials have recognized that the councils as originally constituted cannot be expected to confront conflict. "Who among their members," an appraisal made late in 1971 asked rhetorically, "needs to pick *overt* fights or appeal *overtly* over the heads of their peers without having the coercive power to force events to a satisfactory conclusion and when the cost of the encounter is in the only working currency available, voluntary good will?"[27] Another says: "The entire regional council system in the field and in Washington has been crippled by the absence of a decision forcing mechanism."[28] OMB's response was the President's executive order of February 1972, which established the councils more formally ("institutionalized" them, in OMB's term, and increased "their capacity to influence agency decisions"

27. Taylor memorandum.
28. A. G. Patterson, "Strengthening Council Decision-Making Processes," Dec. 20, 1971; OMB, PCD files.

with the aid of "a strong Presidential mandate"[29]). In addition to giving them a more formal charter, the executive order incorporated two strategies for changing the councils.

The OMB sought to define the councils' functions more precisely and to link those functions to the making of grants. For example, the councils were to encourage "joint and complementary grant applications for related programs." More important, OMB sought to increase central influence over the councils and, by inference, over the agencies the councils represent. The 1972 executive order stated that the President would designate a council member as chairman and that the chairman should "serve at the pleasure of the President." Representatives of OMB were explicitly authorized to participate in council deliberations. The Under Secretaries Group for Regional Operations was established with the deputy director of OMB as chairman; in one form or another, such a group had been functioning for some time. The executive order said that the Under Secretaries Group, under the chairmanship of OMB, "shall be responsible for the proper functioning" of the regional council system. It should establish policy for the councils, give them guidance, respond to their initiatives, and seek to resolve policy issues referred by them.

Simultaneously, OMB renewed an effort, which it had initiated three years earlier, to persuade federal agencies to delegate more authority to their regional directors. From the start of the regional council undertaking, OMB had believed that lack of authority as well as inconsistent amounts of authority for the regional directors would handicap the councils. President Nixon had included decentralization with extension of regional councils and creation of common regional headquarters and boundaries in his announcement of reforms of federal field administration in the spring of 1969, and soon thereafter OMB and nine cooperating agencies initiated the Federal Assistance Review in response to the order to decentralize. But the FAR's objectives were diffuse (they covered many more kinds of decentralization than delegation of authority to regional directors); it was ill staffed and its activity sporadic; and coordination with the Program Coordination Division of OMB, which was shepherding regional councils, was poor. There was no

29. "Fact Sheet on Regional Councils."

substantial delegation of authority to regional directors between 1969, when the regional council system was started, and 1972, when the PCD tried to accelerate the councils' development.

To the PCD, the regional directors' limited and divergent amounts of authority continued to seem a serious problem. HUD and OEO came closest to what PCD saw as the model of delegated authority. On an organization chart, both are straight-line organizations with a single regional structure under a director who has sign-off authority on grants and reports to Washington. Subregional units report to Washington through the regional director. The chain of command is clear and the regional director's scope of authority is agencywide. With certain exceptions the regional directors in both agencies have authority to hire personnel up to the level of GS-14 without approval from Washington. The Environmental Protection Agency's director is similarly powerful. In HEW, which OMB views as the agency most urgently in need of reform, numerous regional and subregional structures report directly to Washington. The regional director is supposed to coordinate program units and see that the secretary's policies are carried out, but he does not have line authority or the right to sign off on grants. His authority to hire is limited to his immediate staff.[30] Whereas executive direction at the regional level has been weak at HEW (which is the leading target for reform mainly because its program volume is so large), in Labor and Transportation it has

30. HEW officials have questioned whether their department's actual situation is so different from that of other departments. Deputy Undersecretary Frederic V. Malek wrote to Kenneth Kugel, OMB, Nov. 25, 1969 (OMB, PCD files):

"It is more useful to work toward a regional director's power to influence events rather than the conventional bureaucratic concept of 'authority.' Little effective influence would accrue to the HEW regional director if he were simply given the sign-off authority for the thousands of project grants and contracts in his region. Appropriate power will accrue as regional agency executives are given decision making authority and the regional director secures their conformance with priorities and policies of the Secretary. Planning analysis, review, and adaptation of regional operations are more influential than signatory performance in grants-in-aid.

"In contrast to smaller departments, it is not physically possible for a regional director of HEW to make individual judgments about dozens of grants made each day in his region. He can, however, direct planning, monitoring, and evaluation systems to assure appropriate decision making.

"At the risk of destroying a popular myth, there is no convincing evidence that HEW's field operations are less 'integrated' than those of HUD or Labor, for example. It is now clear that Secretary Finch expects his regional directors to manage field operations. That provides the necessary strengthening of the regional director's position."

been nonexistent. The Department of Transportation had no regional director until a weak "secretary's representative" was created in 1970 when the department joined the councils. Nor has Labor had a regional director, and its representative to the regional councils in their early years was the regional manpower administrator, the regional official most involved in giving grants for social purposes. When Labor did create a regional director in 1971, his authority was so limited that PCD feared the change would be a step backward.

Regional directors of course agree with OMB that they should have more authority, but their own analysis of the councils stresses obstacles to coordination other than the individual members' lack of authority. From their perspective, the chief problem is the lack of incentive to subordinate agency goals to the needs of the council. At a meeting of the Chicago council, for example, the chairman remarked that "OMB must recognize that each Council member has individual agency priorities that he will not, and cannot, put aside for Council activities."[31] A task force of former council chairmen, assembled by OMB to consider how the councils should be run, made the same point more elaborately. The task force noted that regional directors ordinarily expect to be rewarded for accomplishing agency objectives, and if they are to serve the councils instead, they must be assured of reward from their Washington superiors for that. Exhortations from OMB will not suffice:

The individual Regional Council Members must know that their superiors, especially the Under Secretaries but also the other principal headquarters officials, are really committed to the Regional Council system. This entails more than setting forth a position on a piece of paper. It requires some real effort on the part of top agency management to let the Regional Director know that their commitment is more than lip service. In addition to verbal statements, top Washington officials must produce meaningful evidence of support and interest in Council activities. A significant part of the evaluation of a Regional Director's performance could be based upon his Regional Council activity.[32]

Agency officials in Washington have still another perspective. They see the obstacles to coordination as embedded in law. When OMB proposed the executive order early in 1972, the undersecre-

31. Minutes of the meeting of the Chicago Federal Regional Council, Oct. 19, 1971.
32. "A Statement on the Management of a Federal Regional Council," September 1971; OMB, PCD files.

taries "expressed concern that strengthening the FRC system should not result in strains disruptive to the legislatively mandated responsibilities of the agencies."[33]

Councils must rely on OMB. What they do depends on what OMB can induce the member agencies individually and the councils collectively to do.

OMB's conduct toward the councils has been so carefully restrained that its influence, one might argue, has yet to be tested. It has conspicuously refrained from telling councils what they should do or what issues to consider. Although it assigns a staff member to each, he has not sought to lead his council. He has been an observer or informal participant. But this very restraint is a sign of OMB's deference to agency power and prerogatives. The more active OMB is, the greater the danger of arousing agency resistance and destroying the whole effort.[34]

OMB has risked asserting itself in Washington more than in the regions, perhaps because more is to be gained there (regional directors will take cues from headquarters) and because central action is acknowledged to be OMB's legitimate sphere. The nearer OMB is to the President, the less likely is the legitimacy of its action to be challenged. OMB began to chair the USG in 1970 when its representatives to regional councils were only informal participants at meetings. The guidance that USG issues to the councils actually originates with OMB; agency representatives have ordinarily done no more than comment on what OMB has proposed. When this relationship has produced tension, OMB has defended its prerogatives. In responding to a critical paper from departmental representatives, an OMB official said that he detected "a slight undercurrent of limiting OMB," and added that "there may well be times OMB will have to persevere despite a negative vote from the Working Group or even the Under Secretaries."[35]

Although Washington offers OMB a relatively wide sphere for

33. "Mission Statement USG Task Force on FRC Functions," enclosure to "Task Force Report on Regional Council Functions," memorandum for the Under Secretaries Group from William H. Kolberg, Feb. 2, 1972; OMB, PCD files.

34. For criticism of OMB's restraint, see Melvin B. Mogulof, *Federal Regional Councils: Their Current Experience and Recommendations for Further Development* (Washington: Urban Institute, 1970), pp. 56 ff.

35. Kenneth Kugel to Pierce Quinlan, Working Group representative, HUD, May 20, 1971; OMB, PCD files.

legitimate action, legitimacy does not guarantee effectiveness. OMB has had only mixed success in asking agency headquarters to facilitate actions by the regional councils. Issues that come from the councils, such as those of the Hunts Point multiservice center in New York and equal employment opportunity enforcement in the Kansas City region, have not warranted direct intervention by the President. Management officials in OMB can only appeal to the agencies for cooperation; sometimes they get results and sometimes they do not. If, like program officials in OMB, they could threaten sanctions in the form of budget cuts, they would get cooperation more often; but program officials have shown little interest in PCD's goals, and PCD lacks the power to enforce sanctions of its own.

The obstacles to the agencies' cooperating with one another or with OMB originate in law and, beyond the law, in the agencies' needs to sustain their respective programs, to serve distinctive clienteles and distinctive conceptions of the public interest, and to satisfy congressional supporters. Agency separatism and functional specialization, deeply embedded as they are in American government, are precisely the problem that OMB seeks to attack by fostering interagency coordinating committees in the regions. Like the doctor who treats the patient's fever when he cannot cure the disease, OMB attacks the symptom—chaos at the point of administration—because the cause—the pluralism of interests in American politics and of institutions in American government—is inaccessible. But its ability to alleviate even the symptom is limited.

### The Councils as Agents of Decentralization

The councils are supposed to develop a real partnership with state and local governments, especially with governors and mayors, as distinct from functional specialists in administrative agencies, and they are supposed to develop strategies for responding to state and local needs; but OMB did not define the content of these functions before 1972, and the councils were slow to become engaged in intergovernmental relations. As one OMB evaluation noted late in 1971:

"Real partnership" is just too much. What [the councils] do . . . is visit and become acquainted, offer good will, work with systems such as A-95 [an OMB circular designed among other things to permit statewide and substate regional clearinghouses to comment on projects submitted to federal agencies], and seize such opportunities as occur for ad hoc help.[36]

More recently, OMB has searched for ways to involve the councils systematically in intergovernmental activities. Early in 1973 it asked them to brief state and local officials on the federal budget for fiscal 1974. It also asked them to play a part in coordinating relations between the federal government and cities where HUD is trying "planned variations" of the model cities program; to work with various cities in integrated grant administration (IGA), an experiment in which local governments use a single application to obtain funds from several federal programs; and to develop "annual arrangements" with local governments defining federal funding commitments.

There is a danger that the councils' efforts at interagency coordination of grant administration will be purely formal and will complicate rather than simplify intergovernmental relations. For IGA, for example, Federal Regional Councils may assemble approvals of grant applications just as interagency coordinating committees in the field of water resources had assembled agency project proposals. "It is all too easy," an interagency task force said of IGA in 1972, "to create pseudo-interagency relationships with State and local governments by having the State and local agencies staple together their several programs, plans, and applications and deliver them as a pseudo-unit to the Federal Regional Council; then have the Federal Regional Council unstaple them and deliver them to the several Federal agency responses; etc. This simply creates an extra layer of bureaucracy with no benefit to anyone."[37]

In drafting the executive order of 1972, OMB seemed to strive for modes of coordination that would be more than purely formal. One draft called for the councils to "plan interagency and intergovernmental resource allocations, including setting priorities among programs in response to the needs of States and local communities." This would be a very important function for the councils if it were feasible. The final version of the order called instead

36. Taylor memorandum.
37. "Interagency Task Force on Regional Council Functions," enclosure to "Task Force Report on Regional Council Functions," memorandum for the Under Secretaries Group from William H. Kolberg, Feb. 2, 1972; OMB, PCD files.

for the councils to develop long-term strategies for resource allocations. Commenting on this language, an interagency task force said that expectations should be "very modest." Councils could do nothing without "extraordinary support" by headquarters, and "agency chauvinism," the task force noted, "seems stronger in Washington than in the field, particularly in agency headquarters program offices." It is the headquarters offices that formulate budget and program proposals.[38]

OMB appears to assume that federal interagency coordination will serve state and local needs in and of itself. The original critique of federal grant administration that OMB and others formulated in the late 1960s stressed the burden of confusion that state and local governments were being asked to bear. The critique said that the federal government had too many programs administered by too many agencies with too many different field offices to work through and too many different requirements to meet. As a result, it was said, intolerable strains were being placed on state and local governments; it followed that improvements in federal field administration, such as the coordination sought through regional councils, would serve those governments' interests.

The experience of regional councils shows, however, that OMB's expectations of the councils and the expectations of state and local governments are very likely to conflict. State and local governments are important claimants on the federal treasury as well as partners in the administration of shared programs. They—or at least their elected chief executives, whom OMB hopes especially to serve— are less interested in improving interagency and intergovernmental coordination than in enlarging their supply of federal funds. But a council that responds to their interest in getting federal funds is likely to find itself at odds with OMB.

The Seattle regional council was caught in this dilemma. In July 1970 it convened Seattle, Kings County, and state officials to design a program for the Seattle area economy. This effort came to be known as HELPS (Healthy Economic Life for Puget Sound). The task force was chaired by a regional council staff member, as were several of the subcommittees. Its report, containing dozens of recommendations for increased federal assistance, was published under the auspices of the regional council and personally delivered to the

38. Ibid.

associate director of OMB by the mayor of Seattle. OMB officials were profoundly embarrassed. They flew off to Seattle for talks with state and local officials. Two days later the Seattle *Post-Intelligencer* reported that the "feds didn't produce anything and that made the governor very, very unhappy." According to the paper's source, " 'The feds encouraged the whole thing, and now you can hardly get a response from them about it.' " The mayor of Seattle later reported to the U.S. Conference of Mayors that only a few specific proposals had been approved. "These have come on a piece-meal, departmental basis," he wrote, "demonstrating that the Federal government, and OMB, have so far been unable or unwilling to approve this report as a whole or work toward implementing it. This unusual, rapid experiment . . . has thus been disappointing." [39] Privately, OMB regarded the task force report as a compendium of federal projects "masquerading as an economic plan." [40]

Following the HELPS incident, OMB prepared a "critique" (not to be confused with "criticism," it said) of the Seattle council's effort, which OMB said raised many of the principal issues about the role and function of a regional council. This report, reviewed and approved by the USG, commended the council for initiative in a pioneering effort, but fundamentally objected to the council's role:

The Seattle effort . . . resulted in a situation where the Federal field agents were inadvertently encouraging and actively participating in the development of a local petition for Federal action and funds which were generally beyond the feasibility of the Federal Government to respond to. The identification of the Federal field staff became somewhat blurred due to their direct and intimate involvement in the development and transmittal of the plan. The Federal Regional Representatives partially assumed the appearance of petitioners and applicants to their own agencies in Washington. [41]

OMB did not object to the councils' cooperating with state and

39. "Role and Function of Regional Councils in the Development and Implementation of Area Economic Plans," enclosure to memorandum of same title from Arnold Weber to regional councils, Dec. 17, 1970; Seattle *Post-Intelligencer*, Nov. 12, 1970; Wes Uhlman to executive director, U.S. Conference of Mayors, March 9, 1971; all in OMB, PCD files.

40. Kenneth Kugel to Arnold Weber, Nov. 12, 1970; OMB, PCD files.

41. "Role and Function of Regional Councils in the Development and Implementation of Area Economic Plans," Dec. 17, 1970; OMB, PCD files. Technically, this paper was a product of the Working Group of the Under Secretaries Group.

local officials in preparation of economic plans, but the leadership should be supplied by state and local governments and private participants. Federal officials should avoid "integral identification and precommitment." The proper federal role, OMB reminded the councils, was to review and evaluate state and local proposals.[42]

Even when federal regional officials have carefully avoided seeming to promise funds, their involvement with state and local officials has led to expectations of financial aid. Early in its history, the New York council launched a project to improve the technical competence of local officials in the village of Spring Valley, New York. The council was careful not to raise expectations beyond what the member agencies were prepared to meet. But a draft of the final report on the project said that "the major finding in this type of project, in which sophisticated planning skills are imparted, seems to be that the community leaders are unable to give up the belief that funds will somehow be following and that funds alone will solve their problems. In short they feel that, given the funds, none of the training would be necessary."[43]

The OMB seems to sense that the regional councils will not develop into vigorous and effective organizations unless in some way they do serve the needs of state and local governments. They cannot play an important role in the administration of federal grants if the grantees ignore them. Hence OMB is anxious that state and local officials address appeals to the councils, preferably appeals for administrative improvements. But state and local officials will not address appeals to the councils unless they can get definitive and relatively prompt responses and are confident that such responses will not be overruled in Washington. As OMB's assistant director for program coordination observed to a group of federal officials:

You can be certain that state and local officials know where all the power levers are. And if they want something done, they will pull all of them. If things aren't functioning properly, they have a Congressman, two Senators, friends in the region, and friends in Washington. One of our biggest chores is to develop a type of decentralization in which all avenues are exhausted at the regional level before other appeals are

42. Ibid.
43. New York Federal Regional Council, "Evaluation of the New York Regional Council Local Area Project," November 1969 (draft); OMB, PCD files.

made. Too often state and local officials aren't willing to do this. We must develop the capacity to say "No," in Washington and let the issues be settled in the region.[44]

State and local officials, knowing that councils do not have power to make program decisions or to resolve those intrafederal conflicts that they might like to have resolved, such as the dispute in St. Louis between the community action and model cities agencies, will not bring such matters to the councils. And even if the councils' authority was enlarged, state and local officials would not bring them those intrafederal conflicts that it is not in the local interest to resolve. Chaos in the grant system is not all bad from the local point of view: the more sources of funds the better.[45] If HUD and OEO, without each other's knowledge, are both giving money to a legal services project, as was the case in Denver, local sources are not likely to lodge a complaint.

## The Future of the Councils

Because regional councils already cover the country, the question of duplicating them in other places does not arise. The question for OMB is how far and how successfully the functional development of the Federal Regional Councils can be promoted.

OMB's strategy for promoting the councils seems to call for slowly and steadily enlarging their functions, increasing the authority of the regional director (a "generalist" rather than a "functional specialist"), and increasing the role of central (OMB) supervision at both the Washington and the regional levels. Beyond that OMB hopes to cooperate through the councils with the chief executives of state and local governments. The aim, as the Budget Bureau's deputy director said in 1969, is to "pierce the walls" of the agency programs—in effect to form a vertical alliance of generalists from Washington down through the federal regional offices to statehouses and city halls, and to check through the working of this alliance the many parallel alliances of functional specialists.

44. William Kolberg, "The New Federalism: Regional Councils and Program Coordination Efforts," speech presented to the Federal Executive Institute, 1973.

45. Melvin B. Mogulof also makes this point. See "The Federal Regional Councils: A Potential Instrument for Planning and Joint Action," *Social Service Review*, vol. 44 (June 1970), pp. 132–46.

OMB frankly views the councils as a medium for establishing a presidential presence in the field. According to its assistant director for program coordination, the provision that the President will designate the council chairman was in many ways the most important aspect of the executive order of 1972. This was a change "intentionally made to alter the power situation in the field" by ending "laissez-faire secretarial domination of the regions." It brought protests from department heads on that account, but these had no effect on OMB because "somehow or other the President as the head of the Executive branch of the federal government has a responsibility to see that goals are accomplished and work is done in the regions."[46] The question is whether the President, meaning in practice OMB, will have power commensurate with this responsibility. OMB's unsuccessful attempts to induce the councils to resolve issues and its inability to help them achieve resolutions in specific cases, such as the Hunts Point multiservice center and equal employment policies for the Kansas City region, suggest the limits of its power as a central coordinator.

Historically, as the President's principal staff agency OMB has been preoccupied with budget review and legislative clearance functions and with advising the President on how to organize the federal executive branch. Since the late 1960s it has been attempting a new function, operational coordination, one test of which has been its sponsorship and supervision of the Federal Regional Councils. Simply by their existence, let alone their functioning, the councils testify to the limits of OMB's power. OMB has had to use this indirect approach to establishing a presidential presence in the field and to play a cautious observer's role within the councils. The executive order of 1972 is a sign that OMB is being less cautious than before in its sponsorship of the councils, but whether it can grow more effective as a central coordinator operating within them and through them remains to be seen.

46. Kolberg, "The New Federalism."

# [8]

# Action on a Regional Scale

IF FOR THE SAKE of analysis it is assumed that regional organizations are desirable, what form ought they to take? And within American government what forms can they reasonably be expected to take? This chapter compares the merit of various forms of regional organization as performers of governmental activities—development operations, management, planning, or coordination—on a regional scale; analyzes the common difficulties encountered by regional organizations in adjusting to the organizational environment; and discusses briefly the feasibility of reproducing various forms.[1]

## The Forms Contrasted

As an instrument for developing a river basin, the Tennessee Valley Authority has been incomparably more successful than the Delaware River Basin Commission, and form goes far toward explaining the difference. The autonomous, unitary character of the TVA has made it an exceptionally effective instrument of action, the special authority par excellence in American government. In contrast, the DRBC has been seriously inhibited by its dependent, multipartite character. It can do nothing except what member governments agree it should do and are willing to pay for, and that has not been much. The effects of form are reinforced by differences in the bureaucratic environment. The TVA entered a relatively uncrowded universe of relatively undeveloped state and federal or-

1. The first two parts of this chapter, though not the concluding discussion of feasibility, omit the Federal Regional Councils. See p. 10, above.

ganizations, with a clear legal right to displace the Corps of Engineers. Thirty years later and in a very different setting, the DRBC found it much harder to get established. Even its charter was full of ambiguity. Although the DRBC has comprehensive authority to act, the compact explicitly protects the authority of federal, state, and local agencies to plan, construct, and maintain projects and facilities.

As an instrument of action, the DRBC, because it is so dependent on member governments, is ill conceived. As noted in chapter 3, the Syracuse University study that preceded the founding of the DRBC recommended that a federal agency be created first to develop the river and that a federal-interstate compact commission follow to manage what had been developed. Because the purely federal instrumentality was unacceptable to state governments, the management form emerged first, but in the absence of major development there has not been much managing for it to do. Hence it is difficult to compare the TVA and the DRBC as managers. The DRBC does not, like the TVA, regulate the flow of a river or the levels of water in a complex series of reservoirs, if only because the physical facilities for doing so do not exist on the Delaware. It does perform certain management functions, such as monitoring oil spills and taking responsibility for water supply functions at federally developed reservoirs. The organizational characteristics of the DRBC that inhibit major development or regulatory functions do not equally inhibit management functions, which in general are less costly and more technical, and some of which at least (such as the water supply function of state and local governments attendant on development of federal reservoirs) are not jealously protected by any existing federal or state agency. It is possible that a federal-interstate compact commission could successfully perform a wide range of management functions, but it is not fair to compare DRBC with TVA in this respect.

To conclude that the TVA is vastly superior to the DRBC as a development agency is not to say that TVA is superior in performing any and all functions on a regional scale. The presence of the states' representatives means that the DRBC can be a medium for settling interstate differences, a function for which TVA is innately unsuited. As such, the DRBC proved successful in its one serious test, the drought of the 1960s. It also helped to bring about interstate agreement on pollution control standards for the Delaware in the late 1960s. If the form of the DRBC appears defective, that is because the organization has been given so wide a range of functions that no one form could possibly suit them all. A federal development agency would have been no help to the basin in dealing with the issues brought on by the drought.

As regional planning organizations, the Title II commissions are somewhat more plausible than the commissions for economic development. However slow the process and whatever the quality of the results, the Title II commissions do oversee the preparation of documents that are treated as if the contents might someday affect what governments do. Responsibility for planning is contested within the Title II commissions, as in the New England River Basins Commission's consideration of its southeastern New England study and the Great Lakes commission's consideration of the Maumee study. The participants act as if something is at stake—planning funds and jurisdictions at least and, more remotely, the contents of plans. By contrast, planning for action on a regional scale is all but nonexistent within the Appalachian Regional Commission (ARC), which has delegated planning to the states, and it has been lackadaisical within the Title V commissions, which deferred planning for as long as they could and then treated it, realistically enough, as a purely formal requirement of the law and the secretary of commerce. To some extent, the difference is accounted for by differences of form. To leave planning with operating agencies, as does the Title II form (the "forum of peers"), makes planning relatively plausible. Where planning is separated from the execution of plans (as with the "catalyst"), the organizational type depends for accomplishment on acquiring its own spending program, as the ARC has done. The ARC's delegation of planning to the states tends to reunite planning with execution, but it compromises the regional character of the program.

Still, it is not just form that accounts for the economic development commissions' retreat from regional planning, and it would be wrong to infer that adding federal agency representatives would improve their performance in this respect.[2] There are important

2. Function follows form. If the commissions for economic development had had representatives of a number of interested federal agencies rather than a single federal member, they would not have evolved into grant-in-aid administrators with a potential

differences of function and institutional environment between the Title II commissions and the commissions for economic development.

In function, the commissions for economic development are roughly analogous to a federal line agency that administers grants. Whereas the Title II commissions are compelled to engage in planning because they have no alternative, for the commissions on economic development there is a more attractive alternative—spending. Because the kind of spending they support is primarily a state responsibility, the most realistic procedure is to leave planning to the state governments, as executives of the ARC recognized instantly and as administrators of the Title V program found out. The Title II commissions, since they are precluded from operating functions and are concerned with activities for which federal agencies are primarily responsible, must engage the participation of those agencies.

The economic development commissions do not engage federal agencies in planning for another reason. The commissions' purpose is nominally distinct from that of the line agencies, yet it is operationally indistinguishable. They are promoting "economic development," but to do this they supply funds to the states for projects that are usually similar in kind to those the federal line agencies fund, such as highways, vocational schools, and hospitals. The line agencies have no incentive to concert actions through a planning agency in support of an objective, economic development, which is ill defined and which, if it has any meaning at all, requires them to adapt their own programs to development standards. Giving them representation within the regional commission would not alter these circumstances. In the Title II commissions, on the other hand, federal agencies with definite yet overlapping functions come together to try to meliorate the consequences of the overlapping. The Title II commissions do not purport to have a distinctive development function; they, like their member organizations, are engaged in water resources development. Within that broad sphere of activity, the commissions' specialty is coordination of planning.

Still another reason for the relative inability of the commissions

---

for rivaling line agencies. Agency representatives would have had no interest in aggrandizement of the new organization. The single federal member, loyal first of all to the regional organization, does have such an interest.

for economic development to plan for action on a regional scale is the lack of a federal incentive. For the ARC, grant-in-aid funds have been available without any evidence of regional planning or interstate cooperation, whereas in the Title V program Commerce Department and Budget Bureau officials began by insisting on elaborate regional planning but made no promises that plans would be funded. In the Title II commissions, funds are supplied to the commissions and to member agencies specifically for regional (river basin) planning, and for nothing else. These funds furnish an incentive to plan even if there is not much prospect that plans will affect the course of development.

Finally, the commissions for economic development have had the handicap of ill-defined and often heterogeneous areal jurisdictions. The Title II commissions ordinarily oversee planning for a river basin, which is a discrete, identifiable natural unit. Where the boundaries of economic development should be drawn has not been at all clear.

It is not possible to abstract from these cases a model of a regional planning organization for the United States, but experience suggests certain guiding principles. Powerful inducements to regional planning must be supplied, presumably by the federal government. Planning should not be sharply separated from governments or agencies with which the relevant operating functions are lodged; it will gravitate to them anyway, and the separate planning organization will be left with nothing to do or will find a substitute for planning. Organizations "for planning" should be denied opportunities to engage in alternative activities that may displace the planning function, which is likely to be unattractive. The "regional" area for which planning is supposed to be done must have a clear and compelling rationale. Otherwise, there is no chance of resisting the inertia of existing jurisdictional arrangements.

To focus on formal functions risks misjudging organizations that do not do exactly what their charters say they shall. Formal functions and actual functions often differ. Among regional organizations, the DRBC and the ARC best demonstrate the point, the former being something less and the latter something more than their respective laws envisaged. The DRBC should perhaps be judged as a planner and coordinator rather than as an operating agency, whereas the ARC should be judged as the operating agency that in some measure it has become. (The analysis of regional organizations as coordinators here is to be distinguished from the analysis in the next chapter of techniques for achieving federal interagency coordination. Regional organizations as coordinators usually respond to the presumed need for interstate and federal-state coordination, at least. Conceptually, there is no limit to what they are supposed to coordinate within their jurisdictions.)

As a planning and coordinating agency, the DRBC has the advantage of having much broader authority than a Title II commission. It has planning powers with sanctions, which is unusual in American government. Not that the DRBC can compel operating agencies to carry its plans out, but it can prevent others from carrying out plans that it has not approved. It has the power of veto. The DRBC's right to review all projects substantially affecting water resources in the basin enables it to bring its distinctive areal perspective to bear on several hundred public and private actions a year. This makes its coordinating functions more comprehensive than those of the Title II commissions or the commissions for economic development. A Title II commission has the right to coordinate *plans* only, and the plans it produces bind no one to anything. It cannot veto an action that is inconsistent with one of its plans, as can the DRBC. A regional commission for economic development in theory can coordinate *actions*, by using grant-in-aid funds to induce federal and state agencies to collaborate in its strategy of economic development for the regions, but the number of public actions affected within the region is small, limited by the amount of money available to the commission. Because the DRBC's coordinating powers are negative, consisting of the right to clear and review, its influence on projects is marginal, consisting of whatever may be negotiated in the course of clearance; but the coordinating influence of the commissions for economic development is marginal too. The grant with accompanying conditions is just one influence among many on the state or local agency that is deciding whether to undertake a certain public works project and where to locate it. In sum, the organization with binding and comprehensive powers of review, exemplified by the DRBC, appears to be the most effective as a regional coordinator.

As an operating agency, the ARC cannot readily be compared with other regional operating agencies (the TVA, the DRBC). Its

operations have been too different. Whereas the TVA and the
DRBC are concerned mainly with developing and managing the
water resources of a major river basin, the ARC has been concerned
mainly with building highways and other public works and with
running health and child development programs. Unlike the TVA
and the DRBC, the ARC administers grants-in-aid. In effect, it has
won the right to spend a portion of such grants within its region,
yet this right remains abridged. The ARC must divide responsibility for grant-in-aid administration with federal line agencies
having national jurisdictions; while it defines guidelines, they continue to make and to monitor expenditures. Also, like any administrator of grants-in-aid, the ARC depends on the states. Its functioning as a regional operating agency is therefore circumscribed
and ambiguous. More accurately, it is a channel for the flow of
extra federal funds to the states in a deprived region, a medium for
interstate bargaining over allocation of the funds, and a skilled
lobbyist on behalf of the region. As a regional operating agency, it
has no distinctive advantages.

So far, this analysis has compared regional organizations according to what they do rather than according to how regional they are.
Their regional character might be taken as a given or fixed feature
since all do have regional jurisdictions, or regionalism may be
treated as a variable to be judged by the relative success of the
organizations in maintaining a regional orientation, in fostering
or responding to a regional consciousness, or in aggregating interests within the region and articulating distinctively regional goals.
By these criteria, it is hard to tell the organizations apart.

With the possible exception of TVA, all are handicapped by a
lack of regional identity, and TVA might be handicapped too but
for its ability to draw heavily on national support and to be self-
sustaining. In many cases there has been confusion over how boundaries should be defined, and boundaries have shifted in response
to political circumstances or the aspirations of the organization.
When the states belong, there is a recurrent debate over whether
boundaries should conform to state boundaries. None of these regional organizations grew out of a widely shared sense of a regional
interest. Even where the initiative for formation developed within
the region, as with the DRBC and the ARC, it rested with a small
group of public officials or political activists. And even where re-

gional consciousness is relatively high, as in New England, it has not been high enough to affect the functioning of a regional organization. The Title V commission in New England has not been visibly more successful than other Title V commissions—possibly the reverse. The Title II commission there has been more active than the others, but the explanation for this lies in the chairman's personality and the comparatively modest and tractable character of the federal public works establishment in New England, not in a greater sense of shared regional interest.

Since an independent regional consciousness is generally lacking, the organization must create one by the force of its own activities or of its assertions of a regional interest. No regional organization, again with the possible exception of the TVA, has yet been able to do this. Where the states belong to the organization and have an important part in conducting its business, the regional organization becomes a medium for distributing federal benefits to individual states or bringing about mutual adjustments among states, as in the DRBC, which negotiated interstate disputes over water allocation, and the ARC, within which states negotiate the division of federal funds. Instances of interstate collaboration, while not nonexistent, are few. Where the states do not belong, as in the case of TVA, the "regional" organization has been primarily an instrument for realizing the ideological aim of a national coalition. In its grass-roots partnerships, TVA has fostered state and local activities rather than trying to create institutions or cooperative activity on a regional scale. At the same time, the highly visible effect of TVA's own activities has probably generated some degree of regional consciousness in the Tennessee Valley.

If a regional organization is to become the vehicle for responding to or inducing regional consciousness, a location within the region is probably desirable, if only to foster regional orientation of the staff. It is a disadvantage of the commissions for economic development that they have functioned mainly as Washington-based service and lobbying agencies.

## The Need for Adjustment

Whatever their differences, regional organizations have a common handicap in being unusual cases, deviant new growth in a governmental landscape whose enduring and predominant features are fifty state governments and a number of federal departments and bureaus with national jurisdictions. None is a general-purpose government, with the full range of powers that such a government would possess. Each has been superimposed upon the region to carry out selected activities that constitute only a small fraction of the total of government activity. Regional organizations must get established in a crowded, competitive universe, and this requires adapting to other government organizations rather than trying to change them. Invariably, the activity of the new regional organization is constricted in some way. By the standard of what it is authorized to do, the activity of each organization is specialized or subdued.

The regional organizations stand in varying relation to established organizations, depending on their own forms and functions, and therefore have faced very different problems of adjustment. Regional organizations with operating functions are meant to supersede other organizations in the performance of some or all of their activities. The catalyst as coordinator is meant independently to induce changes in the conduct of other organizations. The forum of peers is meant to represent other organizations on matters in which their activities or interests overlap. Each type has a different potential for adaptation.

The type that would seem least compelled to make costly adaptations is the autonomous operating organization with a broad grant of authority, as illustrated by TVA. Yet TVA abandoned the idea of becoming a comprehensive social and economic planner for the valley, specializing instead in the generation and sale of electric power. It is hard to say whether specialization of function is inevitable in a regional organization granted a wide range of operating functions; one case certainly does not prove it. But it seems likely that any such organization will strongly prefer some types of operations over others, particularly those that produce revenue or minimize the costs of jurisdictional conflict. The DRBC's choice of pollution control as a specialty is consistent with this.

The catalyst, because it depends on influencing other organizations, is theoretically in a less advantageous position than an operating agency. Moreover, the premise on which the catalyst rests is likely to be at least somewhat false from the start. Proponents of a new organization in American government usually must agree in advance not to diminish the authority or functions of established organizations: the price of achieving entry into the universe of organizations is a promise not to disturb that universe. Unless the functions of the new organization can be made to appear innocuous (one way to do this is to say that its function is "coordination"), the opposition of threatened organizations is likely to kill it. Although the ARC and the Title V commissions are apparently supposed to exercise comprehensive influence within their regions and induce a wide range of public and private actors to collaborate in carrying out a plan for regional development, it has never been clear how they were to do this. The concept of the catalyst as coordinator was never realistically worked out. The commissions for economic development have been faced with a choice between trying to plan and coordinate comprehensively within their regions (soliciting the collaboration of other organizations on the broadest possible scale) and limiting their activity to whatever programs of expenditure they could claim as their own. The choice of independence—which has been made successfully by the ARC and less successfully by the Title V commissions—may seem the inevitable result of any organization's "natural" quest for autonomy. In fact, it was also arrived at by experience. In both the ARC and the Title V programs, early efforts to elicit collaboration from federal agencies failed. Efforts to influence others proved to be an inefficient use of executive time. External resistance deflected the organization from coordinating in a large sphere.

For the forum of peers, as exemplified by the Title II commissions, the need to adjust to other organizations is inherent in the form. Being dependent on contributions of activity by others, whose primary purposes are pursued outside the forum, and lacking inducements to offer these others, this type of organization finds it hard to sustain any sort of activity at a high level. The Title II commissions have not completed the comprehensive, joint, coordinated plans they are supposed to prepare, and they have not set project priorities.

In short, while particular adaptations to the organizational environment vary widely from one type of regional organization to another, the common result is either specialization of activity or a low level of activity. Regional action proceeds within a narrow sphere or at a slow pace.


## The Feasibility of Regional Organization

If only because regional organizations are unusual forms, an analysis of how they function and which function best must be supplemented with consideration of what is most feasible. Regional organizations are structural innovations by definition. Then what kinds of innovation are possible, and under what circumstances? It is striking that the "strong" forms of regional organization remain unique occurrences, or nearly so. The organizations that have been widely reproduced are the "weak" ones, confined to planning or co-ordination. Is there then some systemic obstacle to generalizing the strong forms, and if so, how do they occur at all? Is it inevitable that generalized forms be weak?

The main thing to be said about the strong organizations (the leading cases) is that they are political accidents, the product of ad hoc coalitions whose success was fortuitous in important respects. Each resulted from circumstances that singly and in combination were quite special and contained a large element of chance. Natural or social conditions created a singular opportunity for initiatives. The existence of the Muscle Shoals plant on the Tennessee River happened to raise the issue of ownership, out of which came an unusual proposal for developing the river. A Supreme Court decree in 1954 and a major flood in 1955 precipitated action in the Delaware basin. The discovery of Appalachian poverty by politicians and the national media in the early 1960s and a severe flood in the spring of 1963 gave state officials an opportunity to appeal for special aid. In at least two of the cases, fortuitous events in national politics were ultimately essential to success: for the TVA, Roosevelt's victory in 1932; for the ARC, Kennedy's victory in 1960 and then the Democratic landslide of 1964. In all three cases, intensely motivated leadership helped overcome the normal obstacles to change. One or a few persons were fervently committed to creating the new organization and prepared to persist against unfavorable odds. It happened also that for a variety of reasons the predictable opposition of federal line agencies could be overcome. In the case of TVA, the Corps of Engineers, which was the only agency immediately and obviously threatened, apparently had neither the time nor the opportunity to mount a defense early in 1933. Three decades later the executive agencies did try to kill the DRBC, only to be overruled by the White House, whereupon they rationalized acceptance on the ground that the occurrence was unique. In the case of the ARC, the new organization did not initially appear to be a threatening alternative to federal agencies. In sum, regional organizations as major innovations are political accidents, and accidents are not likely to happen twice. The fortuitous combination of opportunity, determined leadership, catalytic events, and weak or distracted opposition that accounts for the appearance of the leading cases cannot be expected to recur repeatedly.

The generalized organizations, on the other hand, are the product of central planning. All were planned by the Bureau of the Budget, as the principal staff agency of the President and his adviser on organization and management. The Bureau took the initiative in proposing the Federal Regional Councils and the Title II commissions, both of which arose out of its enduring interest in improving federal interagency coordination. The Title V commissions, however, were essentially the product of political forces over which the Bureau had no control. It engaged in drafting Title V to prevent the Senate from generalizing the Appalachian program and organization: if generalization were to occur, the Bureau wanted to take charge of the design. What it produced was consistent with its designs for the Title II commissions and the Federal Regional Councils.

The Bureau's proposals for regional organization, though sweeping in application, which is to say nationwide, have otherwise been modest. They have included only limited departures from what is established and routine, whether in intergovernmental or interagency relations. The organizations the Bureau has proposed have all been restricted to planning and coordination. It has never proposed a regional organization with the right either to spend money for anything but its own administrative needs or to make commitments of expenditure on behalf of the federal government. It sought to prevent an operating role for the DRBC and ARC.[3] It has never proposed a regional organization in which interested federal agencies would not be directly represented or whose actions the agencies would not have a right to review. Its view of intergovernmental relations prescribes a clear legal and functional distinction between federal and state agents. The regional organizations it has designed were clearly to be federal instrumentalities, subordinate to federal executive supervision, no matter what their composition. It either has not included state members (the Federal Regional Councils), has given the President the right to appoint state members (the initial proposal for Title II), or has refrained from promising federal membership (the initial proposal for Title V).

There appears to be a trade-off between depth of organizational change on a regional scale and breadth of change. It has been possible to create organizations that depart substantially from established forms and that command important resources of authority and revenue, but only in isolated cases. Such change has not occurred systematically and comprehensively. When forms are created through central planning and are inaugurated throughout the system, the federal government's autonomy vis-à-vis the states is protected, the prerogatives and interests of federal executive agencies are taken into account, and actual or anticipated commitments of federal funds are curtailed. Innovation is much more limited.

A consideration of federal coordination problems and of federal-state relations, to which the next two chapters are devoted, will help explain why the Office of Management and Budget acts so conservatively. Evaluating the regional organizations' responses to the need for federal interagency coordination and for decentralization of federal executive action also will provide additional basis for judging regional organizations.

3. The Bureau was twelve years old in 1933 when the TVA was created, and still part of the Department of the Treasury, very small, and engaged only in budget review. Its management and legislative clearance functions were yet to develop fully, and it took no part in considering the TVA bill. Later, it was the source of the Government Corporation Control Act, which imposed a variety of financial controls on government corporations, including TVA. On the evolution of the Bureau's clearance function, see Richard Neustadt, "Presidency and Legislation: The Growth of Central Clearance," *American Political Science Review*, vol. 48 (September 1954), pp. 641–71.

# [9]

# Federal Coordination

THIS CHAPTER assesses various responses to the need for coordinating federal agency actions. None of the different approaches to coordination embodied in the regional organizations is sufficiently superior to the rest to make it preferable. Nor is any particular approach so clearly successful as to contribute substantially to justification of the regional form.

## The Single Federal Member

The single federal members do many things. They represent the regional organization in relations with Congress, the Office of Management and Budget (OMB), and other parts of the federal government. They defend budget requests, seek new legislation, and defend the organization in jurisdictional disputes. Some of them perform a share of executive functions such as definition of goals and of staff tasks. They also perform lateral coordination with federal line agencies. The federal member often functions as a leader and central coordinator of the state members, providing services to state governments, rewarding them with federal benefits for participating in the organization, inducing them to conform to federally inspired policies, and negotiating differences among them. But the one thing the federal member almost never does is be a leader and central coordinator of federal executive agencies. What is theoretically his main function is the one he is least able to perform.

He is unable to perform because his status as presidential agent and putative central coordinator is of little or no use to him as a means of influencing federal agencies. Although he is a presidential agent, he does not outrank department heads, who are presidential agents too. He is either coequal or lower in rank. And although in theory he is supposed to be the central coordinator of agency actions, this theory is not universally shared or fully believed in. In particular, it is not shared by OMB, the organization whose cooperation is presumably most needed if the theory is to become reality. For the federal members of regional organizations to make use of presidential power to influence line agencies would require their having access to that power; they would need to have at their disposal, at least indirectly and implicitly, the sanctions and rewards of the President's principal staff agency. However, OMB has shown no interest in using the federal members as agents or allies in central coordination. Federal members, should they be inclined to venture forth and settle interagency differences, have no reason to suppose that OMB would be behind them.

The explanation for OMB's indifference can perhaps be found in the origins of the organizations. Regional organizations with a single member as agency coordinator have been foisted upon OMB and are definitely not its notion of how to improve coordination. When the Delaware River Basin Commission (DRBC) and the commissions for economic development made their appearance, management officials in the Budget Bureau were concerned mainly that they not be in conflict with federal line agencies. Hence the Bureau sought to narrow their functions and to arrange lateral clearance between them and line agencies. Title II commissions did begin on the initiative of the Budget Bureau, or at least of its deputy director in the late 1950s, but there were important differences between what the Bureau designed and what Congress enacted, with the result that the commissions did not evolve as instruments of presidential control. Their accountability is diffuse, and OMB has shown no subsequent interest in promoting their evolution.

It might be argued, then, that the single federal members fail as interagency coordinators because they get no backing from the presidency. In relations with the agencies, they cannot exploit the hierarchical superiority of the President or their presumed special relation to him because in fact they have no special relation. OMB, which would have to be a partner in this relation, either ignores them or treats them and their organizations as part of the coordination problem, to be subjected to central checks and scrutiny just as are officials in line agencies specialized by function. As a description of the relation between federal members and OMB, this is accurate, but as an interpretation of why the members fail as central coordinators, it is inadequate, for it presumes that OMB could be of great assistance to the federal members if only it wanted to be, and that its institutional habits and inhibitions (or whatever prevents its standing behind them) alone keep them from drawing on the powers of the presidency. The case of the Federal Regional Councils suggests that this presumption errs in overestimating the power and misconceiving the present role of the President's principal staff agency.

## The Interagency Council

It is commonly recognized that the interagency council has serious limitations as a coordinator, and the experience of the Federal Regional Councils confirms this.[1] The councils tend to avoid conflict, cannot resolve the conflicts they cannot avoid, and are inactive or active mainly on matters that are of marginal interest to the member agencies, such as disaster relief. What is interesting about their particular experience is that it constitutes a fairly clear test of OMB's powers as a central coordinator of federal agency operations. While OMB does not chair the councils, they are its chosen form for interagency coordination at the regional level. Without OMB's efforts, they would disappear, but despite its best efforts, they continue to display the standard defects of the coordinating form. OMB has not been able to induce them to resolve conflicts in grant-in-aid administration, nor has it been able to help them at the Washington level the few times they did try to cope with agency differences or to work out a common regional policy, as in the cases of the Hunts Point multiservice center and equal employment opportunity in the Kansas City region.

The President does not have by law the right to say what the federal policies for citizen participation should be in St. Louis, or

1. For general appraisals of the form, see Harold Seidman, *Politics, Position, and Power: The Dynamics of Federal Organization* (Oxford University Press, 1970), chap. 6; and Basil J. Mott, *Anatomy of a Coordinating Council* (University of Pittsburgh Press, 1968).

what the equal employment policies should be in the Kansas City region, or what policies ought to guide the granting of funds by the Department of Health, Education, and Welfare or of Housing and Urban Development in a Puerto Rican area of the Bronx. His staff agency therefore has no such right. OMB has no authority to determine national policies, and no claim to the kind of political competence needed for deciding their application to particular places and circumstances. When the law is unclear and line agencies having discretion come into conflict in the use of their discretion, OMB may try to prescribe the content of settlements. Its reluctance to do so seems to be compounded of several elements: a wish to maintain institutional neutrality, thereby serving the enduring interest of the presidency in executive coordination while avoiding too deep an engagement in the choices of any particular president; a limited ability to invoke the President's name in resolving issues that all participants know are not important enough to engage his personal attention; and a reluctance to commit the prestige of the presidential office to actions that it lacks sanctions to enforce. Hence management officials in OMB prefer a detached role and confine themselves to exhorting and cajoling agencies to arrive at coordinated positions. Playing even this much part in field administration is something new, dating from a commitment in the late 1960s to engage in operational coordination. OMB's power continues to reside in the functions of budget review and legislative clearance, and to be negative and critical. This power is not readily convertible to use in settling policy or jurisdictional disputes between agencies at the point of grant-in-aid administration. Whereas OMB is able to perform budget review and legislative clearance functions by sitting in judgment on matters that reach it routinely, operational coordination requires a far greater degree of initiative and willingness to take risks. Because of the limits of OMB's power as operational coordinator, its sponsorship and continuing interest have not been of much help to the Federal Regional Councils, whose experience as coordinators has been typical of the form rather than distinctively successful. Nor, presumably, could OMB be of greater help to the single federal members of other regional organizations. What it cannot do itself through the medium of the councils, it cannot enable others to do.[2]

2. The lack of top program coordination has frequently been identified as a defect

Unhelpful though the OMB's negative powers are to the Federal Regional Councils, when viewed against the broader background of the regional organizations' history they are effective and important in managing the coordination problem. This study has approached regional organizations as if they were a means of improving coordination, but they can just as plausibly be viewed as contributors to the problem. *Any* new organization is potentially a contributor, on the assumption that the essence of the coordination problem is the multiplication of specialized yet interdependent organizations. The size of the coordination problem increases with the size and variety of the organizational universe. If the new organizations' functions overlap those of existing organizations, as is true with the leading regional organizations, the difficulties increase further. And if they challenge the very principles on which the organizational universe is ordered, the difficulties are compounded again. Regional organizations with operating and management authority, by substituting area for function, would revise the most fundamental principle of federal administrative organization. In the words of a Water Resources Council task force:

all the . . . Cabinet Departments and independent agencies perform certain functional responsibilities over the whole of the nation. It would create intolerable duplication and confusion if the nation were now to establish a series of river basin commissions throughout the United States, with management and operating responsibilities, to conduct and operate regional projects in the very same areas in which the national functional departments are now operating.[3]

The same could be said of the commissions for economic devel-

---

of American government. These findings from regional organizations illustrate the familiar point. See Herman Somers, *Presidential Agency: The Office of War Mobilization and Reconversion* (Harvard University Press, 1950), chap. 7; and Arthur Maass, "In Accord with the Program of the President?" *Public Policy*, vol. 4 (1953), pp. 77–93. The Heineman task force (President's Task Force on Government Organization), created by President Johnson in 1967, recommended that an Office of Program Coordination be created in the Executive Office of the President for this purpose. A minority dissented, arguing that the Bureau of the Budget should perform the function. The report was not made public, nor were its recommendations adopted. In the late 1960s the Bureau of the Budget committed itself to engaging in operational coordination, and this new commitment has been reaffirmed with an ever-increasing emphasis on management functions and on operational coordination as one aspect of management.

3. "The Position of the Federal Government on the Consent Bill for the Susquehanna Basin Compact," Report of the Task Force on River Basin Management Institutions, April 17, 1969; Water Resources Council files.

opment if their function were to overlap those of federal line agencies and be independently funded in large amounts. OMB's negative powers of central coordination are used to contain the chaos. Through legislative clearance, it is able to limit entries into the organizational universe and to bargain for acceptable forms. Through budget review, it can scrutinize the activity of the actual forms that gain admission.

Without OMB's defense of organizational doctrines, the organization of American government would be even more chaotic than it is. OMB has tried to preserve certain elemental principles of administration and management. It has tried to sharpen the division of functions among departments and to group related functions within the same department, to preserve and clarify accountability to the President, to keep the President's span of control narrow, to improve internal management of agencies, and to develop standard administrative procedures.[4] These principles have led it to oppose regional organizations whose functions duplicate those of federal line agencies and to oppose making such organizations independent of line agencies, with federal members reporting directly to the President. If it were not for OMB's efforts to prevent federal coordination from becoming worse, there would be more regional organizations in American government with bigger budgets and broader powers. In particular, the Title V commissions would have followed the pattern of the Appalachian Regional Commission (ARC).

To those who have a taste for innovation and are prepared to pay the cost in chaos, OMB's positions on organizational matters may seem too rigid. Adherence to doctrine makes it conservative, and this conservatism has been reinforced, with respect to regional organizations anyway, by an overriding and pervasive commitment to economy. The Budget Bureau tried very early to head off the Appalachian program, not because it feared a new regional organization, which was a long way off and not the chief worry, but because it anticipated a large new claim on the Treasury. It also

4. Seidman, *Politics, Position, and Power*, especially chap. 1; and John D. Millett, "The Division of Administrative Management in the Federal Bureau of the Budget: A Description and Evaluation" (prepared for the Institute of Public Administration under contract to the Commission on Organization of the Executive Branch of Government, June 1948; processed).

feared, this time incorrectly, that the DRBC would be the source of irresistible claims for expenditures. Its effort to keep the Title V commissions within a line agency is motivated partly by a desire to keep their spending under control.

Doctrinal conservatism is reinforced by procedures and constituency relations. It is OMB's standard practice to solicit reactions to new bills from the federal departments. It clears legislation only after seeking a consensus among them. Organizational innovations that run counter to their interests are obstructed in this way, as well as by OMB's independent application of management doctrines. The odds may seem to be hopelessly against such innovations, yet that supposition does not quite square with the history recounted here. If the proponents of new and unusual forms have enough support from Congress and the President, organizational doctrine goes down the drain, as it did when the DRBC was approved. OMB exists in a political milieu. Like everyone else there, it bargains for what it can get.

The contest over new forms does not necessarily end with their adoption, and OMB's budget examiners may keep a close watch on cases that are expected to present a coordination problem. How successful they are in preventing new regional organizations from developing operating functions and encroaching on line agencies depends in part on the fidelity of the federal member to central supervision and on his finesse within the regional organization, to which he owes loyalty too. It also depends on the organization's support in Congress. The DRBC, which has neither an independent source of revenue nor a congressional constituency, has not encroached on the federal departments. The ARC, with powerful support in the Senate Public Works Committee, has acquired most of the administrative responsibility for the special Appalachian program and has extended that program into departmental domains, particularly with its efforts on behalf of child development.

In sum, OMB is able, through the use of its negative powers of legislative clearance and budget review, to influence the composition of the organizational universe and to constrain the behavior of some members so as to reduce overlapping jurisdictions and keep lines of authority and responsibility more or less clear. It is far less able to initiate measures of central coordination so as to improve consistency among ongoing departmental programs. Its powers, though considerable, are imperfectly adaptable to the demands made on it and to the tasks it has set for itself.

## Decentralization as an Approach to Coordination

If central coordination in the federal government is weak, it may be preferable to avoid dependence on a central coordinator and to decentralize coordination of federal functions. This can be done either by delegating the coordinating function to the chief executives of other governments altogether—the states or their local subdivisions—as occurs in the ARC, or by combining a wide range of federal functions within one relatively autonomous organization having a subnational jurisdiction, as in the Tennessee Valley Authority (TVA).

The first of these alternatives has found great favor in Washington in recent years. It is an important part of the rationale for revenue sharing, the model cities program, and administrative actions by OMB that give state and local chief executives a chance to review and comment on federal grants-in-aid within their jurisdictions. In their mildest form, as exemplified by such review and comment or by the simplification of grants, these actions are designed to open federal programs to state and local executive influence and to avoid federal determination of state and local program choices. The argument is that state and local chief executives have their own priorities, which should not be distorted by narrowly categorical financial offerings from the federal government. In their extreme form, which is revenue sharing, these measures put federal funds at the unrestricted disposal of state and local governments. The coordination problem is dealt with by default. The need to order federal purposes in importance, to harmonize conflicting federal programs and purposes, or to integrate them with local programs and purposes is avoided by the federal government's act of self-denial—it enunciates no purposes.

The proponents of such measures recognize that this is coordination by default, and they supplement proposals for decentralization with proposals for improving the "planning" or "management" or "coordinating" capability of state and local chief executives. Specifically, these usually take the form of grants-in-aid to hire planning or management specialists. If the federal government is going to increase its dependence on other governments, these other governments should be made better, and they are to be made better by enabling their chief executives to behave as ideal-typical chief executives in a modern liberal government, which is to say a government committed to problem solving. The governor or mayor should be able to identify social problems and needs; to decide, according to some criteria of rationality or political responsibility, which problems "ought" to be solved and which needs ought to be met; and to allocate expenditures according to these choices, coordinating administrative organizations as necessary. His choices should not be determined irrationally, by the inertia of bureaucracies or by federal financial incentives that may be inappropriate to the particular circumstances of his government. As an effort to improve the structure or rationality of state and local governments, this is tactically analogous to efforts of a generation ago that prescribed merit systems of personnel for state administrative agencies and concentrated responsibility for achieving federal objectives in state line agencies. In substance, however, it is a reaction against such efforts, for these earlier requirements are now deprecated for the power they imparted to professional specialists at the expense of politically responsible (because elected) chief executives and are regarded as contributors to the coordination problem.[5]

Although no regional organization was designed specifically to incorporate this particular theory of coordination, the joint organizations constitute in varying degrees a test of its feasibility, for they all rest on the assumption that a single state agent can enunciate the state government's position. The single state agent in the

5. Selma J. Mushkin, "Decentralized Decisionmaking of New Fiscal Federalism," in *Regional Planning Issues*, Hearings before the Subcommittee on Urban Affairs of the Joint Economic Committee, 92 Cong. 1 sess. (1971), pt. 2, pp. 263–74; Seidman, *Politics, Position, and Power*, chap. 5; Deil S. Wright, *Federal Grants-in-Aid: Perspectives and Alternatives* (Washington: American Enterprise Institute for Public Policy Research, 1968), chap. 8; Advisory Commission on Intergovernmental Relations, *Fiscal Balance in the American Federal System*, vol. 1 (Washington: ACIR, 1967), pp. 200–35; David B. Walker, "Curbing the 'New Feudalists,'" *The Bureaucrat*, vol. 1 (Spring 1972), pp. 42–45; The President's Advisory Council on Executive Reorganization (the Ash Council), *Memoranda for the President of the United States: Establishment of a Department of Natural Resources; Organization for Social and Economic Programs* (1971), app. 8, pp.147–50.

joint organizations is analogous to the single federal agent and is similarly dependent on the functioning of central planning and coordinating mechanisms within his government. In the ARC alone, the strategy has been made explicit and forms an important part of the organization's self-conception and rationale for existence.

In no case is this theory of coordination by the state chief executive tested fairly. Joint regional organizations have not been nearly important enough compared to all the other claims on the governor's attention for him to take much interest in what they do. This has been especially the case for the water resources organizations; state governments have little stake in regional planning for water resources development. The commissions for economic development are a somewhat fairer test since grants-in-aid give the states a tangible stake in the organization, the governor or his designee represents the states, and, within limits, the governor has discretion with respect to the use of the funds. Yet even in the ARC, with its relatively large amounts of money and its reliance on the governor as central coordinator, the regional commission remains of slight interest to most governors, who have made no attempt to use it as a base from which to effect central coordination.

Indeed, the whole notion that the state or local chief executive ought to be a priority setter and central coordinator seems to be based more on the perceptions of management theorists in Washington than on the felt needs of state or local chief executives. While governors and mayors are bewildered by the incomprehensibility of federal grant programs and greatly annoyed by red tape, it does not follow that they seek to enlarge their own responsibility for choice.[6] Nor would a capacity for central choice and coordination follow from the desire. No one claims that state or local chief executives have such a capacity now; the purpose of federal planning and management grants would be to impart it. In effect, federal grants would induce formation of counterpart agencies to OMB, just as grants from federal line agencies have induced formation of state and local counterparts. President Nixon's Advisory Council on Executive Organization (the Ash Council) actually recommended that OMB administer the management grants. It

6. For data on their attitudes, see Seidman, *Politics, Position, and Power*, pp. 154–56.

seems unlikely, however, that state and local counterparts of OMB would surpass the parent organization's own techniques of program coordination.

Giving other governments more discretion in the use of federal funds may be good or bad but will not "solve" the federal government's coordination problem, unless to transfer it is a solution.

The remaining technique is that exemplified by TVA: to incorporate within one highly autonomous regional organization related functions that elsewhere are distributed more widely. Theoretically this idea is appealing, and its embodiment in TVA doubtless accounts for much of the Authority's acclaim. Certainly, TVA's form precludes the gross manifestations of conflict that occurred between the Bureau of Reclamation and the Corps of Engineers two or three decades ago. One organization alone has been responsible for developing the river. There were no competing, incompatible plans for the Tennessee. The Authority developed the river for a variety of purposes—flood control, navigation, and generation of power—and sought to harmonize them when to do so was unusual in American government. Inevitably, coordination problems were internalized; though the form precluded interagency rivalries in their classic and extreme manifestation, TVA experienced sharp interpersonal disputes in the governing board, and to some extent these were reproduced throughout the organization. The response to internal conflict was mutual adjustment through specialization and decentralization. At first each of the three directors assumed control of a particular aspect of policy and administration. Later the personal and policy differences within the board were subdued and the administrative functions of the three members were taken over by a single official, but the major elements of the organization continued to maintain a high degree of independence from one another. There was nothing out of the ordinary in this. TVA's response to internal conflict was of a kind common enough in heterogeneous organizations. On the other hand, there was nothing here to suggest the incomparable superiority of the autonomous regional corporation as an integrative instrument. Eventually, electric power operations came to predominate overwhelmingly, although an ideal of coordination would probably have called for harmonization of a wide range of related activities. Also, because

TVA's displacement of federal line agencies was only partial, external coordination problems developed, especially in the field of agriculture.

In view of the limited effectiveness of the organizations as coordinators, the justification for regional organizations must be what they do on a regional scale rather than their alleged improvements in federal executive coordination. Whether the Federal Regional Councils, which are primarily coordinators, are worth sustaining on that ground alone may be debated; but while the gains in coordination are slight, the potential costs are slight too, inasmuch as the councils represent federal agencies rather than rivaling their operations.

## Reflections on Coordination

While the organizations embody different techniques of federal coordination, they rest in common on a perception of coordination as a problem of organizational relations, to be remedied by organizational means. The problem to which they are addressed is lack of coordination among federal executive agencies in planning or in administration, and they respond either by displacing old organizations with a newly comprehensive one (TVA); by bringing representatives of established organizations together in a coordinating forum (Federal Regional Councils and Title II commissions); or by creating a single coordinating agent within an organization whose functions are defined by area (the DRBC, the regional commissions for economic development, and again the Title II commissions). Their deficiencies in turn tend to be explicable on organizational grounds. The new multipurpose organization on the model of TVA is unable to displace or significantly influence a large number of established organizations, and tends to specialize in one or a few areas that are relatively open to its jurisdictional claims. The coordinating council depends on the willingness of member organizations to make mutual adjustments. The single federal agent in a regional organization is deflected from a coordinating role by the innate resistance of line organizations, which he has no means of overcoming, and by the claims of his own organization to activity on its behalf before Congress and OMB. For the single federal member, maintaining his own organization inevitably takes preference over influencing others.

Defined as a problem of interagency relations in the performance of executive functions, the coordination problem is real enough but inadequately comprehended. Underlying it is a different yet related problem: that of defining federal purposes so as to guide executive behavior down common or compatible paths and to circumscribe the scope and intensity of interagency differences. Interagency conflict is a symptom of this larger coordination problem, even if it is treated as though it were the original cause. This larger problem of unclear or inadequate federal policy is illustrated in both of the major areas of activity with which regional organizations are concerned. In the past two decades, substantial progress has been made in elucidating criteria for calculating the benefits and costs of federal water resources projects and for allocating the costs among purposes and prospective beneficiaries, but there has been no comparable progress in determining what values should be attached to competing purposes.[7] In programs of regional economic development, "fundamental questions relating to rationale, objectives, and strategy have not been resolved in the legislative mandate or in the administrative process," according to a leading regional economist with experience in both the Appalachian and Title V programs. "The simplest questions of 'what,' 'why,' and 'how' still beg for unequivocal answers."[8] Lack of purpose has been one of the major causes of demoralization in the Title V commissions. When the Department of Commerce tried to develop guidelines for the commissions in the late 1960s, it soon gave up. The country was too diverse and the development problems were too varied. The ARC began with a strategy of sorts—that investments should be concentrated in areas with potential for growth—but has paid steadily less attention to this.

Lack of clear policy guidance from a central source is one of the important limitations on the conduct of the single federal mem-

7. Peter O. Steiner, *Public Expenditure Budgeting* (Brookings Institution, 1969), pp. 91–102.

8. Benjamin Chinitz, "National Policy for Regional Development," in John F. Kain and John R. Meyer, eds., *Essays in Regional Economics* (Harvard University Press, 1971), p. 22.

ber as central coordinator; not only does he lack influence over the agencies, he lacks a specified set of objectives to pursue. If he is a vigorous executive with clear programmatic objectives of his own, he may personally supply the lack, since his freedom is considerable, but that is an exceptional occurrence. In sum, the common experience of regional organizations suggests the importance of viewing the coordination problem also as a problem of definition of purpose, which is a legislative function. So conceived, it is no easier to "solve" than conflict in interagency relations. Its true source is the heterogeneity of opinions and interests in American society, and the openness of government to a variety of influences— an openness that is not matched, and never can be, by the capacity of government to rationalize and make consistent either legislative or administrative acts. The point is that any attempt at rationalization must take in a much larger universe than executive agencies and a wider range of techniques than executive reorganization.

# [10]

# Decentralization

DECENTRALIZATION may be viewed as one way of facilitating definitions of federal purpose. One explanation for deficiencies in making and applying federal policy is the variety of local circumstance. The need to make federal statements of purpose universally applicable means that it is difficult to make them clear. If the country could be divided into a few relatively homogeneous areas, the parochialism of state and local governments might be transcended and federal policy liberated from the presumption of uniformity and thus improved. Such, at least, has been one of the rationales for organizing on a regional scale.

As a class, regional organizations are a technique of decentralization, and the types within this class incorporate additional techniques, of which the most common is jointness, as found in the Delaware River Basin Commission (DRBC), the Title V commissions, and the Title II commissions. By bringing state and federal officials together in a single organization, jointness systematically opens federal executive decisions to the influence of other governments. The results depend both on the states' ability to exploit this opportunity and on the authority exercised by the regional organization. The states are at a disadvantage within joint regional organizations in comparison to the federal members or the staff, but a more important constraint on the effects of jointness is the limited power of the organizations themselves.

## Jointness

Perhaps the best way to test the states' ability to make use of jointness would be to examine the results of federal-state conflict.

When the two sides are at odds over policy, who wins? Are the states able to secure federal adaptations to particular regional conditions or interests? These questions cannot readily be answered because no pattern of federal-state conflict exists. In the Appalachian Regional Commission (ARC) the recurring differences have been among the states, over allocation of funds for programs in which no formula has existed (health care demonstrations, child development), and between the staff and the states, over the conditions to be attached to grants, with the staff seeking to impose restrictions that the states have resisted. In the DRBC the first major issue, over allocation of water, pitted the states against one another. In the decision on water quality standards, the federal member, three states, and the staff were on one side, with the fourth state on the other. Nor is there a pattern of federal-state conflict in the Title V and Title II commissions. It turns out that whether these joint organizations enable the states to win their battles with the federal government is a moot point, since they have very few battles. Thus to judge the consequences of jointness one must look at the respective roles of the principal components of the organizations—federal member, state members, and staff—rather than at the outcome of conflicts.

In general, the pattern of federal-state relations that prevails outside of joint regional organizations is reproduced within them. In theory the two levels of government meet as equals, but the federal side tends to be "more equal" than the states. Some of the advantages of the federal member are formal; for instance, that the federal government need not be bound by decisions of the DRBC and that it holds the chairman's office in the Title II commissions. Formal differences are reinforced by informal ones. Jointness does not alter the fundamental fact that the federal government gives grants whereas the state governments get them, or the fact that federal agencies carry out most water resources development and hence do most of the planning for it.

Major initiatives usually come from the staffs. The disadvantages of the state members in relation to the staffs are those common to any group of part-time policy makers: they assemble infrequently to attend to the business of the organization and in the interim are engaged in many other activities. Whether they are heads of departments or attached to the governor's staff, the state members of regional organizations are likely to have a large amount of demanding other business. In contrast, the single federal member serves full time and is thus able in varying degrees to share in the day-to-day policy making and executive direction of the organization.

The staffs of both the ARC and the DRBC, which are the most active of the joint organizations, inevitably have had a major impact on organizational choices and in general have been progressive in their choice of policy positions and reformist in their orientation toward state governments. This orientation, like the inability of state members to participate actively in the daily conduct of the organizations, tends to make state governments objects of action by the joint regional organizations rather than independent, highly influential actors within them.

The value of jointness to the states is limited by the handicaps they bring to the organization or encounter there; but a more fundamental restriction is the limited power of the organization as a whole. The benefit to the states in being part of a joint organization is determined initially by what the organization does. Having access to the uses of federal authority is no asset where not much federal authority is being put to use. Sharing in trivial or superfluous decisions is no great privilege.

In fact, the regional organizations have very limited rights to act on behalf of the federal government. While the executive branch has acquiesced to the formation of a number of joint organizations, it has never concurred in principle to the creation of joint organizations having operating, management, or regulatory functions, and it has declined to cooperate in the exercise of such powers when granted, as in the DRBC.[1]

1. Whereas the DRBC is unable to exercise its powers fully, the ARC exercises more than the law originally gave. Why, if jointness has inhibited the DRBC's functioning as an operating agency, has it not had the same effect on the ARC? In part, the explanation is that the combination of jointness with broad powers in the Delaware compact alerted federal opposition at the outset. Taken at face value, the Delaware compact, a weighty legal instrument, would have given a regional agency the power to bind the federal government or to act in its stead. Although the Appalachian Regional Development Act created a joint commission, this was done by a federal law, the commission appeared to receive no important powers, and it was incidental to the spending program, which would be carried out by line agencies. Besides, the two organizations engage the interests of federal line agencies in very different ways. The DRBC appears to supersede federal natural-resources and regulatory agencies in the Delaware basin. At least initially, the ARC gave no sign of superseding or rivaling federal agencies, but was simply a means of their receiving more funds for categorical

In view of the resistance of the executive branch to jointness, it is probably less pertinent to examine the results in specific cases than to ask what the cases show about the merits. The wisdom of joint organization is still an issue in intergovernmental relations, but the issue has never been publicly debated, and the positions of the interested parties remain unarticulated. This is unfortunate, for jointness involves an important question of principle in the federal system: are the federal and state governments distinct and independent governments with obligations to distinct electorates or are they interdependent parts of what actually has become a unitary system though federal in form? It might be argued that in the course of evolution to a unitary system, the various governments have lost their separate identities and functions, and the states have become administrative agents of the federal government. If the two levels of government are sharply distinct and independent, joint organizations are obviously an anomaly that should be removed from American government. If the two levels are thoroughly integrated as in a unitary system, jointness is of no great importance and should pose no serious problems. In reality, the condition of the federal system is between these extremes. The levels of government are neither fully independent nor fully integrated. Jointness has developed more or less as an experiment and, as is characteristic of American government, without much debate or reflection. It does pose problems, especially for the federal government, which has most at stake.

One federal objection, originating with the Department of Justice, has a constitutional foundation. It holds that the federal government may not constitutionally delegate federal authority to an agency in which the federal government can be outvoted. In the case of the federal-interstate compacts, this objection has been met

---

grant programs—far from displacing them, it enlarged their budgets. It has tended to evolve in the direction of displacement or at least competition, but this has been a relatively subtle process and is not far advanced. Finally, differences in supervision account for the differing evolution of the two commissions. The DRBC is more fully integrated with the executive branch than is the ARC, inasmuch as the federal member is a department head (the secretary of the interior), and it is more closely supervised by federal executive agencies, either the Water Resources Council or the Office of Management and Budget. The federal member of the ARC holds no other federal office and is free of departmental supervision in policy matters.

by giving the federal government a veto. Because it cannot be bound against its will, its powers are protected.

The other principal source of opposition to jointness has been the Office of Management and Budget, which has both spoken for the Justice Department and had reservations of its own. Until the early 1960s, the Budget Bureau opposed formal federal membership in interstate organizations, no matter how limited their powers.[2] After the Delaware compact was enacted, the Bureau changed its position and acquiesced in the formation of joint organizations with planning and coordinating functions only. The basis of the Bureau's objections to jointness is hard to trace, but resistance appears to have been grounded in interpretation of the President's powers of appointment, which this agency is thoroughly committed to protect. In OMB's view, administrative agents who spend or plan for the spending of federal funds should be federal agents, unambiguously accountable to the President. He should appoint them or one of his appointees should appoint them. It seems, then, that what is at stake in jointness is the principle of accountability, which for some time management specialists in the Budget Bureau sought to preserve in pure form.[3]

Yet what seems to be merely a defense of dogma has deeper purposes. The OMB's overriding and pervasive commitment, shared by all parts of that organization, is to the control of expenditures. In its eyes, the universe is composed of claimants on the Treasury. To control expenditures, it cannot rely on only the formal processes of budget review, which are nearly a last resort. It needs also to discourage development of new and powerful sources of demand. It must prevent federal agents from entering into commitments that it may be unable to limit or reverse. This in part explains its attitude toward joint organizations. It rightly sees state governments as major claimants on federal funds—a class of claimants constitutionally immune from presidential direction. It sees federal line officials, especially those in the field, as claimants on the Treasury

2. Harold Seidman, *Politics, Position, and Power: The Dynamics of Federal Organization* (Oxford University Press, 1970), pp. 244–50; *Delaware River Basin Compact*, Hearings before Subcommittee No. 1 of the House Judiciary Committee, 87 Cong. 1 sess. (1961), pp. 69–71.

3. See Seidman, *Politics, Position, and Power*, pp. 73, 245–50.

too, eager to build, expand, and spend. Although these officials are formally subject to presidential direction, in fact the Bureau's power to reduce or reject their spending proposals is limited; and if they enter into alliances with state officials in support of particular spending proposals, the combined force of their demands, if backed by Congress, may be irresistible. OMB therefore suspects all organizational arrangements that foster alliances between federal field officials and state and local officials. It dislikes organizational arrangements that may lead to implied or express promises of federal funds. In short, it dislikes arrangements that build on the centrifugal force of American politics at its own expense. It therefore dislikes joint regional organizations. The state members are inherently uncontrollable, and the federal members are too likely to become captives of state interests that want funds.

If the case against jointness remains largely unarticulated, so does the case for it. In truth, sponsors of joint regional organizations want federal participation mainly because they want the access to federal powers or funds that will come with it. Without federal membership and support, no regional organization today is likely to amount to much. When justifications for jointness are offered, they are cast in general, indisputable terms such as "improved Federal-state coordination" and "more effective" government action. Thus, for example, when the Title II commission chairmen wrote to OMB in defense of their organizations, they declared:

Effective natural resources policy cannot be approached on the assumption that Federal activities and state activities can be planned and administered in isolation from each other. On the contrary, it can be stated categorically that the physical environment and natural resources of the country will not be effectively conserved, developed, and utilized unless the action of all levels of government are purposefully shaped into coordinated programs.[4]

There is here the germ of a serious justification for joint organizations, a justification that might be expected to have considerable appeal to management officials in OMB. Increasingly, the federal government depends on state governments for realizing its pur-

4. Frederick O. Rouse et al. to Kenneth Kugel, Office of Management and Budget, Program Coordination Division, no date (1972); New England River Basins Commission files, Boston.

poses. Whatever improves integration between the levels of government might be expected to improve realization of federal programmatic aims. Jointness is a technique that the federal government might turn to advantage; joint organizations could be a medium for federal influence over state governments as well as the reverse. Proponents of joint organizations ask OMB to accept that view.

Which assumption about the joint organizations is more nearly correct? Do they become uncontrollable claimants on federal funds, more demanding and powerful as a result of being joint? Or do they improve realization of federal purposes?

Results vary among the cases, which suggests that the effects of jointness are marginal. In determining how they function as claimants and as federal-state coordinators, what the organizations do is more important than how they are structured. In particular, those that administer grants-in-aid must be distinguished from those that plan and coordinate the use of water resources.[5]

The commissions for economic development, whose reason for being is to deliver federal funds to selected states, inevitably function mainly as claimants on their behalf. The ARC has been able to do this very successfully, and jointness has contributed to the organization's considerable capacity to maintain itself. Having a joint headquarters structure, with one chief executive who is employed by the states, gives the ARC exceptional freedom. The states' regional representative, being free of obligation to the executive branch, can lobby at will for new benefits.[6] When the Nixon

5. Federal management experts appear to make a distinction themselves. The President's Advisory Council on Executive Organization (the Ash Council), which President Nixon created in 1969 to make recommendations and which received information and advice from the Bureau of the Budget, made no reference to the DRBC or Title II commissions but recommended that the commissions for economic development be abolished. The council said that their "continued existence . . . creates strong pressures for increases in budgets and generates requests for additional commissions" and that they are "an unnecessary administrative layer in the Federal grant process." However, the council's recommendations on natural resources reorganization did imply abolition of the Title II commissions. The report called for creation of a Department of Natural Resources within which planning and evaluation functions of the Soil Conservation Service, Corps of Engineers, and Bureau of Reclamation would be consolidated, both for river basin planning and individual project planning. *Memoranda for the President of the United States: Establishment of a Department of Natural Resources; Organization for Social and Economic Programs* (1971), pp. 69, 151–57, 26–29.

6. It might be argued that this situation differs only in degree from what is usual in American government. It has often been observed that the President's nominal sub-

administration threatened to end the special Appalachian program and substitute rural-development revenue sharing, the ARC was able to mobilize the region's governors in its own defense. For the ARC, the governors are more than a powerful constituency: they are members of the organization and beneficiaries of its method of grant administration. Yet jointness has not enabled the Title V commissions to secure large programs. They had to start from scratch, and resolute budget-cutting by OMB kept them small, whereas the ARC had the great advantage of starting with presidential support and a large spending program, which in turn generated its own support in Congress and the state governments. The jointness of the administering organization may help make it a powerful claimant, yet a federal line agency with a similar amount of money to spend and comparable congressional support would do well too.

As instruments for realizing federal purposes, the commissions for economic development function in a manner analogous to a federal line agency that gives grants, though with a very different structure. Federal-state coordination is secured by offering inducements to the states to carry out federally inspired policy. States are expected to conform to guidelines in order to receive grants—at least, that has been the pattern in the ARC. The Title V programs have been so small and the Commerce Department's supervision has been so slight that no spending guidelines of substance have developed and the states' discretion is total. For the ARC, guidelines have incorporated locational criteria, but the criteria are very general. State discretion, which ordinarily is wide even in a program conventionally administered, is if anything increased by the states' presence in the administering organization, which enables them to bargain with the federal member and/or the staff for reduced restrictions. Also, responsibility for securing federal objectives rests with one man, the federal cochairman, rather than with the organization. His personality and bargaining skill are therefore crucial to the realization of objectives. In a joint organization, guidelines for

---

ordinates—bureau chiefs, say—are able to win independence of hierarchical supervision by building support among congressional committees, client groups, and lobbies, some of which in turn owe their power to a base in state and local governments. A joint organization in which the federal member shares executive functions with state members, who can exploit their independence of federal discipline for the organization's purposes, carries this phenomenon to an extreme and makes it legitimate.

grant expenditures may be better coordinated than usual in the procedural sense that they have been mutually agreed upon by federal and state agents, but this agreement does not produce more refined statements of purpose.

Logically, one might expect that organization of grant-in-aid activity on a regional scale would result in a more precise statement of federal objectives and therefore a more effective supervision of state activity. Presumably, a region of states is much less diverse than the nation and the states making up the region have something in common—something that matters for public policy—or they would not be distinguished as a region at all. From the federal government's point of view, this should be the advantage of decentralization, yet the ARC has developed with virtually the opposite rationale, stressing more freedom for the states from the burdens of federal supervision. In sum, a joint regional organization does not seem to improve the realization of federal purposes over conventional methods of grant-in-aid administration.

Unlike the commissions for economic development, the river basin commissions are not primarily engaged in distributing federal funds and their claims for direct federal support are modest. Insofar as they make such claims, jointness may be of some slight help. Among Title II commissions, the New England River Basins Commission has been able to get funds for planning studies despite OMB's denial of budget requests, and the federal chairman may have been a bit freer to arrange this and a bit more able to draw on the governors' backing than if he had headed a federal line agency. Still, these joint planning and coordinating organizations are hardly powerful lobbies or big spenders. The early fear that the DRBC would morally bind the federal government to development expenditures has proved unfounded.

As federal-state coordinators, the river basin commissions have found themselves in circumstances very different from those of the commissions for economic development because the pattern of federal-state relations is different. While federal and state governments have had overlapping interests in water resources, functions have been relatively distinct and interdependence has been limited. The federal government has carried out major development itself rather than through grants-in-aid. Until the last decade, it had little interest in pollution control, which it left to state and local governments. In such circumstances there could be no argument for jointness as a way of improving the realization of federal purposes. The rationale was, rather, that because federal development activity affected the interests of state governments they had a right to participate in development planning. Since the mid-1960s, however, the federal government has expanded its interest in water resources and increased its dependence on the states. Federal laws have given them large new responsibilities and large sums of money for pollution control and, more recently, for coastal zone management. The need for vertical coordination has increased, and the usual technique is being employed—the grant-in-aid, with accompanying regulations, administered by a federal line agency in direct relations with each state. The river basin commissions have no part in administering grants. If anything, the growing federal-state interdependence in water-related activities has weakened the river basin commissions, whose state members are so busy meeting obligations to their new federal patrons that they are less able than ever to contribute to the activity of a regional organization.

Whether jointness improves realization of the federal purpose depends on the ability of the federal agent in the regional organization to enunciate purposes and offer inducements to the states to comply. For jointness to pay off for the federal government, its agents must be better able to pursue federal goals than conventional line agencies, but line agencies, as federal coordinators of state actions, have all the advantages. They have the statutory responsibility for realizing federal goals within their program specialties and the funds to offer as inducements to state governments to cooperate. What distinguishes federal agents in joint organizations is that they are not tied to programmatic specialties. This virtue is supposed to enable them to transcend the parochial aims of bureaus or departments and to speak for the federal government or its executive branch as a whole. In reality, it means they cannot speak for anyone, since the executive branch *as a whole* has no purposes. If there were a central executive agency from which the federal members of joint organizations could derive authoritative guidance on policy and if that policy could be backed by sanctions and rewards from this central source, then federal-state coordination might occur, and perhaps even be improved, through the joint organizations—but that is not the case, as chapter 9 has shown.

If the federal government does not stand to lose as much from joint organization as its executive agencies have sometimes feared, neither does it appear to gain anything of value. The promised improvements in intergovernmental coordination and in effectiveness of federal programs are remote and problematic. Joint organizations add little if anything to standard techniques of vertical coordination. On the other hand, losses in accountability are immediate and visible, at least in the case of the ARC. Unless or until OMB or some other presidential agency can exploit the potential uses of joint organizations as instruments of federal purposes, OMB cannot reasonably be expected to promote their development. And as long as the executive branch is unwilling to cooperate in their development, joint organizations will be of limited value to the states as agents of decentralization.

## Purely Federal Organizations

Constitutionally, TVA and the Federal Regional Councils are conventional forms. Their relative acceptability to the executive branch makes them more feasible than joint organizations as a technique of decentralization, but how effective they are is still a question. Being purely federal, they raise no novel questions of intergovernmental relations for the Department of Justice and OMB to be concerned about, but neither are they inherently accessible to the influence of other governments.

If the criteria of decentralization are the *amount of federal authority* effectively available to the regional organization and the *accessibility* of that authority to nonfederal interests, TVA has to be rated well. As a possessor of federal authority, it is vastly superior in its actual operations to all other regional organizations. While its structure does not guarantee nonfederal interests systematic access, TVA has constructed an organizational ideology out of accommodation "at the grass roots," and has actually made numerous adjustments to state and local governments. It has deferred to them in its choice of activities, refraining from acts of displacement. It has provided services. In its agriculture program, it has relied on them as agents of its purposes. In the power program, it has enlisted their cooperation as retail distributors of its product.

TVA's case especially demonstrates the impact on a regional organization of decentralizing forces in the environment, which is to say the American political system as a whole. This federal corporation, inherently independent of the state governments and expected by some of its New Deal founders to challenge them, has nevertheless been quite circumspect. The explanations lie in the constitutional system itself—in the combination of legal structure and parallel social structures that make the states durable political communities, and in national institutions, such as the structure of Congress, the electoral college, and the party system, that help perpetuate them as political communities and as governments.[7] Governmental practices reinforce the institutional strength of the states —in particular, the federal government's reliance on them for execution of national programs. There was never any real prospect that TVA would substantially displace the states. Their legal status as independent governments in the federal system makes them all but invulnerable to displacement, at least in its extreme form, which is abolition; and the habits and institutions that reinforce their legal independence make it hard to displace them as performers of major governmental functions. Legally, the federal executive agencies are much more vulnerable. Having created them, Congress can abolish them or reassign their functions. This is what happened with TVA: Congress could and did displace the Corps of Engineers, but not the state of Tennessee.

The inertia of governmental arrangements made it likely that TVA would duplicate earlier patterns in intergovernmental relations, as it did in the agriculture program, to the states' advantage, and in its development program, to their disadvantage. The result was a considerable measure of decentralization (as the term has here been defined) yet with some inconsistency in the pattern of TVA's accessibility to nonfederal interests. TVA has been accessible only in ways and in programs more or less of its own choosing. Thus, while environmental forces can probably be counted on to induce decentralizing adjustments from even a purely federal regional organization, the effects of these external forces are likely to be haphazard and to permit some selectivity of response on the part of the regional organization, unlike the effects to be expected of joint-

7. Daniel J. Elazar, *American Federalism: A View from the States* (Crowell, 1966); James W. Fesler, ed., *The 50 States and Their Governments* (Knopf, 1967), chap. 1.

ness, which makes decentralization inherent in the form and therefore preferable as a means of securing accessibility.

Of themselves, the Federal Regional Councils can hardly be considered a technique of decentralization at all. They are primarily coordinating organizations; as such, they depend on, without themselves embodying, substantial delegations of authority from the headquarters of federal departments to their regional directors. OMB's effort to establish the councils as regional-level coordinators of federal grant-in-aid programs has coincided with an effort to induce federal departments to decentralize authority to field locations, especially in grant-in-aid programs. This technique of decentralization—redistributing authority within the present framework of federal executive organization rather than creating new types of regional organizations—is OMB's preferred method. So far, however, it has been unable to induce major acts of decentralization by the departments. As in their supervision of the Federal Regional Councils, management officials in OMB have found it hard to take initiatives, and they lack ways to reward the agencies for compliance with management objectives. In any case, they seek a more limited decentralization than that of the regional organizations. Mainly, they have urged federal agencies to decentralize decisions about awards of grants in specific cases but not the responsibility for determining the content of grant-in-aid regulations or of regional plans for spending. OMB's willingness to experiment with decentralization inside executive departments, like its willingness to experiment with new forms of regional organizations, is diluted by apprehension that federal field agents will prove all too responsive to state and local interests, particularly those that seek federal funds.

As with the various techniques of federal interagency coordination, none of the approaches to decentralization represented by these regional organizations appears to be clearly superior to the others. The regional operating agency on the model of TVA is attractive for the range of its authority, but broad authority without guaranteed accessibility for external, proximate interests is inadequate and possibly self-defeating as a technique of decentralization. Whether such accessibility is sufficient and whether the interests attended to are the proper ones are especially important questions in TVA's case because of the scope of the organization's powers.

Like all special authorities, TVA is relatively insulated from scrutiny from any source. Jointness guarantees that state governments will have access but has been self-defeating in a different way: the more authority the regional organization has, the less willing the federal executive branch has been to acquiesce in jointness. In general, centrally planned decentralization has not occurred within executive departments, and the kind of decentralization OMB seeks, which would give field officials authority to sign off on grants, is limited. Again, as in managing problems of federal interagency cordination, none of the forms or techniques analyzed is so clearly successful that the regional organization can be justified on grounds of decentralization alone. The distinctive value of regional organizations is whatever value they have as responses to problems of scale.[8]

## Reflections on Decentralization

Regional organizations raise the questions whether and in what sense excessive centralization is a problem at all. The experience of these organizations shows that state governments are not atrophying. They have plenty to do, and more all the time. One of the genuine obstacles to sustaining regional organizations is that state governments are so busy managing direct relations with the federal government and meeting responsibilities under grant-in-aid programs that they have no effort to spare for regional activity. The inertial force of state activity is so great and the states as claimants for federal funds are so powerful that it is impossible for regional organizations to transcend the states in defining regional goals. Organizations that distribute federal funds, such as the commissions for economic development, therefore become mediums for interstate bargaining. If failure to transcend the states is thought to be a defect, the solution ought to be the purely federal instrumentality modeled after TVA. However, it does not fully transcend the states either—certain of its activities are integrated with theirs. In short, the states continue to be powerful claimants on federal resources, to be objects of federal deference, and to perform a wide range of governmental functions. They persist, and political decentraliza-

8. See chapter 1.

tion persists, in the sense that dispersed centers of power, often based in state governments, successfully make and defend claims on federal resources and retain considerable discretion in disposing of those resources according to local values.

What has been occurring in American government is not the displacement of state governments by the federal government, but an increase in cooperation between the two with the result that state governments are more and more subject, as recipients of grants-in-aid, to federal executive regulations. Federal executive agencies increasingly make decisions that affect state governments or promulgate rules that they are supposed to follow, but unlike Congress, the agencies are not inherently open to state and local influence. What most of the regional organizations are designed to achieve, the joint ones in particular, is decentralization of federal executive decisions, at the stage either of planning programs or of formulating grant regulations, so that federal executive agents will accommodate to preferences of state executives. Were *political* decentralization less than it is, the executive branch, represented by OMB, would be more willing to experiment with *executive* decentralization. Only as the federal government's capacity for central discipline and direction of its own executive agents increases can it afford to give them broad discretion in relations with state governments.[9]

9. Compare the parallel point made by Grodzins: "if the political parties were centralized, then an ordered decentralization of government would be possible." Morton Grodzins, *The American System* (Rand McNally, 1966), p. 315.

# [11]

# Conclusions

ISSUES about regional organizations occasionally arise as choices among forms. There may be, at certain times and in certain places, agreement on the need to create a regional organization, and the question then becomes which type is best. But actual choices very often are of other kinds—between a particular proposed regional organization and no regional organization; between duplicating a particular form and not duplicating it; between administering a federal program such as economic development through regional organizations and administering it more conventionally through a line agency with a national jurisdiction; or between regional organizations as means of decentralization or federal interagency coordination and some altogether different technique. Proponents of replicating the Appalachian Regional Commission (ARC) in the early 1970s claimed that it was better than revenue sharing as a technique of decentralization. They argued that giving funds to the states through a regional commission would increase the states' discretion while retaining some measure of federal supervision by reason of the federal member's presence.[1]

This brief concluding chapter attempts to extract from the common experience of regional organizations some general lessons about their formation, recognizing that, in view of the variety of regional forms and the necessarily contingent character of any recommendations, such lessons are hard to state. Organizations are

1. For a detailed analysis of proposals and issues concerning regional organizations in the early 1970s, see Advisory Commission on Intergovernment Relations, *Multistate Regionalism*, Report A-39 (Washington: ACIR, April 1972), especially chap. 6.

instruments of purpose, and they ought not to be judged apart from the objectives they purport to serve. Thus, for example, whether Title II commissions are useful organizations cannot be separated from whether comprehensive planning for river basin development is a valuable public activity. In form, Title II commissions may be better instruments for regional planning than the commissions for economic development, but that does not establish that the millions of dollars spent on comprehensive river basin planning through Title II commissions and similar coordinating organizations in the past decade is money well spent, or that river basin development is somehow better than it would have been without such organizations.[2] In the case of the commissions for economic development, surely the chief question for policy is not the form but the plausibility and relative merit of public works spending for regional development or national development or whatever. The proposed Public Works Development Act of 1972, which would have duplicated the ARC across the nation, would have authorized $7.5 billion for public works in the first three years. On the basis of the experience of the ARC and Title V commissions, the results of such a program would probably not be very different if it was administered by joint regional commissions than if it was administered by a federal agency through grants directly to the states. The main issue ought to be the merit of the spending for the particular purpose. Organizational forms are also contingent upon setting and circumstance. The Tennessee Valley Authority, for example, worked well in the Tennessee Valley in the 1930s, but even its most sympathetic analysts have doubted that this performance would have been duplicated in other river basins. And even if the effects of environment are discounted, it is not possible to predict accurately from one case of regional organization how others patterned after it would perform. In quality of leadership, quality of staff, and organizational esprit, the TVA, the Delaware River Basin Commission (DRBC), and the ARC have all benefited in some measure from being new and experimental. Imitations would not have the

2. See Arthur Maass, "Public Investment Planning in the United States: Analysis and Critique," *Public Policy*, vol. 18 (Winter 1970), pp. 211–43, especially pp. 213–17, in which Maass argues that "the technique of multipurpose planning has grown over the years into a caricature of itself."

qualities of the original, some of which have come precisely from being new and unique.[3]

In view of the need for caveats, it is tempting simply to repeat the advice of the National Resources Committee in 1935: that the selection of an organizational type should depend on the functions to be assigned, the area of operation, the location of the constitutional powers required, and the incidence of benefits and costs. In other words, the only policy is pragmatism. Still, thirty years of experience must say something.

The principal thing that experience suggests is that pragmatism is the *best* policy: it leads to the most effective regional organizations. It is no accident that the leading cases of regional organization are accidents. Any one of the executive organizations of government needs to be sustained by some constituency or underlying set of interests as well as by the force of the formal instrument that created it. Or it needs to be autonomous: it must have the means to sustain itself. For a regional organization, which runs counter to the deep institutional grain of American government, these needs are especially exigent. To win the fight for existence and a significant share of public functions, it must have extraordinary constituency support or extraordinary means of self-support. These conditions can be met, if at all, only in very special circumstances, when there is a fortuitous coming together of opportunity, leadership, and political backing, so that it becomes possible to go against the institutional grain and create a genuinely new form. If the conditions for such an act of organizational innovation develop at all, they may persist long enough to enable the new organization to get well established. Clearly, this happened with TVA, which survived initially by exploiting presidential support and ultimately by becoming autonomous. Quite possibly it is happening with the ARC, which seems likely to survive with the aid of a powerful constituency consisting of a sizable number of governors and high-ranking members of the Senate Public Works Committee. It is not so clear that it is happening with the DRBC, whose failure to secure revenue from the development of pumped storage at Tocks Island meant

3. See Roscoe C. Martin et al., *River Basin Administration and the Delaware* (Syracuse University Press, 1960), chap. 17, for a more elaborate discussion of the contingent features of regional organization.

that it would not be self-sustaining, and which has no powerful constituency in the state governments or in Congress.

Not all the accidental cases, then, are highly successful cases; but for a regional organization to be centrally planned is practically a guarantee that it will be weak and ineffectual. The forms that emerge from central planning are certain to be dependent on federal line agencies, to have no functions that conflict with those agencies' functions, and to have no substantial claim on federal funds. Defenders of these forms over the more innovative, accidental ones argue that they are preferable precisely because they do make concessions to the principally affected interests, especially the federal executive agencies. Thus a Title II commission is said to be more realistic politically than the DRBC, yet the difference is one of degree. A Title II commission, like the DRBC, lacks the necessary base of interested support. Federal agencies accede to the centrally planned forms, but neither they nor the states have much incentive to sustain them. The form reflects the interests and preferences of the central planner, the Office of Management and Budget, and even the central planner is not much interested in regional organizations except as federal interagency coordinators.

It may be said that OMB should be more interested in novel forms of organization, more willing to experiment in organizational matters, and more willing to compromise doctrines, especially when new forms provide a setting for federal agents with a generalist perspective who are potential allies and instruments of a central coordinator. This argument would be far more persuasive if OMB or any other presidental staff agency were able to make use of such instruments. As it is, OMB must calculate whether the more innovative regional forms, with a joint structure and single federal member, are more likely to reinforce the centrifugal tendency of American government or counteract it. It has taken the more pessimistic view, which is as much a realistic recognition of its own limitations as central coordinator as it is a manifestation of doctrinal rigidity.

Given the odds against the formation of "strong" regional organizations and the widespread latent resistance to them, the past decade is notable for the emergence of a leading form, that of the ARC, which gives promise of being generalizable. The explanation of its relative feasibility lies in its function. The ARC began as a medium for additions to the grant-in-aid expenditures of federal agencies, and these additional funds both enabled it to surmount the predictable opposition of federal agencies and constituted an inducement to the states to participate. Moreover, the logic of political processes tends to produce generalization, as the Title V program shows. A program started as a special benefit for one lagging region, Appalachia, immediately began to be extended. This occurred not because a majority coalition had developed for regional organization, but because a majority had enacted the Appalachian program, and other, less-than-majority interests successfully bargained for extension of the regional form. By 1972 the partial extension had reached all but eleven states, and the Senate Public Works Committee was considering a bill for "wall-to-wall regions," a comprehensive generalizing of the ARC.

If regional organizations on the model of the ARC were the only possible channel for increasing the flow of federal funds to the states, or if they were the channel preferred by the executive branch, then they would be formed. However, other channels exist—the traditional categorical grant-in-aid and since 1972 revenue sharing —which are more acceptable to the federal executive agencies than are joint regional commissions. Augmenting federal aid through categorical grants or revenue sharing does not raise, as do joint regional commissions, the jurisdictional problems for federal agencies that come with superimposing rival organizational types on the present pattern of executive organization.[4] Also, both tech-

---

4. Areal specialization would produce major jurisdictional conflicts within Congress as well as the executive branch, since congressional organization is specialized by function too. If the ARC were generalized and the volume and purposes of expenditure much enlarged, Congress would probably have to reorganize for purposes of supervision. Overseeing the ARC has been a responsibility of the Public Works committees, to which the Appalachian bill was referred in 1964 because it contained mostly new authorizations for public works. Responsibility has remained there even as the ARC has expanded into other activities. It was the Senate Public Works Committee which declared in 1969 that the Appalachian region should be a national laboratory for child development. A study of the House Public Works Committee's oversight of economic development programs has found that the committee has carefully scrutinized the activities of the Economic Development Administration, a federal agency, but not of the joint regional commissions. The ARC in particular has escaped scrutiny. The author of the study speculates that the intergovernmental (joint) character of the commission accounts for this. He found that "the whole ARDA [Appalachian Regional Development Act] program seemed to be viewed [by the

niques are more consistent with OMB's management doctrines than jointness is, for they preserve a clear distinction between the federal government as supplier of funds and other governments as recipients. Although revenue sharing alters the terms of the federal-state relation to the states' advantage, agencies of the federal government remain free to pass judgment on the other governments' proposals and uses of federal funds, insofar as Congress elects to have them do so.

If joint regional commissions were the channel for federal aid preferred by state governments, they would probably be formed; and if such commissions substituted for federal line agencies, they would be highly attractive to the states. But that is not a realistic possibility. As superstructure upon the more traditional structure of federal-state organization, they are a complicating feature, attractive to the states for whatever money and services they yield, but not for their own sake.

Questions of feasibility aside, regional organizations ought to be fully generalized only if they show promise of making general, which is to say systematic, improvements. But the systemic problems to which they are addressed—federal lack of coordination and excessive centralization—do not appear to be substantially ameliorated by any form, with the possible exception of TVA. The distinctive virtue of regional organizations is that they are suited to respond to particular needs or problems isolable on a regional scale and somehow peculiar to an area as a natural or social or economic unit. For example, managing water quality in river basins is such a need, currently of public concern, and economists have advanced strong arguments for creating regional organizations for that purpose.[5]

In the ARC's case, to generalize the form fully would undermine its distinctive regional purpose, which is to augment federal aid to

committee] hardly as a Federal program at all." Douglas K. Bereuter, "Investigative Oversight of Economic Development Programs by the House Committee on Public Works (1964–1972)," seminar paper, Harvard University, 1973. The wide variation in ARC programs probably also discourages oversight by the Public Works committees, which cannot claim a special competence to examine a child development program, for instance.

5. Allen V. Kneese and Blair T. Bower, *Managing Water Quality: Economics, Technology, Institutions* (Washington: Resources for the Future, 1968); and Marc J. Roberts, "Organizing Water Pollution Control: The Scope and Structure of River Basin Authorities," *Public Policy*, vol. 19 (Winter 1971), pp. 75–141.

"a region apart" from the rest.[6] It is a means of distributing aid to a needy area that does not conform to state boundaries, and it is the area's advocate and ally in the conduct of relations with the federal government—a "broker," in the ARC's phrase, that can make federal programs work for the benefit of the needy region. If this is the peculiar virtue of the form, as ARC officials have sometimes contended, it should not be extended to the whole country, since this would again place the needy region on a par with others while giving extraordinary help to places whose need for it has not been demonstrated. Conceivably, special help should be given to other depressed regions, as the proponents of Title V have contended, but if the aim is to aid depressed regions, some principle of exclusion is required.

This analysis of the ARC is consistent with the earlier conclusion —that in the formation of regional organizations with operating or regulatory functions the best results are likely to be achieved ad hoc, in response to particular needs that can be shown to require organization on a regional scale and to require it so urgently that the inevitable costs in administrative confusion are worth paying.

As an approach to regional organization, only that sponsored by OMB is fully generalized while avoiding the costs in coordination that come with radical departures from the functional pattern of federal executive organization. Perhaps OMB's actions to date— the delineation of standard regions, the attempts to induce decentralization of authority within departments, the creation of interagency councils, presidential designation of a council chairman, and participation of an OMB staff member in council deliberations—are first steps in substantial development of federal administrative activity at the regional level. Perhaps in a decade or two or three, Boston, Denver, and Seattle will rival Washington as centers of such activity. State and local officials will speak of getting decisions out of New York, Kansas City, and San Francisco, and others will understand them to mean decisions of the federal executive branch. Men will covet jobs as the President's regional representative, the official who mediates interagency disputes, secures interagency collaboration in attacking state and local problems, presides over the preparation of regional program budgets, and

6. The phrase is from *Appalachia: A Report by the President's Appalachian Regional Commission* (1964), p. xv.

arbitrates state and local trading of funds among program categories. Federal regional officials, because they will have a wide range of discretion, will be able to treat state and local governments differentially, without being bound by uniform national regulations designed to apply to all places but in practice ill suited to many. Federal executive action, as a result of these developments, will be more expeditious, effective, efficient, and adaptable to needs expressed by particular state and local governments.[7]

This evolution would require a major assertion of presidential power in relation to Congress and the line agencies. OMB, acting for the President, would have to compel the change. Moreover, unless there is such centralization of power in the presidential office, the change to a predominantly regional administration may not be desirable. Without strong central supervision, federal field officials are likely to join with state and local officials in pressing indiscriminately for federal expenditures. Far from rendering federal programs more efficient, administrative decentralization might make rational choices among programs even more difficult. Moreover, in the absence of clear policy guidance from a central source, greater discretion of field officials might be used in arbitrary and capricious ways, increasing the burden of federal administrative intervention on state and local governments without improving the realization of federal objectives. Greater discretion for field agents is desirable only insofar as Congress, the President, and departmental headquarters can make reasonably clear the goals that the use of discretion should serve.

7. For full statements of the rationale underlying this outline of regional organization, see Charles L. Schultze, *The Politics and Economics of Public Spending* (Brookings Institution, 1968), chap. 7, and James L. Sundquist, *Making Federalism Work: A Study of Program Coordination at the Community Level* (Brookings Institution, 1969), chap. 7.

# [APPENDIX]

# *The Organizations*

| Organization | Created | Composition | Headquarters |
|---|---|---|---|
| Tennessee Valley Authority | 1933, by act of Congress | Corporation governed by three directors appointed by President | Knoxville, Tenn. |
| Delaware River Basin Commission | 1961, by federal-interstate compact | Federal member appointed by President and governors of Delaware, New Jersey, New York, Pennsylvania | Trenton, N.J. |
| Appalachian Regional Commission | 1965, by act of Congress | Federal member appointed by President and governors of Alabama, Georgia, Kentucky, Maryland, Mississippi, New York, North Carolina, Ohio, Pennsylvania, South Carolina, Tennessee, Virginia, West Virginia | Washington, D.C. |
| Title V commissions for regional economic development | 1965, by act of Congress (authorization only) | Federal member appointed by President and governors of member states, listed below | |
| Ozarks | 1966 | Arkansas, Kansas, Louisiana, Missouri, Oklahoma | Washington and Little Rock |
| New England | 1967 | Connecticut, Maine, Massachusetts, New Hampshire, Rhode Island, Vermont | Washington and Boston |
| Upper Great Lakes | 1967 | Michigan, Minnesota, Wisconsin | Washington |
| Four Corners | 1967 | Arizona, Colorado, New Mexico, Utah | Washington and Farmington, N.Mex. |
| Coastal Plains | 1967 | Georgia, North Carolina, South Carolina | Washington |
| Old West | 1972 | Montana, Nebraska, North Dakota, South Dakota, Wyoming | Washington and Rapid City, S.D. |

| | | | |
|---|---|---|---|
| Pacific Northwest | 1972 | Idaho, Oregon, Washington | Washington and Vancouver, Wash. |
| Title II commissions for river basin planning | 1965, by act of Congress (authorization only) | Federal chairman appointed by President; representatives of interested federal departments, appointed by agency heads (typically, departments of Agriculture, Army, Commerce, Health, Education, and Welfare, Housing and Urban Development, Interior, and Transportation, Federal Power Commission, Environmental Protection Agency); representatives of member states (listed below), appointed as provided for in state law; one representative of each interstate compact agency with jurisdiction in basin; and, at President's discretion, one member of U.S. section of any international commission established by treaty with jurisdiction over basin | |
| Pacific Northwest | 1967 | Idaho, Montana, Oregon, Washington, Wyoming | Vancouver, Wash. |
| Great Lakes | 1967 | Illinois, Indiana, Michigan, Minnesota, New York, Ohio, Pennsylvania, Wisconsin | Ann Arbor, Mich. |
| Souris-Red-Rainy | 1967 (terminated 1973) | Minnesota, North Dakota, South Dakota | Moorhead, Minn. |
| New England | 1967 | Connecticut, Maine, Massachusetts, New Hampshire, New York, Rhode Island, Vermont | Boston |
| Ohio | 1971 | Illinois, Indiana, Kentucky, Maryland, New York, North Carolina, Ohio, Pennsylvania, Tennessee, Virginia, West Virginia | Cincinnati |
| Upper Mississippi | 1972 | Illinois, Iowa, Minnesota, Missouri, North Dakota, Wisconsin | Twin Cities, Minn. |
| Missouri | 1972 | Colorado, Iowa, Kansas, Minnesota, Missouri, Montana, Nebraska, North Dakota, South Dakota, Wyoming | Omaha, Neb. |
| Federal Regional Councils (ten) | 1969, by executive action | Regional directors of the departments of Agriculture, Interior, Health, Education, and Welfare, Housing and Urban Development, Labor, and Transportation; Office of Economic Opportunity; Environmental Protection Agency; Law Enforcement Assistance Administration | Boston, New York, Philadelphia, Atlanta, Chicago, Dallas–Fort Worth, Kansas City, Denver, San Francisco, Seattle |

# Index

Ackerman, Bruce, 59n
Adkins, Roger, 125n
Advisory Commission on Intergovernmental Relations, 3n, 102
Agriculture, and TVA, 36, 37, 39
Agriculture, Department of, 29, 121, 136–37, 152–53. *See also* Soil Conservation Service
Alonso, William, 3n
Anderson, Clinton P., 140–41
Appalachia, 76, 77, 78; effort to extend boundaries of, 111n; states included in, 83. *See also* Appalachian Regional Commission
Appalachian Housing Fund, 85
Appalachian Regional Commission (ARC), 4, 129, 130, 201, 226; aim of, 76; appropriations and staff, 15, 83, 84; authority of, 80–81; as "catalyst," 120, 191; and centralization, 12; compared with DRBC and TVA, 188; compared with Title V commissions, 123–24, 125, 131–33; conflicts within, 210; and coordination problem, 10, 11; effect of programs, 104–06; feasibility of duplicating or generalizing forms of, 106–07, 227–28, 229–30; federal cochairman, 98–101; and federal funds, 215–16; form and functions of, 7–8, 81–86; and governors, 11, 101–04, 216; and jointness, 85–86, 91–98, 211n; as leading case, 15, 192, 193; location of investment, 91–94, 97–98; as operating agency, 186, 187–88; origin of, 1–2; and staff, 85–86, 93–95; and states, 87–91, 184, 188; states' regional representative, 96
Appalachian Regional Development Act (ARDA), 77–78, 80, 82, 87, 98, 108, 110n, 123

ARC. *See* Appalachian Regional Commission
ARDA. *See* Appalachian Regional Development Act
Area Redevelopment Administration, 77, 99
Arkansas-White-Red Basin Inter-Agency Committee, 135, 136, 144
Army, Department of the, 67, 152–53
Artman, J. O., 37n
Atlanta, 161; Federal Regional Council in, 169, 170
Atomic Energy Commission, 56

Banfield, Edward C., 6n, 19n, 23n
Barber, Blue, 85n
Barton, Weldon V., 14n
Baxter, Samuel S., 61–62
Bereuter, Douglas K., 228–29n
Blatnik, John, 113
Bolton, Chester C., 44n
Boston Federal Regional Council, 169, 170
Boston *Globe*, 117
Bower, Blair T., 6n, 50n, 59n, 229n
Brown, Lawrence D., 120n
Buchanan, Roger E., 87–88n
Bureau of the Budget, 52, 71, 128, 136, 137, 138, 139, 154, 186; and ARC, 82, 83, 98, 100; and DRBC, 66, 196, 201; development of, 194n; and jointness, 213; and origin of Federal Regional Councils, 158–63; and origin of Title II commissions, 134–39, 196; and PARC proposal, 77, 78, 79, 80; proposal for Title V commissions, 109–10; and regional organizations, 193–94; and Title V commissions, 112, 113–14, 118, 122,

WHITMAN COLLEGE LIBRARY

WESTMAR COLLEGE LIBRARY